ROBERT L. MILLS, J.D.

THE *LAWYER* WHO BECAME A *WRITER*
FOR BOB HOPE REMEMBERS

The
LAUGH
MAKERS

A Behind-the-Scenes Tribute to
Hope's Incredible Gag Writers

Foreword by Gary Owens

Acknowledgments

My thanks to each and every writer, producer, director, and staff member of the Bob Hope Show who made my comedic journey so much fun. If I've forgotten anyone, please pencil yourselves in. You know who you are.

Gene Perret, Martha Bolton, Jeffrey Barron, Gig Henry, Seaman Jacobs, Fred Fox, Doug Gamble, Charles Lee, Bill Larkin, Elliott Kozak, Bob Alberti, Barney McNulty, Keith McNulty, Don Marando, Melinda Manos, Nancy Gordon, Maggie Kleir, Ken Kantor, Bob Keane, Sheldon Keller, Howard Albrecht, Richard Albrecht, Sol Weinstein, Brian Blackburn, Frank Leiberman, Buz Kohan, Jim Mahoney, Ron Burla, Onnie Morrow, Ellen Brown, Marcia Lewis, Al Borden, Bob Arnott, Harvey Berger, Marty Farrell, Kathy Green, Geoff Clarkson, Bob Alberti, Rick Ludwin, Lee Hale, Chris Hart, Stan Hart, Jack Haley, Jr., Hal Kantor, David Letterman, Chris Bearde, Charles Issacs, John Harlan, Brandon Tartikoff, Howard Koch, Phil Lasker, Casey Keller, Gail Lawrence, James Lipton, Dick McDonough, Bob Banner, Bob Keene, Bryan Blackburn, Steve Perani, Mel Shavelson, Paul Pompian, Peter Rich, Devoney Marking, Tom Shadyak, John Shea, Ken Welch, Mitzie Welch, Marshall Flaum, Hal Collins, Howard Koch, Andrew Solt, Eddie Rio, Walter C. Miller, Bob Wynn, Don Ohlmeyer, Jim Henson, Frank Oz, Jimmy Frazier, Carl Jablonski, Geoff Clarkson, Pacy Markman, Dorothy Proper,

Phil Savenick, Onnie Mortrow, Linda Hope, Elle Puritz, Kip Walton, Dale Huffstedler, Kevin McDonough, Frank Reo, Chuck Gouert, Harry Flynn, Bob Hussey, Tim Kiley, Sil Carranchini, Malcolm Leo, Jane Upton Bell, Warden Neil, Dick Vosburgh, Gary Chambers, Paul Abeyta, and Jan Morill.

My thanks to guests of the *Bob Hope Show* whom I came to know and whose stories are included in the book: Jonathan Winters, Howard Keel, Don Rickles, Barbara Mandrell, Loni Anderson, Jack Lemmon, Glen Campbell, Florence Henderson, Barbara Eden, Charo, Bernadette Peters, Jim Coburn, Glenn Ford, John Marcus, Mikhail Baryshnikov, Big Bird (Carroll Spinney), Morgan Fairchild, Betty White, Red Skelton, Sammy Davis, Jr., Dean Martin, Mac Davis, Brooke Shields, Marie Osmond, Jim Henson, Mickey Rooney, Robert Urich, Andy Williams, George C. Scott, Perry Como, Phyllis Diller, Sugar Ray Leonard, Marvin Hagler, Lee Marvin, Pat Boone, Charlene Tilton, Dick Cavett, Joe Montana, Howie Long, Mr. T, Gerald Ford, Angie Dickenson, Henny Youngman, Danny Kaye, Catherine Bach, Richard Burton, Olivia Newton-John, Bonnie Franklin, Loretta Switt, Boy George, Raquel Welch, Twiggy, Emmanuel Lewis, Sir Lew Grade, Audrey Landers, Lola Falana, Crystal Gayle, Roseanne Barr, Debbie Reynolds, Howie Long, Tony Randall, Linda Evans, Steve Lawrence, Frank Oz, Eydie Gorme, Danny Thomas, George Burns, Carol Lawrence, Alan Shepard, Norm Crosby, Jack Carter, Barbara Rush, Milton Berle, Pat Boone, Placido Domingo, John Forsythe, Cindy Crawford, Johnny Carson, Christie Brinkley, Leslie Uggams, John Denver, Morgan Brittany, Donna Mills, Tommy Tune, Gordon McCrae, Robert Preston, Ann Jillian, Kenneth Mars, and Elizabeth Taylor.

Special thanks to Hope's longtime agent-producer, Elliott Kozak whose information on the inner workings of the Hope organization was invaluable to the book's factual integrity, and to Louise Nicholson for its typographical accuracy.

Finally, to Don Sherwood who set the course for my incredible journey by showcasing my material on KSFO, San Francisco. To Carolyn

Raskin and Dinah Shore for my first job in television, to Steve Allen for the second, and to producer Greg Garrison and head writer Harry Crane for my first network assignment, *The Dean Martin Celebrity Roasts*, which prepared me so well for my years with Bob Hope. My gratitude is boundless.

To Madeline & Ralph — Hope you enjoy reading about these adventures as much as I enjoyed living them — my best,

6-15-09

Dedication

To my beautiful, loving wife, Shelley, who shared the dream, and helped it come true by keeping us financially afloat during the lean times. For typing the first draft of this book. For proofreading, spell-checking, and monitoring it for neatness, originality and aptness of thought, while providing invaluable advice on questions of taste, political correctness, and the laws governing libel and slander. For pointing out anachronisms and identifying passages better left unsaid and words or phrases considered inappropriate for mixed company — and all the while keeping me in clean socks and underwear.

And to my brother, Dave Mills, who was, from the very beginning, my most loyal fan who never ceased encouraging me every step of the way.

BearManor Media
P O Box 71426
Albany, Georgia 31708
www.bearmanormedia.com

ISBN 1-59393-323-1

Printed in the United States of America.

Book & cover design by Darlene Swanson of Van-garde Imagery, Inc.

Contents

foreword

I've known Bob Mills for years and when I was told he had finished a book about Bob Hope's writers, I was happy to hear he was reading again — I knew he was having trouble with the big words. But *then* — then they told me he had *written* the book... well, you could have knocked me over with a feather dance — uh, duster.

In *The Laugh Makers*, Bob Mills takes us on a delightful, side-splitting journey back to the slapstick sketch comedy of television's Golden Age — a long-ago era of variety, song-and-dance, brilliant patter and a seemingly endless parade of laughs — sprung from the genius of "gag men," that talented group of wit-blessed wordsmiths to whom the book pays well-deserved homage. I was part of it and I have to admit at the time, I didn't notice — I mean the "golden age" part. Back then, it just seemed like your ordinary, run-of-the-mill age. Hey, what did I know?

What we have here is a failure to communicate — oops, sorry — that's from a cartoon remake of *Hud* I've been working on. Actually, what we have is a priceless collection of heretofore unpublished recollections revealing untold secrets and goings-on behind the scenes on the *Bob Hope Show*. It's a never-before-seen look at the previously classified inner workings of Hope's well-known comedy assembly line that for decades proved as efficient as any in Detroit.

The Laugh Makers is the book we've all been waiting for. It's jam-packed with stories, anecdotes and un-retouched photos from a fondly remembered past, recalling often hilarious, sometimes heartwarming, and always touching tales of legendary stars, near-legendary stars and one or two complete failures — which happens in show business. You can look it up in your Funk & Wagnalls.

I must confess that I couldn't put the book down. That fly paper on the cover was a clever touch, but I probably wouldn't have put it down anyway. The book, like its author, is truly one of a kind.

So sit back... relax... prepare to laugh and enjoy *The Laugh Makers*. I know I did. I may even call the library so I can keep it another two weeks.

Gary Owens

Preface

I first laid eyes on Bob Hope in person when I was seventeen. He came to my hometown, San Francisco, in 1954 to promote his recently published book, *Have Tux, Will Travel*. A friend and I rode the streetcar from the fog-enshrouded Parkside District where we lived, through the Twin Peaks Tunnel, past the soon-to-be-famous Castro District to Market Street.

Within sight of the Bay and just a few blocks from the Ferry Building, one of the city's largest department stores, The Emporium, stood grandly in the heart of downtown.

As we waited in the midst of the small crowd of expectant celebrity-watchers that had gathered along the curb, our hearts beat like trip hammers — we were about to meet our first movie star!

Since I had held the undisputed title of class clown at St. Gabriel Grammar School, it was no surprise that, just before I left the house, I grabbed a paperback copy of Bing Crosby's autobiography, *Call Me Lucky*. I couldn't wait to see Hope's reaction when I asked him to autograph it instead of his own book.

Soon, a black stretch limo glided up to the store's ornate entrance and out stepped the instantly-recognizable, matinee-idol-handsome, 52-year-old Hope. As everyone in the crowd applauded, whistled or cheered, he quickly combed back a still-generous shock of brown hair that had been suddenly rearranged by a gust from the Bay. "Where am I? *Chicago*?" Laughter joined the sound of passing traffic. He was funny in real life, too!

As the star made his way through a path across the sidewalk that had parted for him like the Red Sea, we dutifully followed him to the book department. A special author's table had been set up on a riser with stacks of *Have Tux* strategically stacked nearby.

A queue quickly formed and I got into it, my copy of Bing's book clutched securely for action. Hope began signing, and, as he asked each person's name, would add a little joke or comment — "O'Callahan. Jewish, huh?" — an accommodation that slowed the process, but one that presaged something in his nature that, years later, I would observe time and again: whenever he had the chance, he made fans and supporters feel that they were somehow special. It was the mark of a consummate salesman which, I would someday learn, he was.

I reached the head of the line and said, "Hi, Bob." He nodded. Then, in that smart-alecky way only teens can handle just right, I said, "I can't afford your book, but will *this* do?" He looked at the dog-eared paperback, held it up for the others in line to see — it had a picture of Bing with his pipe on the front — and tossed it straight up, where it hovered momentarily at mezzanine level and then fluttered to the floor like a wounded pheasant, landing beside a Hoover upright on sale in the adjoining housewares department. The crowd reacted just as I thought they would. My visual gag produced a spontaneous, genuine laugh. I had created my first comic routine for Bob Hope!

I had no way of knowing then, of course, that some two decades later, he'd hire me to write thousands of them. There would be a few detours during my journey, but for a brief, fleeting moment I was in show business — and I *liked* it.

* * * *

When I grew up, the traditional path to happiness and riches included a college degree—for me it was San Francisco State University—followed, ideally, by graduate school—University of California, Hastings Law. A career in the law looked okay on paper, but eventually I realized I had less in common with Perry Mason than *My Cousin Vinnie*. I dragged myself to the office in Palo Alto (a suburb of San Francisco that would become the heart of Silicon Valley) for what gradually became a daily grind.

Then, one day, while I was exploring the depths of my professional doldrums, the Comedy Fates suddenly and unexpectedly tilted their golden scepters in my direction. Some jokes I had submitted to a San Francisco radio disc jockey named Don Sherwood — stuff I'd jotted down while staring blankly out the courthouse window — landed me an introduction to his agent, Charles Stern. Seeing something in my work, Stern pointed me in the general direction of Hollywood where dwelled a staff writer on the *Carol Burnett Show* named Gene Perret, a genial, kind-hearted and generous man of my own age who soon became my mentor. Gene had been freelancing monologues for Bob Hope while working on *Burnett* and welcomed a little help that I was more than happy to provide. Ten years later, Gene and I would again work together when he joined Hope's staff full time.

Arriving in Burbank with my wife, Shelley, in December 1975, I would gain valuable experience on the staff of *Dinah!*, a 90-minute day-time talk show, and the *Dean Martin Celebrity Roasts* before being in-ducted into the Hope comedy fraternity two years later.

When I was born, Bob Hope was thirty-five and already a star who could boast a vaudeville career that dated back to 1924, a stint on Broadway in *Roberta*, seven short films beginning with *Going Spanish* in 1934 and a starring role with Jimmy Durante and Ethel Merman in *Red, Hot and Blue!*, which had been a highlight of the Great White Way's 1937 season.

When, forty years later almost to the day, Hope hired me to write for him, he had dominated the airwaves in radio and had starred in fifty-two movies. (The sudden death of Bing Crosby just two months later would scuttle plans for yet another, *The Road to the Fountain of Youth*.)

Hope had been visiting America's living rooms, first on kinescope and later on tape, for almost three decades. Yet, at the age of seventy-five, he was in many ways just hitting his stride and would, over the next fifteen years, produce and star in over eighty-five television specials, many of which would rank among his best.

When you signed on with Bob Hope, it was akin to entering an ancient, tradition-laden religious order where you agreed to forego the temptations of the secular world in exchange for a life of unwavering loyalty, absolute obedience and, I have to admit, more thrills and excitement than anyone could possibly imagine.

First, there was great professional satisfaction in being a "Hope writer." In those days, a contract to write for him was considered gilt-edged—the comedic equivalent of a degree from Harvard.

As for the work itself, he might have been the pope and you a cardinal commissioned by the Almighty to provide a never-ending supply of wit and drollery for delivery to the masses assembled in Vatican Square. Hope-staff-alumnus Larry Gelbart (*M*A*S*H*, *A Funny Thing Happened on the Way to the Forum*), quoted in the Museum of Broadcasting's *Bob Hope: A Half Century on Radio and Television*, summed it up perfectly:

> "Hope would never fire anybody. If he bought you,
> you were there. He knew pretty much you were
> going to stay. He got his help down to a science —
> people preparing him, massaging him, laying out
> his clothes. It was a little like preparing a bullfighter."

The only difference being, the work was steadier. When a bullfighter dies, you're out of a job. When Hope died, he kept coming back for more.

When you were invited to take a seat at his comedy Round Table (to switch to a less religious metaphor), you were keenly aware that your name was being added to a venerable honor roll of humorists.

Hope had employed more writers over a longer period than any performer in history and among the veterans of "Hope's Army" (so labeled by the press) were Mort Lachman, Mel Shavelson, Larry Rhine, Sherwood Schwartz, Norman Panama, Jay Burton, Jack Douglas, Larry Marks, Si Rose, Mel Tolkin, Al Schwartz, Jack Rose, Les White, Johnny Rapp, Mel Frank, Bill Larkin, Hal Goodman, Marty Ragaway, Ray Siller, Hal Kanter and Milt Josefsberg. To a man, these veteran jokesmiths shared a common talent: the ability to put words into Hope's mouth that appeared to have originated there.

Hope himself was the first to point out that having maintained a staff of the most able writers he could find contributed as much to his sustained popularity and prodigious body of work as the uncommon physical stamina with which he had been genetically gifted.

The unique performer-writer symbiosis that developed between Hope and his comedic entourage was the first — and most likely will be the last — of its kind.

What follows is an inside look at how Hope's system operated — one that I hope will provide clues as to why it did for seventy years.

CHAPTER 1

If You See an Opening, Jump In!

When I won my commission in August 1977, I joined a skeleton crew (for Hope) that included Charlie Lee, a relocated Brit who had been toiling in the Hope vineyards for twenty-five years, and Gig Henry, a Brooklyn Polytechnic grad who had worked for U.S. Intelligence during World War II and had been with Hope for two decades — save for a brief period in the seventies after Texaco prevailed on Hope to let his longtime producer and writing staff go. (Charlie and Gig were quietly rehired several months later.)

Billed as a "consultant," Norman Sullivan, a seventyish, red-cheeked Irishman who had been with Hope all of his adult life beginning in radio, lived on a sailboat docked at Malibu and several times a week delivered monologue jokes sealed in Manila envelopes.

Gig, Charlie and I worked under a forty-week contract to provide material for the television specials as well as Hope's personal appearances which at the time averaged three a week. In the summer we were given the option to continue working under a separate contract covering only personal appearances. When Charlie retired in 1979, Hope hired a pair of variety show and sitcom veterans, Seaman Jacobs and Fred Fox (*I Love Lucy, The Red Skelton Show, F-Troop, The Addams Family*) to assist Gig and me on the TV side. When Gig retired four years later, he was replaced by Gene Perret who had been freelancing monologue material for

Hope while working on *Laugh-In, The Carol Burnett Show; The Bill Cosby Hour; Welcome Back, Kotter* and *Three's Company.* (The latter three he co-produced with his partner, Bill Richmond.)

In 1986, Martha Bolton came aboard. She had been a cartoon caption writer for Bill Hoest, creator of the nationally syndicated *Howard Huge* and *The Lockhorns.* She also wrote religious-themed books (*A Funny Thing Happened on My Way through the Bible*) and would be the only full-time female writer Hope would ever hire. Jeffrey Barron, a University of Chicago graduate and former staff writer on *SCTV* in Montreal who had worked on various Hope specials in the seventies, joined us a year after Martha.

Writers brought in by the various producers included Harvey Berger, Howard Albrecht, Sol Weinstein, Bob Arnott, Bryan Blackburn, Marty Farrell, Chris Hart, Stan Hart, Casey Keller, Richard Albrecht, Gail Lawrence, Peter Rich, Pacy Markman, Steve Perani, Paul Pumpian, Charles Isaacs, Dick Vosburgh and Gary Chambers.

Freelance contributors to the television monologues included over the years Joe Madieros, Ron Burla, Cathy Green, Doug Gamble, Tom Shadyac, John Markus, Dennis Snee, Phil Lasker, Pat Proft and Bob Keane.

These were the Laugh Makers.

Gig Henry and I working on the script for my first Hope special *On the Road With Bing.* Gig was very helpful in acclimating me to Hope's workaday foibles and idiosyncrasies. Soon, I would travel with him to Perth, Australia; Peking; and London. Prior to my arrival, he had been paired with Charlie Lee who didn't care much for travel so my bags were always packed.

Seaman Jacobs and Fred Fox had been together for a decade. Fred, a UC Berkeley grad, had worked as a radio disc jockey despite a stuttering problem that mysteriously disappeared when he spoke into a microphone. Si, a graduate of Syracuse University, had been a press agent in New York and knew almost everybody in show business.

Martha Bolton, Jeffrey Barron and Gene Perret would help staff the specials beginning in the mid-eighties. Gene, who had begun his career submitting jokes to Phyllis Diller while in middle management in Upper Darby, Pennsylvania, began contributing to Hope's monologues in 1969. Later, he and I would travel with Hope to London, Stockholm and Tahiti.

Little Ol' Line Makers

Working individually, we prepared eight-to-ten pages of topical jokes for each of Hope's live performances — his standard fee for *Bob Hope in Concert* had climbed, by the mid-eighties to $85,000 — laced with local references prepared with the aid of questionnaires provided by local contacts. It was a process that had served Hope well for years — allowing him to "personalize" each appearance with opening lines tailored to current happenings in that town or city. ("Nice to be here in Pitiful Falls — the gateway to Nowheresville. I thought I'd visit your former mayor. What time are the jail visiting hours?") After a half-dozen or so local references, he'd segue into his regular material and the entire two-hour routine would seem "fresh."

A call from Hope could come from anywhere in the country — or the world, for that matter — and we'd spring into action like so many comedy firemen responding to an alarm. He'd have spotted some news items for us to "jump on." (His longtime producer, Mort Lachman, had dubbed the calls N.A.F.T.s — "Need A Few Things.")

We'd usually have several hours to come up with the jokes, and then one of us would call him back and recite them one-by-one, as he'd scribble his picks on the backs of envelopes or hotel stationery. Returning home, his secretaries would retype the lines for inclusion in his joke file. The process was tedious, and we rejoiced at the arrival of the fax machine that did away with the lengthy calls.

Once on Hope's payroll, you were tethered to him with an invisible telephone cord. If he knew you were accessible by phone, he relaxed. But if he thought you were out of Ma Bell's reach — even if you were on vacation — he'd quietly panic. Each summer, Gig would spend several weeks in Europe, but no matter where he'd go and despite his attempts to keep his itinerary secret, Hope would somehow track Gig down. So one year, he decided to book his tour under his given name, Henry Rosenfeld. Checking into a hotel in Paris, he ran into actor Gig Young, whom he knew slightly. "Gig, would you mind telling Hope where you are?" said Young. "He keeps calling *me!*"

Gig Henry (whom Hope called "Igor" after his Quasimodo-like crouched walk) with Hope in Toluca Lake. This may have been the Christmas party when Hope leaned down to pet his guard dog's week-old puppies and got nipped on the nose. "Snow Job" was granted a pardon and grew up to succeed his mother on the security detail.

In vaudeville, catching trains on-the-run to get from one booking to the next, napping in railway depots or hotel lobbies when short of cash, Hope had become accustomed to operating with little or no sleep — or rather, the amount of sleep most people require. Actually, he *got* enough sleep but in small increments, just as Thomas Edison reportedly did. He could nap at will, nodding off almost instantly. It was a rare ability I would witness time and again. Because of his unorthodox lifestyle, he got used to *working* when other mere mortals were exploring Lullaby City. The primary victims of his odd hours were his writers.

A story had been kicking around for years — about a writer named Cy Rose whose marriage was threatened by Hope's late-night calls. Si's exasperated wife finally says to him, "This has to stop. The next time he wakes us up, *I'll* answer the phone." Thinking she intended to deliver an ultimatum, he agrees. Several nights later, the phone rings around two in the morning, and she answers. "Sorry to bother you at this hour," says Hope, "but I've got to speak to Cy right away." "He's not here," says the wife. "He told me he'd be with *you* tonight." Without missing a beat, Hope replies, "Oh, yeah, here he comes now!" And hangs up.

So on the day Hope asked me to join the staff, I decided to level with him right up front and explained that I'm a *morning* person. He said, "What time do you turn in?" I said, "About ten o'clock — almost *every* night." He seemed unfazed. "I can live with that," he said. "I'll make sure I call you before ten." Over the next seventeen years, he missed the deadline only once. I answered the phone one night around ten past ten and, without saying hello, he says "Am I too late?" I said, "Well, you're lucky we're watching the news, so I'll let it slide." Then I paused and said, "But don't take advantage." He let out one of the biggest laughs I ever got from him.

Call Funnyside 777

Once you hitched your wagon to the Hope star, you could be called upon at any time and under any circumstances to provide fodder for Hope's comedy cannon. Material could be sought for any conceivable event from receptions to political rallies, sales conventions, award ceremonies, college commencements, ribbon cuttings, book signings, ground breakings, ship launchings, golf tournaments, weddings, christenings, bar mitzvahs and funerals.

On the night of October 14, 1977, only two months after I had joined the staff, the phone in our Burbank condo rang. It was Hope calling from New York's Waldorf-Astoria Hotel where he had just learned that Bing Crosby had suffered a fatal heart attack while playing golf in Spain. He said he was suffering from the worst headache he'd ever endured, had canceled the show that was scheduled that night in New Jersey (Bill Cosby subbed for him), and was flying straight home.

News of Bing's death stunned Hope since both were the same age (born twenty-seven days apart in 1903) and, while not the pals the *Road* pictures had led the public to believe — they seldom saw each other socially — they had been inordinately successful business partners and shared a mutual respect. The press was hounding Hope for a statement, so he asked me to write some comments and have them waiting for him when he arrived back home.

It was late and I wouldn't have much time, so I snapped on my IBM Selectric — this was B.C., *Before Computers* — and set to work. I decided to compose the tribute in much the same style as our one liners — "setup - payoff - setup - payoff" — and using this technique came up with:

"The whole world loved Bing with a devotion that not only crossed international boundaries, but erased them. He made the world a single place through his music and spoke to it in a language everybody understands — the language of the heart. No matter where you were in the world, because of Bing, every Christmas was white. And because we had him with us, it will always seem a little whiter. The world put Bing on a pedestal, but somehow I don't think he ever really knew it. Bing asked the world, 'Going My Way?' and we all were. Yesterday, a heart may have stopped and a voice stilled, but the real melody Bing sang will linger on as long as there is a phonograph to be played — and a heart to be lifted."

As a lifelong fan, it was with a sense of sadness that I dropped off the two-page tribute at Hope's Toluca Lake house. The next morning, it was on his secretary's desk with instructions to release it to the wire services without changes. Over the next several days, the quotes appeared in newspapers throughout the country and in Europe as well and have been reprinted many times since. They appear as Hope's tribute in *The One and Only Bing* by Bob Thomas.

I sensed in my embryonic career as a Hope writer that, if I could manage not to stick my comedic foot in my mouth, my job might just last awhile. As things turned out, I was right, but I had no way of knowing then what fantastic adventures lay ahead. In less than a month, I would begin work on my first Bob Hope special, *On the Road With Bing*, produced by Howard Koch, co-writer of *Casablanca* and former head of Paramount Pictures. He would be the first of many distinguished producers that I'd have the privilege of working with.

Hope was no fan of meetings, convinced that we were most effective working at home. He preferred to receive multiple, independent versions of each assignment, without any "collaborating" — a preference that went back to radio. Thus, we usually gathered like this only once to discuss ideas for upcoming specials. (left to right) Seaman Jacobs, me, the CEO, Bob Keane, Gig Henry, Fred Fox.

Grin Reapers

The writers churned out heartfelt remembrances for just about every deceased celebrity's final casting call, but once Hope asked me to compose a last-minute eulogy for the mother of a member of our staff whom he had never met (although I had). I wrote a short remembrance and dropped it off at the house. Later, he called, told me the sentiments were perfect, and asked if I'd mind *delivering* the message at the funeral on his behalf! I agreed, but later managed to convince the minister that it might better be included with the other notes of condolence.

When it came to Hope himself, unexpected reminders of the Robed Man with the Scythe could elicit some surprising reactions. One day, I flew to San Francisco to attend the funeral of an uncle. I left word with

Hope's secretary that I'd be out of action for a few hours. During my absence, Hope returned from a trip, failed to get my message and called me later that evening. "Where were you," he asked. "My uncle's funeral," I explained. "I was a pallbearer."

Without thinking, he asked, "Get any laughs?"

Although on the surface, he was outgoing and gregarious, when caught off guard, Hope could appear to have a fair amount of ice water coursing through his arterial system. In the late eighties, a guest on one of our specials was forced to drop out at the last minute. Hope called a usually reliable fill-in guest, a well-known comedian, who had helped out in the past. When Hope dialed his number, the man said, "Gee, Bob, I'd love to but my wife is scheduled to undergo surgery that weekend. Sorry."

There was a pause and then Hope replied, "We'd only need you for *half* a day."

No surprise that the man never agreed to guest on our show again.

Hope's seemingly unfeeling response resulted from being *surprised*. He was caught off guard by something *unpleasant*, and unpleasantness was something he preferred to avoid.

Apparently that barely perceptible chill in Hope's personality was occasionally projected on the screen, too. In his book, *SCTV: Behind the Scenes* (McClelland & Stewart, 1997), author Dave Thomas relates an incident regarding a letter he received from Steve Allen. Allen, who was then researching one of his *Funny People* books, wrote: "Dave, it seems to me that you have captured with your impersonation of Bob Hope the essential coldness behind the man. I wonder if I could interview you for my book and talk about this." (Thomas had recently appeared in several SCTV sketches playing Hope.) He declined the interview on the grounds that, since he didn't know Hope personally, he was hardly an expert on the matter.

Perhaps Hope's British reserve contributed to the perception among some that his feelings were on the chilly side. In truth, he was something short of the "hail-fellow-well-met" that he appeared to be on the screen, but hardly the icy tycoon that some imagined him to be — and that Bing Crosby actually *was*.

Yours Truly, Bobby Dollar

Through the years, stories circulated that Hope could be insensitive in his relationship with his writers. Admittedly, I joined him relatively late, but I never saw any evidence of it. A story still circulates that he had a habit of delivering paychecks to his writing crew by making paper airplanes and sailing them from the top of his staircase while "the boys" in the foyer scrambled for them like Mexican coin divers. I was told that it happened, but only once in the fifties. The bit got a big laugh and entered the land of the apocryphal.

But Hope's reputation for being inordinately close to the greenbacks in his wallet was not entirely unfounded. While he had no problem peeling off a $6 million check for the Eisenhower Medical Center or the Motion Picture Country House and Hospital in Woodland Hills (and did just that more than once), he did appear to be somewhat attached to the currency that resided in his pocket — the ones he could *see*.

In the mid-sixties, Bill Larkin was the only bachelor on the staff. Late one afternoon, he got a call from Hope. "How fast can you get to LAX?"

"Fast," Bill said, "but why would I go to the airport?"

Hope told him that he was flying to Paris to discuss a picture deal and wanted some company — could Bill join him for a weekend in Europe?

Was he *kidding*?

Two hours later, they're off to France. After checking into the hotel, they're taking a stroll down the Champs Elysees when Bill says, "Bob, we left LA in such a hurry, I didn't have a chance to visit the currency exchange."

Hope assures him that he's covering Bill's expenses so he'd have no use for francs.

Bill replies, "I know, Bob, but I'd feel more comfortable if I had some *walking around* money — you know, in case I need a pack of cigarettes or something."

Hope stops walking, pats Bill on the shoulder, and says, "You know, Bill, you *really* should give up smoking."

And walks on.

That's the story Bill told me and it rings true. I think it went back to Hope's early days in vaudeville when, as he once recounted to me, he was often forced to survive on tomato "soup" concocted from ketchup and hot water he'd cadge from the Automat — with the free oyster crackers floating on top.

When someone says, "It's not the money," you can bet your Social Security check *it's the money*. But with Hope it really wasn't the money so much as the *competitiveness* that's necessary to acquire great wealth and somehow manage to keep it. I believe he saw the rich as those who had recognized an advantage and had been shrewd enough to capitalize on it. He told a reporter once, "I could have bought the Rams." What he was really saying was he now recognized an opportunity that he somehow had overlooked — while someone else hadn't and now owned a franchise worth a fortune. It wasn't his loss that concerned him so much as the other person's *gain* — at his expense.

Zero-Mostel-like Jeffrey Barron was a bachelor who slept all day and wrote at night. He had his own table at Lowry's House of Prime Rib; and while with *SCTV* in Montreal, lived in a hotel for two seasons "... for the room service," as he explained it. Jeff was a shrewd investor who owned several houses in Beverly Hills, though he lived in a small apartment. One evening, while collecting rent, he was questioned by a couple of Beverly Hills cops. "What are you doing here," they demanded. "I own that house," Jeff replied. "Next time take a cab. Nobody walks in Beverly Hills."

Hope never wanted to be the one who missed out. Here's an example. In the late-eighties, when fax machines first came on the market, we all decided that since I was the most computer-savvy, I should check out what was available and negotiate a "fleet price." After a little research, I bought four Panafax 150's (I still use mine), at a $200 discount per unit.

A few weeks later, Hope asked "Hey, how come you didn't let me in on your fax machine deal?" Surprised, I explained that his machine needed bells and whistles that ours didn't, like a paper cutter (originally all fax paper came on rolls) — that he'd be sending and receiving faxes while we would just be sending and could get along with machines that were less complex. He seemed to have been following the logic — but there was a pause and then he said, "How come I need a separate telephone line?" I was back where I started — but remember, I was talking to someone born before the invention of the airplane.

Linemen for the County

While assignments like eulogies and commencement addresses were included in our job description, the bulk of our creative output was devoted to Hope's stage act and the television specials. And when it came to television, our services weren't limited to his own shows. Whenever he was booked on someone else's show, he made sure to request a script well in advance to give us ample opportunity to "punch up" his lines. The standing rule was that we couldn't tamper with the speeches of other performers but were encouraged to submit as many alternate lines for him as we could. If for example, we were asked to punch up a sketch for *The Pat Boone Show* in which Hope is cast as an Indian attending the first Thanksgiving dinner — a perfect example since he actually did this one year — we might come up with the following exchange:

PAT   (as a Pilgrim): What's the matter, Chief? Don't you like
           roast turkey?

HOPE: Turkey fine, but I think I'm sitting on a giblet.

Now as long as we leave Pat's straight line alone, we can conjure up a wide variety of responses, providing that they don't affect the plot:

- White man still finding ways to give Indians the bird.
- Anything with this many feathers we usually marry.
- Chief just bit into part of turkey that jump over teepee last.
- Don't say the word "turkey" to me so soon after my last show.

The problem was that Hope would arrive at the taping armed with his own secret arsenal of punchlines that no one else on the show would hear until he actually delivered them. To make matters worse, he'd try a different line on each retake — a practice that produced panic in directors and had fellow cast members furiously rechecking their scripts.

It was no surprise that there were more than a few variety shows on which Hope was not welcome. Producers tended to resent guests who volunteered their own material rather than that provided. The plain fact was that Hope didn't trust writers who weren't on his own payroll; and from long experience, he knew that the script didn't exist that couldn't be improved. And Hope figured that the more comedic ammunition he could lob at the audience, the more bull's eyes he'd score. He and Bing had done the road pictures this way, and it had proved a winning formula; although Dorothy Lamour admitted years later that she resented the boys allowing their writers to suggest lines between takes. Maybe because she didn't have her own writers.

Dorothy recalled an incident on the set that took place after the cast had broken for lunch, during which Bob and Bing had huddled with their writers for some last-minute script revision. When they resumed shooting, Dorothy said she didn't recognize a word and thought she was in the wrong movie. At this point, according to Dorothy, Bing turned to her — with the camera still rolling — and said, "If you see an opening, Dot, jump in!"

While I missed Hope's feature movie career by five years — his final film, *Cancel My Reservation,* was released in 1972 — in 1986 he co-starred in a movie for television called *A Masterpiece of Murder* with Don Ameche, Jayne Meadows, Stella Stevens, and Anne Francis. Every day

The A-Team (sans Freddy) taken backstage at NBC. (Clockwise left to right) Seaman
Jacobs, Martha Bolton, Gene Perret, me, Jeffrey Barron and what's his name.
Martha was the only woman on the staff. Used to his ol' boy crew, before repeating
some locker room joke he'd heard, Hope would say "Close your ears, Martha," and then
launch into it before she could even take a breath. A Fundamentalist Christian, she
usually was some shade of pink, depending on the raunch level. Martha never
traveled with us since Hope was used to working in his underwear and
sensed that "Leave the room, Martha" wouldn't be a workable solution.

throughout the month-long shooting schedule in Vancouver, we'd receive
pages of the script to comedically enliven. As usual, we did what we were
trained to do — stick in a joke whenever we detected a suitable opening.

Several years later, Jayne Meadows complained to an interviewer that
"Not only didn't [Hope] know his lines, but I always had the impression
that he didn't know what he was saying." The explanation, of course, was
that he was the *only* one who knew what he was saying, thanks to one of
our infamous punch-up jobs.

Ghost Writers In The Sky

Virtually every word that appeared in print attributed to Hope was the product of a comedy assembly line that operated as efficiently as any in Detroit. Every "celebrity quote" that showed up on the feature page of newspapers and magazines — "My favorite joke, place, recipe, etc." — had been plucked from his conveyor belt of tailored witticisms.

Occasionally, we'd be assigned a longer piece such as the essay I wrote for the *Ladies Home Journal* on the occasion of Hope's eightieth birthday in 1983. The article, entitled *The Gift of Laughter*, appeared in the June issue of the magazine's "Last Laughs" page and was illustrated by an Al Hirschfeld caricature. The requirements for such assignments were simple: Make it interesting, fill it with jokes and make it sound like Hope talking to the readers:

> "As I approach my eightieth birthday — eighty is such a
> round number, isn't it? I prefer to think of it as a sixty
> that, like me, has simply put on a few extra pounds."
> Laughter provides that invisible armor we all need to protect
> us from the stresses of life. When you're laughing, it's impossible
> to be angry; those two emotions get along about as well as
> Menachem Begin and an Arab oil minister at an embassy party."

Hope is credited with having authored or co-authored no less than ten books about his life and show business adventures. Except for those that were ghosted ("As told to…") by pros like Carroll Carroll (*I Never Left Home* 1944), Pete Martin (*Have Tux, Will Travel* 1954), Bob Thomas (*The Road to Hollywood* 1977), Dwayne Netland (*Confessions of a Hooker* 1985) Melville Shavelson (*Don't Shoot, It's Only Me!* 1990) and Ward Grant (Ed.) (*Hey, Mr. Prez, I Wanna Tell Ya!* 1996), the books were products of Hope's writers-Print Division.

According to the old-timers I talked to who had churned them out, the process differed little from that used for the television specials — individual chapters were assigned to each writer or team. Hope would edit the material, staple it together and off it would go to the publisher, but not before everyone was issued the challenge of coming up with a catchy title.

My favorite contribution — for what turned out to be his highest earner with profits going to the USO — was the title of a compilation of golf reminiscences he wrote with *Golf Digest* editor, Dwayne Netland: *Confessions of a Hooker*.

May I Borrow A Cup of Punchlines?

Occasionally, our services would be donated to those in need. One day, I got a call from an aide to New York Mayor John Lindsay who said Hope had suggested she call me. Seems hizzoner was scheduled to give a speech somewhere, had run into Hope, and asked if he could impose upon him for a few lines. "Henny Youngman promised the mayor he'd write some, but they weren't suitable," she said.

Thinking I'd get a clue of the type of humor Lindsey didn't care for, I asked, "Like what did Henny write for him?"

"Just a sec," she said. I could hear her rustling papers. "Oh, here they are. Let's see... *A guy goes to the doctor...* "

I was never completely surprised by any request Hope made — punching up grandson Zachary's grammar school valedictory address came close — except on one occasion when he called and said, "I need a few jokes about Pentagon generals. You know, how they spend six hundred dollars for toilet seats — that sort of thing."

I glanced at the schedule that was tacked to my bulletin board. "I don't see any military events this week. Are they giving you another medal or something?"

"Oh, nothing like that," he said. "This afternoon, I'm playing golf with three of them."

It wasn't that Hope was incapable of being extremely funny in real life. He was seldom at a loss for a snappy comeback and enjoyed the give-and-take common among comedy writers. Often, when talking to him, you'd get the feeling you were playing Bing's part in a *Road* picture. Once, when I broke my wrist playing golf, I had the cast put on at the Motion

Picture & Television Hospital in Woodland Hills and went directly to a
meeting at the Hope office. Arriving late, I told him what had happened
and he said, "How do *you* qualify for the Motion Picture Hospital?"

"Why not? I'm in show business," I replied.

He frowned and said, "The jury's still out."

Then he looked at the shorts I was wearing and said, "Does the Red
Cross know about those knees?"

He was a born smartass and related so well to us because most of us
are, too. We just learned how to write it down.

Hope found Fred Fox's speech impediment a wellspring of humor.
He once congratulated him on the recent birth of twins with, "I see you
don't stutter only when you talk."

Once, during a writers meeting, Fred jumped up and began acting
out a sketch idea. "See, Bob, first we g-g-get George Go-go-gobel or may-
may-maybe Mi-mi-mick-ey Roo-roo-rooney and — "

Hope stopped him and said gently, "Fred, don't stand up unless
you're *sure*."

And Hope would laugh just as hard when the joke was on *him*.

I had been on his payroll about ten years, and during contract negotiations one summer, he said, "You know, Bob, I can't pay the writers as
much as I used to."

I said, "Oh? How come?"

He said, "I had to pay *six million* dollars in property taxes last year alone."

I said, "That's criminal. But I've got an idea that could benefit us
both."

"Oh, yeah? How?"

"You know how you pay me by check every week?" He said, "Yeah."

"Well, how about instead of a check, you give me a piece of *Orange
County*."

He chuckled, appreciating my offer to help. But I wasn't finished yet.

"Better yet," I said, "why don't you give me *Orange County*?"

He laughed so hard I think he dropped the phone. And I never heard
another word about his property taxes.

CHAPTER 2

Running Naked Through the Lobby

No matter the theme, location or length of a special, the format that Hope had developed and perfected in radio was as inviolable as the formula for Coca-Cola or McDonald's secret sauce. The show's rundown would invariably look something like this:

- Topical monologue
- Conversation with guest
- Performance by guest
- Sketch featuring Hope and guest
- Hope/guest musical number (when possible)
- "Thank you's" and "goodnights"

The format was simple, consistent, efficient and reliable — and succeeded in keeping the specials at the upper echelon of the Neilsen ratings for over forty years.

Monologuejam

The eight-to-ten-minute topical monologue that began each show was Hope's favorite segment and the one to which he devoted the most care and preparation. He had begun his career as a dancer in vaudeville but one night was asked by a theater owner to emcee when the regular one failed to show up. He enjoyed it and soon began adding jokes to his introductions. He eventually realized that the jokes were his strong suit and abandoned the dancing.

On television, he considered the monologue a hook with which he could snag viewers to keep them from channel surfing during the remainder of the show. Today, talk shows begin with a monologue for the same reason.

On a Hope special, the monologue that the viewer saw was a string of thirty to thirty-five gags — setups followed by punchlines — delivered rapidly. They covered the major news events of the day with particular emphasis on politics, sports, celebrities and pop culture. Though he was born in England, much of the material concerned how Americans lived.

The initial step in building the monologue was choosing the topics. They had to be current and able to remain fresh until the show aired — usually several days following its taping. If an important event was scheduled — a playoff game, say, or the opening of a major movie — we'd write alternate lines covering all eventualities.

We would submit a list of topics from which Hope chose the ten or fifteen he thought had the strongest comic possibilities. Over the next few days, we would churn out ten to twenty lines per topic. Working hours at a time on a monologue took a goodly amount of stamina. I would play a tape of Hope delivering jokes just to get his rhythm, turning on the recorder whenever ideas were slow to come.

After awhile, the jokes would seem to flow automatically as though I was simply writing down what Hope was saying. My wife, Shelley, would hear me chuckling at the keyboard and say, "Laughing at your own jokes again?"

And I'd say, "No. *Hope's.*"

(Not that I never laughed at my own jokes, mind you.)

Hope loved being inundated with lines and we tried not to disappoint. But despite this plethora of material, woe to the scribe who skipped a topic. His phone would ring with an inquisitive comedian at the other end: "What happened? Didn't get my list?"

Of course, the material had to complement the rapid delivery that he had so carefully developed on stage. He leaned toward particular setups, punchlines and a unique cadence that, over the years, became identified with him alone. (Perhaps the reason impressionists seldom attempted to imitate him.)

The monologue might begin with a definition gag that would sound something like this:

> *Hey, it's great to be here in Pasadena. You know what Pasadena is — that's Beverly Hills on Medicare.*

Or, the joke could be in the form of a translation:

> *Here we are in beautiful, tropical Tahiti. Tahiti is an ancient Polynesian word meaning, "Forget the suntan lotion, did you bring the American Express card?"*

The monologue would most likely contain one or two "list jokes" where the final item is the payoff:

> *Here in Las Vegas, if you see a guy running naked through the lobby, he's either a streaker, a loser, or his wife arrived a day early.*

And no monologue was complete without a "that was just" joke:

> *I went to see "Star Wars" and couldn't believe all the weird, alien creatures with purple hair; green, slimy skin; and pods for eyes. And that was just waiting in line to get in.*

Also effective was the "but enough about" setup:

> *This is quite a ship — round-the-clock partying, booze flowing like water, girls hanging from the chandeliers — but enough about the captain's quarters.*

Every word produced by the writers was delivered directly to Hope, which was uncommon in television. On most variety shows, a head writer would review the material and present only what he considered the best of the lot to the star. I had apprenticed on *The Dean Martin Celebrity Roasts* and there, head writer Harry Crane was the final arbiter of all material that appeared on the show.

But Hope wanted to see everything himself, so he never employed a head writer. There could be someone on the crawl with a "Writing Supervised by" credit, but his job was only to make sure that all the material got directly to Hope.

Next, he would go over our submissions, checking off the lines he liked. If he approved a joke, he accepted it "as is" — that is, he never reworded a gag or returned it for a rewrite. Once accepted, the joke would be retyped by his secretary exactly as the writer had submitted it.

The importance of this to a writer cannot be overemphasized. Hope knew from experience that we consider our setups and punchlines nothing short of poetry — each having a distinct structure and rhythm, every word carefully chosen. Adding or deleting even one word, or altering the punctuation, can irrevocably destroy a line. Which is why most experienced comedy writers avoid quoting their own material in press interviews — the possibility of being only slightly misquoted is enormous and the result can be disastrous.

Throughout his career, Hope took pride in his ability as an editor and understood that his talent was in *choosing* rather than rewriting jokes. And he saved every line, storing it in his voluminous joke files for later review. It wasn't uncommon to hear a line he had passed on seasons before crop up in a monologue. To Hope, jokes were currency whose value might not be fully appreciated until later. A line could mature — like a bond.

That's not to say *we* could recycle jokes. Hope's comedic antennae could identify an old line faster than a carnival barker spots a rube. Whenever he suspected someone was sending something through a second time, he'd read the line aloud and say, "This has the distinct odor of nostalgia about it."

Over the next several days, Hope would winnow down the original submissions to a workable 125 to 150 jokes that would be sent to Barney McNulty to print on cards. These were the survivors, the lines the studio audience would hear. At a pace of roughly three to four gags a minute — including laughs and applause — the entire routine would take him thirty to forty-five minutes to deliver.

Following the taping — literally before the applause had died down — he would be in the control room for playback, carefully checking his delivery as well as the audience's reaction to each joke. As he went along, he'd make his picks. From paper to home screen, it was a long, tedious process but one on which he never took any shortcuts. The monologue was his baby, and it had to be just right.

Etch A Sketch

As much a Hope mainstay as the monologue was the sketch, a costumed comedy piece that usually ran eight to twelve minutes on the screen. The sketch could trace its rich theatrical lineage to vaudeville and, before that, to the English music halls, Stratford-on-Avon and the Greek Theater.

It's no surprise that the sketch had achieved such stature in Hope's comedy arsenal. Sketches became popular on early radio because most of the comedians hired to work in the fledgling medium were vaudevillians who had trunks jam-packed with sketches they had performed on stage. That's why to this day, when a comedian delivers old or tired material, he's said to have "gone to the trunk."

A Hope sketch was broadly written, usually a parody of a current movie, television show or a story from the headlines.

Once a show's theme was chosen, we would submit about five single-page sketch ideas. Because of his innate public relations sense, a title alone could sell him on an idea based on how it would look in the show's promotional ads. For a special we were preparing for the Bahamas, I hooked him on an idea with one word: *Nassaublanca*. He thought of a title for a sketch we needed for a special to be taped in Paris. He called me, gave me the title and told me to have everyone work on a story idea that it would fit *The Hunchback of Maitre d'*.

To Hope, the names we gave our specials and sketches were no different from billings — what the public would see and evaluate. He told me how, in vaudeville, he had come to realize the importance of billings. As he worked his way up the ladder from dancer to dancer-emcee to comic-emcee to comic, his name became larger and more prominent on the marquee. Though he still had a way to go to reach household-name status, he was proud of his success every time the letters grew taller. Arriving in a new town, he'd check the marquee on the theater he was playing even before checking into the hotel.

One day, he discovered the manager had misspelled his name! He rushed into the theater, sought out the manager who was adjusting curtains backstage, and said, "I'm Bob Hope, and you have my name spelled wrong on the marquee."

"How did I spell it?" asked the manager.

"*Ben* Hope," said Bob.

The manager went back to what he had been doing and said, "Who'll know?"

(Hope had been sensitive to his billing as far back as 1937 when he starred on Broadway in *Red, Hot and Blue!* with Ethel Merman and Jimmy Durante. Although a relative newcomer compared to his co-stars, he demanded equal billing. Understandably, Ethel and Jim balked, thinking his demand a tad premature. After extensive negotiations, the three agreed to have their names printed in a circle so no one would get top billing!)

Next, we would receive a copy of the approved outline to use as a guide to write a complete, eight-to-twelve-page sketch. The process was another holdover from radio where the writers turned in a complete script for every show. This was unique to Hope. On most variety shows, assignments to write the various segments were spread among the staff. Also, Hope writers worked alone, seldom as a group — as was done on *Your Show of Shows,* Milton Berle's *Texaco Star Theater* and many variety shows. We brainstormed only when coming up with the ideas for sketches and routines, never when writing the segments themselves.

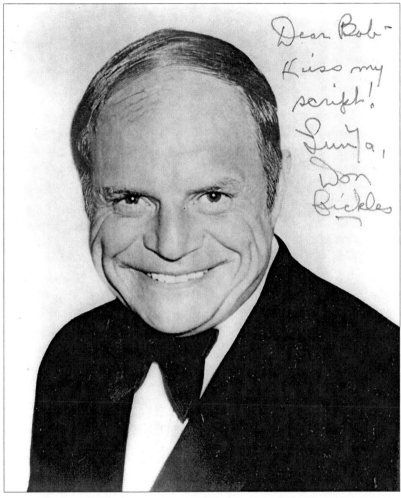

One of the most uniquely talented performers to appear on our show was
"Mr. Warmth" himself, Don Rickles. In a sketch on our Super Bowl show, Hope
and Don — in drag — address the rising cost of Rams' tickets by auditioning for jobs
as cheerleaders. They not only bamboozle the head pom-pommer, Ann Jillian
and assistants Lola Falana and Audrey Landers, but Hope catches the eye of team owner
Merlin Olsen who asks "her" out. In 1999, my wife and I sailed with Don
and his wife, Barbara, to South America aboard the Crystal Harmony. I was
there as a lecturer, and Don took me to task for not inviting him to my
show that included a clip of the cheerleaders sketch. His anger was
feigned, of course — I told him to go have a cookie.

Audrey Landers worked with Hope both on television and on stage,
opening for him as a singer. Best known as Afton Cooper, a role she
played on Dallas for nine years, her salary eventually eclipsed that of clan leader, Larry
Hagman. As a Rams cheerleader, she accuses Hope of being a "hussy"
when she discovers he's landed a date with her boyfriend played by Merlin Olsen.
Audrey told me she enjoyed appearing on Hope specials because it gave her a rare
chance to do comedy. Audrey could sing and act and looked sensational doing both.

The requirements for a Hope sketch were simple. First, there should
be some sort of plot — a barely discernible one was okay, but it had to be
there. Ideally, it should require characters in costume, the most outlandish reserved for Hope himself. Pope Paul II, the Ayatollah Khomaini,
Col. Igor Boris-Morris, former head of the KGB and the Bolshoi Ballet
("I quit when I got tired of all that Bolshoi.") George Washington and a
woman disguised as a cheerleader for the LA Rams (with Don Rickles)
are a few that come to mind.

Everything spoken in the sketch was ideally a setup or a punchline

— we advanced the plot with jokes. Again, in a throwback to radio, Hope considered the spaces between laughs dead air.

With each writer or team delivering eight to twelve pages, pasting a workable sketch together was a formidable task, but Hope took great pride in doing it himself, laying the pages out on his bed and checking off the lines he liked. Usually, the material could be stitched together without visible seams, although once a sketch snuck into the shooting script in which Brooke Shields had *two* entrances!

Those problems aside, the biggest challenge was coming up with a sketch blackout that Hope would accept. The ending, called a "blackout" from vaudeville — where the footlights were actually turned off — shouldn't be that difficult, but is for reasons known only to God and Neil Simon. On every special, Hope's parting words at day's end were "Think of another blackout." Even as the show was being taped, he might drift over to one of us and say, "Have everybody work on another line for me at the end."

When working in Burbank, we usually ate dinner at a landmark restaurant directly across Olive Avenue from NBC called Chadney's. It was one of those reliable, old-fashioned steakhouses with a fireplace, a great bar, a trio playing in the corner, and the best prime rib and scaloni — pressed abalone and scallops — in the San Fernando Valley. When Hope called the union-mandated meal break around five, we'd head across the street to our regular booth which on show weekends was traditionally reserved for us. Often, guest-stars who enjoyed the competitive banter that comedy writers revel in would join the party.

While sampling the eatery's well-known "bottomless" martinis and the best margueritas north of Tijuana, we'd try to come up with replacements for whatever Hope was unhappy with. Whenever we all agreed on something — which would commonly take at least two rounds of adult beverage — we'd jot down our output on cocktail napkins. It became a kind of ritual even though our win-loss record was abysmal.

One night, our creative juices seemed to be flowing faster than the Beefeaters and Jose Cuervo — or so we thought. We rushed back to

Roseanne Barr (shown here with Burt Reynolds) had a remarkable ability to improve scripted material, literally extracting laughs from lines we didn't know were there. She played Maid Marian opposite her (then) husband, Tom Arnold's Robin Hood, displaying a talent for comedy that had distinguished her own top-rated sitcom.

present our brilliance to Hope, now in makeup ready to tape. He shuffled through the notes, let out a sigh, and said, "I wish Chadney's had funnier napkins."

Up Stethoscope!

While on our perpetual quest for the perfect blackout, on rare occasions, one would just land in our creative laps. We were taping a special one year entitled *Bob Hope Salutes the Soaps*. Hope had landed Elizabeth Taylor, known to be addicted to the daytime pot boilers, (Sammy Davis was, too.) and had promised that we'd write her a sketch that would parody her favorite sudser, *General Hospital*.

We set it in an operating room with Hope as a gastroenterologist who's having a torrid affair with his head surgical nurse, Elizabeth. But the randy Florence Nightingale is concurrently scrubbing instruments for a pair of Hope's fellow residents — Anthony Geary (whose marriage to Genie Francis on *General Hospital* had recently made headlines) and movie icon, Glenn Ford.

As the sketch begins, Hope is prepping the patient on the operating table. Liz and an older nurse assist him:

HOPE: (Peeking under sheet) My, my. What a nasty wound.

LIZ: That's his navel.

Morgan Fairchild backstage with Martha Bolton and Jeffrey Barron. Martha was
from Arkansas, was married to a sergeant in the L.A. Police Department and
showed up at just the right time. Considerably younger than most of us,
she brought a softer, more Norman Rockwellian, *Readers Digest* sensibility to
the material that balanced the edgy, smart-alecky tone the old-timers thrived on
and that seemed less and less suitable for a comedian who was, by then, 83.

HOPE: It is? I was never good at navels.

NURSE: Doctor, where's your surgical mask?

HOPE: (Burps) Oh, they gave me a flavored one and I ate it. I wonder what you take for cheesecloth heartburn.

(Liz crosses to the door. Glenn Ford, in surgery togs, is standing there and they hug. Hope cannot see them.)

GLENN: Melanie! Melanie!

(They embrace)

GLENN: I love you!.

LIZ: I love you too, my darling!

GLENN: Then we're going to Acapulco right after the operation!

HOPE: (Busy) Hey, will you turn off that TV! I can't listen to soap operas while I'm operating!

(Intercom:)

VOICE: Calling Dr. Carraway. Calling Dr. Needleson. Calling Dr. Needleson. Calling *Butterfingers*!"

HOPE: (Looks up) Yes?

VOICE: You just lost your patient in 204.

HOPE: Oh, drat. Another funeral I have to attend.

LIZ: (arm around him) Oh, you poor baby.

HOPE: I'm so tired of being stoned by the mourners.

LIZ: Oh, they're sooo mean to you. (kisses him) Your breath smells like wintergreen.

HOPE: That's my surgical mask.

(Tony Geary, in a white smock, emerges from behind a screen. Liz rushes to him and they embrace, again out of Hope's line of sight)

TONY: Are we running off to Acapulco together?

LIZ: You know we are, darling!

TONY: Without a doubt, you are the most beautiful girl in the world.

HOPE: (Busy) Will you please turn off that TV?

           (Intercom:)

VOICE: Dr. Needleson, your patient in 313 has the chills. Please advise.

HOPE: Well, move him in with Miss Fletcher across the hall. She's running a 105 fever.

HOPE: (Steps back) There, that should do it. Through no fault of mine, the operation was a success! (puts down scalpel) You know, we doctors like to get patients back on their feet in a hurry these days. (Pulls back sheet) C'mon, up! Up!

In our original sketch, the "patient" on the table was a bit player with whom, in our story, Liz was also having an affair. During rehearsal, Richard Burton arrived on the set to pick up his wife for lunch. We all looked at him with the same idea. Would he mind lying on the table for a few minutes? We'd write a few lines for him and, since he hadn't been booked on the show, would surprise an audience who had no inkling he was in town. Burton was a big fan of Hope's and a good sport. He agreed and provided us with a blackout the likes of which writers can only dream.

           (The patient sits up. We see that it's Richard Burton. He climbs off the table, takes Liz in his arms and gives her a lengthy embrace — a *very* lengthy embrace.)

As expected, when the audience spotted Richard, there was such a gasp, all at once, the air was sucked out of the studio. When he took Liz in his arms, they whooped and hollered loud enough to be heard in Glendale.

HOPE: Hey, wait a minute! You're stealing my girl! What do you have to say for yourself?

RICHARD: (Shakespearean delivery) 'Tis a far, far better thing that I do than I've ever done before. It is a far, far better rest that I go to than I have ever known. (They start to leave)

HOPE: (grabs Dick) Hey, wait a minute! Where do you think you're going?

LIZ: Well, one thing's for sure. (Looking at each other) It *won't* be Acapulco!

LIZ/DICK: Puerto Vallarta?

(They exit arm-in-arm as Hope and the others look on in disbelief.)

The Stanishopesky Method

While Hope sketches were broad, farcical and in the opinion of some, too silly, he had definite ideas about how he wanted them played. Most of the guests followed his directions to the letter, but once in awhile he'd run into a problem case — one like former model Susan Anton.

Susan was cast on one of our football specials as a scientist hired by the NFL to test the safety of the equipment. Hope answers her want ad for a guinea pig and is put through a series of punishing tests. Susan was going with British actor Dudley Moore at the time, and he was never far away during rehearsal.

During the read-through, Hope had warned Susan not to laugh at her own lines while putting him through the wringer — literally. In one sequence, he's in a stretching "machine" we had designed like a magician's trick. Following our diagram, the prop department built a box with hidden shelves and dummy pants, legs and shoes that would appear to belong to Hope.

But despite his advice, Susan insisted on injecting a series of giggles before, during and after every one of her lines. Bad enough during rehearsal, but later in front of an audience, her giggling if anything, increased. Repeatedly, Hope stopped the taping, called her off to the side and whispered instructions. Then she'd go over to Dudley who'd give her more tips — apparently to keep up the good work.

Finally, Hope surrendered and finished the sketch, hoping that Susan's delivery could be fixed in post. But no amount of editing could save her performance, and we lost a perfectly serviceable eight-minute sketch — not to mention an opportunity to introduce the world to a human-stretching machine that would have made Dick Cheney proud.

Bonfire of the Parodies

Most Bob Hope sketches were takeoffs on popular movies or television shows. In March 1982, I took these photos at the NBC studios in Burbank during the taping of a special entitled *Bob Hope Laughs with the Movie Awards* with guest-stars Lee Marvin, Pat Boone, Ann Jillian and George Burns. We had to use "Movie Awards" in the title even though we meant *Academy* Awards. The latter is a trademark, and we couldn't get permission to use it.

Our first sketch parodied the recent Academy Award winner *Chariots of Fire*. We called our version *Chariots of Ire*.

On the same show, we wrote a sketch parody of the first Oscar winner, *Wings*. In our version, entitled *Thighs,* Lieutenants Hope and Pat Boone are World War I fighter pilots serving in a squadron

Lee Marvin (center with whistle) doesn't seem too impressed with the boys' idea of a training schedule. They're posing here for publicity stills to be used in ads and posters promoting the show. Guest stars were asked to remain in costume for a few extra minutes to accommodate the NBC photographer.

Even posing for the still camera, Marvin demonstrates his superb sense of comic acting just through body language. Remembered now more for his dramatic roles — in my opinion he was underrated as a comic actor — he did win an Oscar for his comic role in *Cat Ballou*.

based outside Paris that's commanded by tough-as-nails Squadron Chief Lee Marvin. Hope and the captain are sweet on the comely flight nurse, Polly, played by Ann Jillian. When Polly continues to display an obvious preference for her ski-nosed lieutenant (She asks him "Where did you ever learn to kiss like that?" and Hope replies, "In civilian life, I blew up blimps for Goodyear."), Captain Marvin decides to increase his odds of winning the fetching Florence Nightingale by sending his competition on a death mission to capture the dreaded German pilot, Baron Von Shtickhoven, better known as "The Red Baron." Of course, complications ensue and Hope not only locates the German ace (George Burns), but befriends him and brings him back to meet his "fiancée" whom Burns, of course, immediately steals. "Come, my dear, and we'll stroll arm-in-arm through the Black Forest!" The two American lads win the war but lose the girl.

I took these shots as our stars were taking their well-earned bows.

Note the authenticity and realism of the movie-quality set. Thanks to a
farsighted contractual arrangement Hope had made with NBC years earlier,
he was getting them at bargain-basement prices. The set for our parody of
Wings was as authentic as the real movie's.

Ann Jillian was a frequent guest in the 70s and 80s. She had been a child star and, as
an adult, saw her hit single "Wind Beneath My Wings" make the top of the
charts. She married her bodyguard, a former policeman.

Protective Custody

Hope went out of his way to treat his guests well and did anything he could to help improve their performance. They, of course, usually welcomed his guidance and suggestions. On the other hand, he could be as protective as a mother bear with cubs if he felt the quality of the show was being threatened.

We were in Fort Lauderdale, Florida taping a special on which Tony Randall was a guest. Tony was by nature genial and gregarious and easily connected with people on a personal level. As we taped each segment over a period of several days, Tony had developed the habit of wandering onto the set in advance to make contact with the audience prior to his performance.

Unfortunately, Tony went beyond the usual behind-the-scenes jokes and "Where are you from?" chatter and began quoting lines from the sketch about to be taped — "Now when I say such and such, you laugh." An audio line to Hope's dressing room was left open, and he overheard Tony's repartee. As soon as he came offstage, Hope was all over him like a baseball manager berates a catcher who's telegraphing the signals.

He was as angry as I'd ever seen him. "Tony, what in the hell are you doing out there? You know better than that! How do you expect us to get laughs if they already know the lines?" Tony, a true gentlemen who had meant no harm, was devastated, his humiliation evident. He apologized and assured Hope that it would never happen again.

But the message was clear. Hope wouldn't hesitate to vent his anger even at a well-known star if he believed the show was being sabotaged, regardless of how innocently.

Before taping a segment, Hope would often emerge to chat with the audience but was careful never to audition the material in the script. When rehearsing the monologue in front of an audience, he'd recite his lines in gibberish. There were no joke previews. So sensitive was he to the possibility of dulling the spontaneous reaction at hearing lines for the first time, he refused to allow them the traditional "audience warm-up," common on all sitcoms taped in front of people. This despite the boredom that sets in when people are asked to remain in their seats for long delays between takes.

Later, I suggested that he play segments already taped so the waiting audience would have something to watch other than technicians making adjustments. He agreed, and that was done for our last five or six seasons.

If Hope wasn't satisfied with a particular performance, you'd know about it — fast. Charlotte Rae, star of a seventies sitcom called *The Facts of Life*, was in a parody of *Dallas,* cast as Miss Ellie. Since Hope watched little television (save for football and golf), he had no idea who the animated Broadway-trained actress was. Delayed at the airport, he had missed the read through, so the dress rehearsal was his first opportunity to appraise his fellow performers. During a break, he came rushing back to his dressing room.

"Who is that playing Miss Ellie?" he asked the producer.

"That's Charlotte Rae. She's a well-known sitcom star."

"Well, tell her to knock off the mugging. She looks like Mickey Rooney."

High praise, indeed, as the Mick is one of Hollywood's legendary scene thieves.

* * * *

Sometimes, a less-than-stellar performance by the usual standards would provide unexpected comedic dividends. There was an actress on the real *Dallas* named Charlene Tilton whom we had as a guest. About five feet tall, she was bubbly and appeared to get a great deal of enjoyment out of life.

We cast Charlene in a parody of the sitcom *Happy Days* opposite Hope as the "Fonz." Like Susan Anton, she consistently telegraphed the laughs, but did so in such a charming and disarming way. Hope realized she brought an additional element of entertainment to the sketch (which, if I recall correctly, it needed). Moreover, when Charlene flubbed a line, she'd break up and go into hysterics, sometimes literally kneeling on the floor.

Whenever Hope sensed he was getting interesting outtakes, he'd tell the director to keep the tape rolling. This was one of those times — in spades. Over the years, he ended up with some priceless flubs and bloop-

Diminutive *Dallas* star Charlene Tilton was discovered by a casting agent selling
T-shirts in a Malibu surf shop. Her role on Dallas gave her scant opportunity
to sharpen her comedic chops, but she made up for it while guesting on one of
our specials, literally rewriting the sketch she appeared in by adding her own,
obviously genuine glee in delivering her lines. Her unique approach won her
appreciation from Hope and extra exposure on *The Tonight Show*.

ers which were used in NBC's promos for the show and on Hope's obligatory *Tonight Show* appearance.

"Save that one for Carson," he'd say.

We got some irreplaceable classics from Miss Tilton.

Jawbone Junction

Unlike monologues and sketches whose family trees were firmly planted
in vaudeville and live theater, the standup, also called a "talk spot," was
strictly a child of radio. And unlike the monologue and the sketch, it

failed to adapt very well to a visual medium. From a writer's standpoint, conversational segments featuring Hope and his guests speaking as themselves limited the scope of the comedy that could be injected into them. They seemed shallow, stilted and phony, but Hope insisted that they be included on every one of his specials. Many of the experienced producers Hope hired, including Ken and Mitzie Welch, Jane Upton Bell, Sheldon Keller and Jim Lipton viewed the spots derisively as "talking-heads" and strongly discouraged them — usually with limited success.

A good many of our guests over the years detested the spots. Richard Burton told me that he was uncomfortable speaking as himself on stage and went along with it only because it was a Hope show. Ditto Tom Selleck who so disliked speaking to an audience of strangers, he insisted that his own show, *Magnum P.I.*, be shot on a closed set. No visitors — unless he *knew* them.

We were in London to tape a special and one day after lunch, Gig and I entered the backstage entrance to the Paladium. As we threaded our way through the darkness, avoiding the ropes, pulleys, sandbags, and other backstage hazards, I could hear a lone voice on the unlit stage in front of the curtain reading lines from our script.

The voice belonged to Richard Burton, and he was experimenting with various inflections — "Yes, Bob... Yes, indeed, Bob... Righto, Bob...". I peeked through the curtain and said, "Dick, you're not actually *rehearsing* that fluff we wrote for you?"

He said in all seriousness, "I am."

I said, "You've probably played King Lear a hundred times on this stage."

And Burton said, "True, but the King never says anything stupid. Richard Burton *often* does."

Hope never seemed to grasp the fact that most actors become actors to hide behind a character. Some of today's leading men won't go near a TV talk show for fear they'll reveal their actual personality which can be nonexistent.

Compounding the built-in static nature of people engaged in conversation, Hope insisted that his guests recite *our* words. We had to imagine what a guest would say, were they amusing in real life. In many cases, this was a tall order.

Guests who actually had a talent for sparkling repartee resented (and with good-reason) the words being forced into their mouths. Jonathan Winters, who can hold his own with anyone, usually solved the problem by ignoring the script entirely. But Jonathan could get away with it. Hey, he's *Jonathan Winters*.

Devoid of anything else to force into the mouth of a guest, we usually resorted to insult lines as in this exchange between Hope and Rhonda Fleming from a 1983 special entitled *Bob Hope's Road to Hollywood:*

RHONDA: Bob, we did *The Great Lover* together right after I'd finished *A Connecticut Yankee* with Bing.

HOPE: Yeah, you came to me to help you salvage your career.

RHONDA: Bing was so charming and sophisticated, he had me walking around in a daze.

HOPE: That wasn't charm. He had Novocain in his makeup.

RHONDA: Now, Robert, there's no reason for bitterness. As a lover, you were completely adequate.

HOPE: And the Rams think *they* took a beating.

Or this bit of verbal jousting with Jill St. John …

HOPE: We had fun making *Eight on the Lam*, didn't we?

JILL: Fantastic. You taught me so much about acting on that picture.

HOPE: Oh, you mean emotion, motivation and technique?

JILL: No. I'd never met an actor who could do a love scene and practice his putting at the same time.

HOPE: Is there a better way to improve my grip?

Though totally scripted, at least these conversations recalled real events from a fascinating era. But such rich topics and legendary stars were exceptions. The challenge was to create entertaining and amusing conversation with little subject matter to work with.

Glee for Two

Another vaudeville-born device we used often was the "comedy duet," where, at several points throughout the number, the performers stopped singing to deliver jokes, usually in the familiar straightline-punchline format. In a 1978 special entitled *A Tribute to the Palace Theater*, our studio had been transformed into a replica of New York's Palace Theater, the Holy Grail of all vaudevillians.

The special was produced by Sheldon Keller, a devoted vaude-affi-

Sheldon Keller goes over a script with Howard Albrecht and Sol Weinstein. The talented trio worked on every Hope special that Keller produced in the 70s and early 80s — and that routinely ranked among Hope's best.

cionado (my word, but descriptive) and the lines throughout the show reflected his distinctive style. His writing partners, Howard Albrecht and Sol Weinstein (a team I had worked with on the *Dean Martin Roasts*), also shared writing credit. The music of this duet performed by Hope and George Burns was written by Sol Weinstein. It's entitled *That's the Way It Was in Vaudeville,* and I consider it a truly remarkable reflection of the spirit of the era it honors.

The set was a small-town railroad depot, circa 1928. The boys wore brown tweed suits and bowler hats. Each had a cane he would use throughout the number. As the gold-ltasseled red velvet curtain rose, they were revealed along with two large steamer-trunks, Hope standing and George sitting. When the music begins, they don their bowlers and move forward to center-stage.

(Music: up)

HOPE/BURNS: *Hat, cane, trunk, train... that's the way it was in vaudeville...* (Softshoe) *Song cue, softshoe, that's the way it was in vaudeville... They loved us in the cities, they loved us in the sticks, we didn't mind the vegetables, but when they threw the bricks...Laughs, frowns, tank towns, that's the way it was in vaudeville...*

BURNS: *Mamaroneck, Saranac, Scranton and Canton...*

HOPE: *Austin and Boston, Racine, yes I mean...*

HOPE/BURNS: *That's the way it was in vaudeville...*

BURNS: *Ashville and Nashville, Nogales and Dallas,*

HOPE: *Detroit and Beloit, Kankakee, don't you see?*

HOPE/BURNS: *That's the way it was in vaudeville.*

HOPE: Vaudeville... what an era.

BURNS: But it wasn't all fun and games. Bob.

HOPE: I know what you mean. Remember some of those small town we had to play?

BURNS: You remember Zyszx, Nevada?

HOPE: Do I remember Zyszx? Just *saying* it used to clear up my sinuses.

BURNS: That town was so small, the trains only stopped there once a week... just to *laugh*.

HOPE: It was so tiny, the electric company was four batteries and a jar of fireflies.

BURNS: But what made vaudeville worthwhile was some of the unusual acts we worked with.

           Like *The Great Maurice*... half-man and half-woman. It was fine until one night he was arrested for making a pass at himself.

HOPE: I remember the case. At the last minute, he dropped the charges. But the most unique act of them all was *Knock-Knees Needleman,* the original one-man-band.

BURNS: Yeah, nobody could follow him.

HOPE: He had a pair of cymbals strapped to his knees, a harmonica in his mouth, base drums on both hips, mallets on his elbows, and if that wasn't enough, he tapped danced on a Wurlitzer to the tune of Tchaikovsky's "Nutcracker Suite."

BURNS: That kid had to belong to about six unions.

HOPE: (ad-lib) That's the longest straight-line I've ever had. But in his prime, the poor guy was struck by a bolt of lightning and died in the key of F.

BURNS: I remember his last request was to be buried dressed in his instruments. And while they were lowering him, a windstorm came up and he played at his own funeral.

HOPE: Where else but in a free America?

           (Music up)

HOPE/BURNS:	*The act was a dilly in Cleveland and Philly... we rocked 'em in Brockton and Troy...What a joy, they went batty in old Cincinnati... They screamed in Moline, Illinois...*
BURNS:	*We had 'em in Chatham...*
HOPE:	*We killed 'em in Wilton. They raved in New Haavden...*
BURNS:	Hold it! Where the hell is New Haav-den?
HOPE:	Somewhere near Conned-id-did-icutt.
HOPE/BURNS:	*That's the way it was in vaude...Listen every son and daughter... Aren't you glad that you have bought a... ticket to a good old vaudeville!*

Sol Weinstein was the most talented song writer I ever worked with. A former jazz disc jockey, he wrote several songs recorded by major artists including "The Curtain Falls," heard for the first time on the *Bobby Darin Show* when Sol and Howard were on his staff in the sixties. Bobby used it to close his act, and it's sung by Kevin Spacey, as Darin, in his 2004 biofilm, *Beyond the Sea.* Hope sang it at the conclusion of *A Tribute to the Palace Theater,* and its lyrics conclude this book.

The comic duet took about an hour-and-a-half to tape. Both men had just returned from long road trips. But since we had the audience already in place for another number, they decided to go out and wing the duet without rehearsing it first.

Several problems were immediately apparent. Since it's an original song and not a familiar standard, it was more difficult to sing. And the words are alliterative — some difficult to pronounce. Also, the routine involved choreography. Singing unfamiliar lyrics while dancing proved to be a killer. And, most important, these guys had been around awhile — they claimed they met while appearing in the lounge on Noah's Ark. At the time, Burns was 83 and Hope was 76.

They had begun the number about three times when Keller told the

George Burns, appeared in many specials during the seventies and eighties. He and Hope even did a personal appearance tour together with Hope, in drag, performing the role of Gracie. Asked once if he would ever retire, George replied, "I've been retired since my first day in show business." He had dropped out of the third grade to form the Pee-Wee Quartet that sang and danced for coins on the street corners of New York.

Like Hope, George had a strong work ethic and remained a star his entire life, rehearsing his act daily (though it hadn't changed in decades) with his longtime pianist Morty Jacobs. George Burns died in 1996 at age 100.

director to keep the tape running even during the flubs. The audience, of course, loved being witnesses to the train wreck. Hope and Burns ad-libbed throughout, ribbing each other while referring to mutual friends they had known in vaudeville.

When Burns drifted off camera, Hope stopped the track and said, "We've got to put a string on him. All at once, I was doing a single." After about ten unsuccessful attempts on the line "The act was a dilly in Cleveland and Philly," George looked at the audience and said, "The act was a dilly? The act was *pathetic*."

The audience roared.

I replay the outtake reel for friends who often ask, "Why didn't you make an entire special out of this?"

With both legends now gone, the tape is priceless.

Cutting Room Floor Sample

On motion pictures and most television shows, post production editing is done by someone other than the director and seldom by the star himself. Working with the director, the producer and a tape editor, Hope guided the fine tuning of his specials with a firm hand, frame by frame, segment by segment. Along with choosing the shots that would appear in the finished show, he also oversaw the *sweetening* process in which canned laughter is added to the sound track.

Contrary to what most viewers believe, sweetening is necessary, not to *add* laughter so much as to smooth out the sound between cuts. In Hope's case, it also involved the removal of excessive applause which, later in his career, audiences felt obliged to insert after almost every joke.

Post production could take up to a week, depending on the length of the show and its complexity. Specials shot in the studio were generally easier to edit than those shot on location where there was less control of sound, light and camera positioning. The editing of *Bob Hope in China* took several weeks.

Editing complete, the show's music would be mixed from pre-recorded tracks and dubbed onto the master tape. Hope oversaw this process as well with his musical director, Bob Alberti. Once the master tape was delivered to the network, it was out of Hope's hands and irretrievably in those of the viewers and the TV critics. Usually.

In July 1969, Neil Armstrong became the first man to set foot on the moon. The eyes of the world were focused on TV screens from Maine to Moscow as Armstrong planted the stars and stripes on the planet's silvery surface and haltingly spoke his momentous words: "One small step for man, one giant leap for mankind."

As Armstrong was shaking the moon dust off of his space boots, at the NBC studios in Burbank, a tape of a Bob Hope special was being beamed by satellite to New York to be aired that night. Hope had taped his monologue the day before, and, while he had referred to the moon shot generally, the landing itself, which NASA had authorized at the last minute, wasn't mentioned.

Immediately, Hope was on the phone to NBC's Engineering — would it be possible to pause the tape during the monologue so that he could insert several jokes *live*? They told him it had never been done, but they felt certain it was technically possible. The writers were put to work on fresh material covering the historic landing. Then Hope reserved a set and assembled his technical crew.

They would have to recreate the stage backdrop and lighting precisely as they looked on the master tape. Hope himself would dress exactly as he was dressed that night and position himself so that when the director cut away during an audience transition shot, he'd appear on camera, insert the new jokes, the tape would resume running and the audience at home would be none the wiser.

Pinpoint timing would be essential. Hope's lines must fit snugly into the hole in the tape created expressly for them. As it had begun, the live insert would conclude with a shot of the audience, which would allow the director leeway of a second or two. The volume level of Hope's voice would have to match the tape's for the ruse to work. And it was not without considerable risk. If anything went wrong, the operation could come off as cheesy and amateurish — and torpedo the entire show.

Luckily, all went as planned and Hope had his updated monologue.

Since every crew member connected with the deception was working on what the craft unions call "golden time" (triple their usual salary), the jokes had to be the most expensive Hope ever delivered — "I'd congratulate the NASA scientists, but I don't speak German."

The process was costly, technically challenging, and, some would argue, entirely unnecessary. Would the audience have faulted Hope for not mentioning the moon landing? Who knows? But the incident illustrates the lengths he would go to ensure that whatever went into America's living rooms bearing his name was the best show that he could produce.

Just the Fax, Ma'am

Hope was interested in new technology even though his knowledge of matters scientific was limited. When facsimile machines first came on the market, we were confident that they would streamline our system of getting material to him on the road. So we decided to use a little drama to introduce him to the new technology. The earliest faxes were installed in hotels for the convenience of their business guests. Ward Grant, Hope's PR man, was the first to put a machine in his office, so we decided to use it to demonstrate their value the next time he called for material.

A few days later, he called me from New York. He was leaving shortly to fly to his next gig in Boston and needed lines on several breaking news stories.

"I'll call you around three your time after I get to the hotel," he said.

Ordinarily, I'd notify the others, and they'd call me back with their lines to deliver to Hope verbally. But this time, we'd deliver our typed pages to Ward's office, and he'd fax them to the hotel in Boston with a request to the desk clerk to deliver them to Hope's room at *precisely* six o'clock.

As always, his call was right on time.

"Have the stuff?" he asked.

"No," I said, "*you* do."

At that moment, I could hear the bellman's knock.

"Hold on, there's someone at the door."

Hope got up, and I could hear the clerk delivering our material.

He returned to the phone. "What *is* this?"

"It's what you ordered, sir."

Well, to say he was dumbfounded would be an understatement. As he leafed through the pages, he was *floored*.

"How did you guys *do* this?"

"Cutting edge technology, Bob. Pretty neat, isn't it?"

He just couldn't believe we could send him pages over a telephone line that looked *exactly* as they did back home.

"How did you get to Boston?" I asked.

"I flew."

"No, you didn't. You sat down in an aluminum tube in New York and got out in Boston. The *plane* did the flying. Do you understand what kept the plane in the air?"

"Well... not really."

"I don't know how a fax works, either — but we're going to *love* it."

CHAPTER 3

Selling Donner and Blitzen to Iran

From the beginning, what set Hope specials apart was his reliance on a unifying theme or topic — a structural device that gave the writers a framework on which to attach the show's various elements. From his first network variety show, a Broadway-style review that aired on Easter Sunday in 1950, Hope specials had covered a broad spectrum of subjects which included a tribute to America's service women in 1952, his fifteenth anniversary with NBC in 1953, highlights from his movie career in 1955, the new TV season in 1965, presidential politics and spy movies in 1968, vaudeville in 1970, the space program in 1971, and TV detectives and the U.S. Bicentennial in 1976.

By the mid-seventies when I came aboard, most of the themes had been pretty well picked over, so beginning with the 1977 season, Hope presented the first in a series of *salutes* — shows that would honor or highlight outstanding people, careers, TV programs, cartoon characters, sporting events, government agencies, and even theaters:

On the Road With Bing (1977)

America Salutes the Queen (1977)

A Tribute to the Palace Theater (1978)

A Salute to the 75th Anniversary of the World Series (1978)

A Salute to the Ohio Theater (1978)

Opening of the Gerald R. Ford Museum (1981)
Stand Up and Cheer for the NFL's 60th Year (1981)
A Pink Panther Thanksgiving Gala (1982)
A Salute to NASA (1983)
A World's Fair Salute (1984)
A Salute to the Soaps (1985)
Hope Salutes the Super Bowl (1988)

If we couldn't salute it, then we looked at it, laughed at it, spoofed it or
lampooned it:
A Comedy Look at TV's Prime-Time Wars (1980)
An All-Star Comedy Look at the New TV Season (1981)
Bob Hope Laughs at the Movie Awards (1982)
A Star-Studded Spoof of the New TV Season (1982)
Bob Hope Lampoons the TV Scene (1986)
Bob Hope Lampoons Show Business (1990)

And if we couldn't salute it, look at it, laugh at it, review it, lampoon it, or
kid it, we did the only thing left — we invited some *all-star* guests (Our
guests were designated *all-stars* whenever possible) — strung up some
streamers, grabbed some confetti and tossed a party:
Bob Hope's All-Star Christmas Comedy Special (1977)
Bob Hope's Merry All-Star Christmas Special (1978)
An All-Star Birthday Party for Bob Hope (1979)
The Bob Hope All-Star Comedy Christmas Special (1980)
An All-Star Birthday Party at West Point (1981)
Bob Hope's All-Star Super Bowl Party (1983)
Bob Hope's All-American Champs (1988)

Though by 1977 he had hit the three-quarter century mark, Hope remained partial to themes that recalled his well-publicized relationships
with former female costars, and we tried to come up with an idea for
one each season. Our motives were partially self-serving, since the shows

relied on clips that generated *residuals*. These specials never varied much but usually posted high Neilsens:

Hope, Women, and Song (1980)

Bob Hope's Funny Valentines (1981)

Spring Fling of Comedy and Glamour (1981)

Women I Love: Beautiful and Funny (1982)

Bob Hope's Road to Hollywood (1983)

Rounding out our roster of specials were programs that featured a story-line in which Hope played himself or a fictional character. Over the years, they had proved to be the least successful of Hope's TV formulas so they were attempted only rarely …

Bob Hope and the Starmakers (1980). Hope stars as Miles Baduc, a down-on-his-luck theatrical agent who becomes romantically involved with one of his clients (Linda Gray) to the consternation of his long-suffering secretary (Bernadette Peters).

Hope for President (1980). At the behest of fans, Hope throws his hat in the ring, but snatches it back when his English birth comes to light.

Hope Buys NBC? (1985). Hope puts a down payment on the pea-cock, but soon concludes that owning a network isn't half as much fun as just taking money from one. (NBC president Brandon Tartikoff played himself.)

NBC Investigates Bob Hope (1987). Spoofing the then ongoing Iran-Contra scandal, Hope faces formal Senate hearings when evidence emerges that he's been secretly selling jokes to NBC's arch enemy, Cable TV.

Almost as important to Hope as a show's theme was its title. He was ever on the lookout for an alliterative, catchy name that would pique the curiosity of readers of *TV Guide*. And length didn't seem to matter as long as the title promised to deliver plenty of fun …

TV's Prime-Time Wars: Will the People Strike Back? (1980)

Bob Hope's All-Star Comedy Look at the New Season:

   It's Still Free and Well Worth It (1981)

Bob Hope's Wicki-Wacky Special From Waikiki (1984)

Hype•ochondria

Show titles were important to Hope's publicity strategy. In the week prior to a show's air date, he'd give scores of telephone interviews to television writers, critics and radio talk-show hosts across the country. Over the decades, he had established strong friendships with many of them, and he knew that he could rely upon them for strong plugs. In return, he was always available to them as a last-minute fill-in guest.

Logging as many as two dozen calls a day, Hope would spend hours giving listeners a preview of the guests, the sketches and even some of the jokes. He'd take call-ins and answer questions on the air. And always, he'd end each conversation with a reminder of the date and time our special was scheduled.

Hope thought that my background as a former lawyer was an interesting angle that might help promote the specials. So he had NBC's publicist send out a detailed bio with photos inviting newspaper columnists to use me as a subject. When requests came in, Hope's publicist, Ken Kantor, would set up phone interviews, scheduling them just prior to a show's air date.

I did eight or ten interviews a season and appeared in papers ranging from the *Washington Post* to the *San Diego Union*, and in magazines like *The American Bar Association Journal* and *Writers Digest*. As it turned out, I was way ahead of my time. Today, you need a law degree from Harvard even to land an *interview* for a writing job on *Saturday Night Live*.

I was always happy to promote the specials, and in the fall of 1978, Hope asked me to help an old friend who had a late-night talk show on the radio in Florida. I thought he meant one of my regular telephone interviews, but this time, instead of working from home, I'd be on the air live from his house in Toluca Lake. To an inveterate ham, it sounded like fun. And I wouldn't have to wear makeup.

When I arrived around quarter of seven (the show would begin at ten in the East), Gig was already there. Hope's buddy, working without an engineer, had patched a telephone hookup to the studio in Miami and had set up the microphones on a small table in Hope's gatehouse. In his

I join Freddie and Gig in the green room at NBC for a rare photo of gag
writers wearing neckties. They had been the standard uniform for writers in
radio, but the practice had long been abandoned by their successors in television.
The picture was taken around 1980.

horn-rimmed glasses and white shirt with rolled-up sleeves, he looked
more like an accountant or an insurance salesman than a radio personality. His gruff New York accent made him sound more like a cab driver
than someone making his living on the radio.

He began the interview, and soon, Gig and I were taking calls from
listeners asking the usual questions about working with Hope. About a
half-hour into the program, Hope came down from the main house and
quietly slipped in through the gatehouse door. He waited until there was
a cutaway for a commercial and said, "Well, how are the boys doing?"

"Great, Bob. I'll introduce you next."

Then Hope turned to us and said, "I see you've met Larry King."

Hope had learned early on a basic tenet of any business — the product is important, but selling it is even more important. And sell he did.

Because of his long association with the network, Hope ran promotional spots during sports events covered on NBC. Throughout the seventies and eighties, it wasn't uncommon to hear announcers like Johnny Miller covering a golf tournament or Merlin Olsen during half-time of a football game drop in a quick plug — "Get ready for laughs tonight at eight Eastern, seven Central as Bob Hope welcomes his guests. . ."

On the Friday night preceding a special, Hope would appear on the *Tonight Show* to promote it. We would provide him with plenty of ad-libs, but Carson obviously took great glee in steering Hope away from the agreed-upon topics. We always felt that Johnny resented the use of his show as a billboard.

Deck the Halls with Peacock Feathers

Taking a cue from Will Rogers, Hope never met a holiday he didn't like. Be it Easter, Thanksgiving, Valentine's, Groundhog Day or the Ides of March, a holiday theme was always as welcome around the production office as a hot buttered rum in a winter snowstorm.

Christmas, of course, was Hope's annual theme champ even during peacetime when his army fatigues were folded away in the cedar chest awaiting the next outbreak of hostilities. Even in the years that he entertained the troops, he usually produced a domestic Christmas special as well and aired the military shows in January.

The Christmas specials had become perennial ratings bonanzas that left high Neilsens in Hope's stocking year after year. Even beyond that, they were television's longest sustaining Yuletide specials, continuing well after Andy Williams, Glen Campbell and Perry Como had packed away the prop fireplace and the flocked Douglas fir.

Whatever mysterious combination of elements made Americans take a break from their last-minute shopping to tune in the mid-December offering, Hope wasn't about to tinker with it. The Christmas show segments were as cast in stone as the Ten Commandments and the format was as predictable as the story of the Nativity itself. Every Yuletide special was made up of these five elements:

- Holiday monologue
- Associated Press All-America Football Team
- Seasonal sketch
- Rose Bowl Queen and Court
- "Silver Bells" duet

Each December, our rhyming dictionaries saw yeoman duty as we struggled to give the headline of the day a *God Rest Ye Merry Gentlemen* spin. Be it Ollie North or a Cabbage Patch doll (strangely similar in many respects), we somehow managed to capture them in a couplet:

> *It's Christmas time once again*
> *But have fun while you can*
> *We just got word that Ollie North*
> *Sold Donner and Blitzen to Iran (1988)*

> *It's Christmas time around the world*
> *A season that's merry to all*
> *But this would be the best one yet*
> *If I could just find a Cabbage Patch doll (1983)*

Next in order came reminders of how the holidays were being celebrated in Southern California, with particular emphasis on the tract housing adjoining Rodeo Drive:

> *They try to have a traditional Christmas in Beverly Hills, but it isn't easy. Yesterday, I saw Santa behind the wheel of a Rolls-Royce being pulled by eight Japanese gardeners. (1978)*

Then we'd make our mandatory stop on Hollywood Boulevard:

> *The fellas celebrate Christmas a little different. Down there, they decorate each other. (1985)*

Today, we'd be picketed by gay rights groups.

Though Santa wasn't due to arrive for another week or two, we had the welcome mat out for him …

> *We're having a typical Hollywood Christmas. Yesterday, Larry Flynt announced that he has secret tapes of Santa doing weird things with the elves. (1983)*

During the Holiday Season, the writers were not unlike elves, battling a deadline to meet our quota of gift-wrapped shopping jokes:

> *A big seller this year is the 'Baby Tears' doll. I asked the sales clerk, 'What makes it cry?' And she said, 'Nothing, but when I tell you the price, you will.'" (1981)*

> *And with all the crowds this year, I've never seen the sales people so nasty. I saw one floorwalker who got rid of his carnation and was wearing a Venus fly trap. (1978)*

And no Christmas would be complete without several reminders of the seductive aroma of turkey and pigskin that would soon waft through most American homes:

> *This holiday season, they're combining the Peach Bowl, the Orange Bowl and the Sugar Bowl. It'll be called the Diabetes Bowl." (1986)*

Dad ∘ Lad

If we had a musical guest on the billboard, we'd try putting a Yuletide spin on a comedy duet as in this segment with Andy Williams. In it, Andy is Hope's pop dispensing fatherly advice. Hope is dressed in a Little Lord Fauntleroy outfit with a huge red tie. (Does that say Christmas or what?)

> (Music: up)

ANDY: *Small fry, struttin' by the pool room...Small fry, should be in the the school room...You'd best change your ways, you hear...Or Santa's gonna pass you by this year...*

ANDY: Let me look at you, Son. (looks) Ugh. I told the doctor when you were born, he was slapping the wrong end. Son, I think it's time that we had a man-to-man talk.

HOPE: Oh, you mean about the birds and the bees?

ANDY: Exactly.

HOPE: I'd be glad to, Dad. What is it you don't understand? (Music: up)

ANDY: *Small fry, watchin' television... Small fry, without my supervision...My, my, the things that you have seen...make* Playboy *look like* Parents Magazine.

HOPE: Tell me, Daddy, were you and Mommy happy when I arrived?'

ANDY: We were delighted.

HOPE: You mean that?

ANDY: Of course. You were cute. You were cuddly. And we needed a *deduction.*

HOPE: Daddy, then how come I'm your only child?

ANDY: For the same reason no one ever bought *two* Edsels.

The day this number was shot, Andy was delayed at the airport so Hope asked me to stand in for him at rehearsal. When Andy arrived, I told him excitedly, "I stood in for you. I think you'll really like this spot."

Andy just looked at me and said, "Then why don't *you* do it?" Stars really know how to deflate someone's balloon.

Jock Shock

Each year, the Associated Press sports writers voted for their college dream team, and Hope would fly the winners to Burbank — at considerable expense, I might add — from all over the country. Their segment was taped in front of a simulated stadium backdrop made of heavy-gauge cardboard that must have dated back to Hope's Pepsodent days — the bit originated as the *Look Magazine All-Americans* in the fifties. It was faded and frayed, but in keeping with Hope's unwillingness to change anything, it was dragged out year after year.

The material we wrote — using voluminous background information on each player sent by his school — was as raggedy as the set as each player would trot out in full uniform and announce his name, college, and position. Then Hope would deliver a joke befitting the guy's size, speed, kicking or passing ability:

PLAYER: Dee Hardison, University of North Carolina, defensive
            tackle.

HOPE: At school, they call Dee "Peanut." That's because when
            he gets through with you, you're shelled, salted and
            stuffed into a jar of Skippy.

This continued until all thirty-two players had been introduced. Occasionally, we'd give a player a sassy remark that would top Hope's. By comedy standards, the spot was static and repetitious, but nonetheless was guaranteed a full eight minutes on every Christmas special we wrote.

As with all sketches, the problem each year was coming up with an ending that wouldn't look like the one we'd used in years past. Hope's favorite was some variation of this:

HOPE: Now, men, you need to realize that the game of football
            requires complete dedication. You must concentrate
            only on the game... focus on the task at hand... don't let
            anything — (A gorgeous girl dressed in a red bikini and
            a Santa hat crosses the stage seductively. The guys spot
            her and follow her off, paying no attention to Hope)

HOPE: (to audience) Are these guys All-American, or what?

My favorite recollection of this segment was the year that a center named William "The Refrigerator" Perry was on the squad. After Hope had delivered his *bon mot* on the appliance's prowess-in-a-crouch, William turned to leave, and the camera caught the portion of his hind-quarter more commonly associated with plumbers. The audience laughter lasted about as long as it took wardrobe to locate the human Frigidaire a larger pair of pants.

Rosebuddies

As comedically uninspired as the football segment was, it was *Your Show of Shows* compared to Hope's interview of the Pasadena Rose Queen who annually showed up on stage with her entire eight-member court. Ranking among our most dreaded assignments, it forced us to do something that went against our very nature and training — think *bland*.

It was difficult enough to dream up amusing repartee between Hope and a starlet, or a politician, or even an astronaut, but it was torture trying to come up with jokes for a *rich high-school kid*. (The royalty was chosen from tony institutions in Pasadena or La Cañada.) After covering her love of horses, dream of becoming a brain surgeon, or her collection of porcelain elephants, we never failed to have the Tiara-ed-one play straight to Hope's self-deprecating AARP-ster in an exchange like this:

QUEEN: Gee, Mr. Hope, you look so young for your age. How do you do it?

HOPE: Well, I attribute it to clean living, a sensible diet, and a makeup man who wants to see his children again.

Or, "a makeup man who has a summer home in Lourdes." We had a drawer full of these responses.

But no amount of pleading — and, believe me, we begged — could persuade Hope to drop the Rose Queen segment. Most likely because it unabashedly hyped the Rose Parade which NBC covered each New Year's Day. Like I should complain. Because of NBC's tie-in with the Rose Bowl Game, Hope received free tickets on the 50-yard line each year. As long as I was on the staff, we never missed one.

Ironically, I am still involved in Rosemania. Each New Year's Day I co-host a live broadcast from the Rose Parade in Pasadena. The three-hour audio description reaches fifty-one radio stations for the blind via NPR satellite. Staffed by volunteers, the program is heard by 2.7 million listeners and is streamed live online at 8-11 A.M., PDT at www.larrs.org.

Further irony — until I began broadcasting it in 2006, I had never seen the parade except on television.

And, before you ask, I don't interview the Rose Queen.

Hearth Invader

The year George Lucas propelled *Star Wars* across America's movie screens, we couldn't pass up an opportunity to spoof it. Our version, entitled *Scar Wars*, starred Olivia Newton-John as Princess Hialeah, Perry Como as Luke Sleepwalker, and Hope as Barf Vader. The epic would recount the abduction of Santa Claus, complete with his sled and reindeer, literally gobbled up by Vader's space vehicle. (We ordered a small model of a space ship with a set of iron jaws in the front from the prop department.)

The Princess learns of the kidnapping and million-dollar ransom demand at Space Police Headquarters by phone — "If you speed, we can clock it, 'cuz we have a cop in an unmarked rocket!" Her deputy, Luke, challenges Barf to show up in person to collect the money. Hope says, "You'll never catch me, you cosmic creeps!" Perry says, "That's easy for you to say ten million miles away, but you'd never say it to my face!"

> (Hope, dressed in a sinister-looking black leotard with a cape and wearing a Darth-like mask, crashes through the wall.)

HOPE: Sorry I'm late. The traffic was nose cone-to-nose cone!

(Music up: "You're the Top")

HOPE: *I'm the pits!*
          I'm an Edi A-meanie!
          I'm the pits!
          I am cold linguini!
          I'm a lunar louse,

Who will tear your house to bits!
'Cuz, baby, I'm Barf Vader!
I'm the pits!

(He turns his back to the camera, and we see printed across his cape: *HONK IF YOU LOVE ROTTEN.*)

Princess Hialeah introduces her sister, the grossly obese Princess Gluttonia, who waddles over to Perry and attempts to kiss him. Perry sings: *It's impossible, to get my arms around you, it's impossible...* (Can you believe the depths to which we would stoop to collect *ASCAP* royalties?)

Following some swordplay with our version of light sabers called *Life Savers*, and the announcement by Barf that he now has an even more powerful weapon than *The Force*, called the credit card force (Did we run out of gas on this one or not?), the festivities conclude with the arrival of the real Luke Skywalker, Mark Hamill, accompanied by some burly, uniformed Los Angeles cops. They cuff Barf and lead him off.

"What's the charge?" asks Hope.

"Public defacement of a marvelous movie!" says Hamill.

After watching this sketch, *we* were on the verge of calling Hope's lawyers to bail us out of jail; but luckily, Mark was only kidding and the cops were extras. But why take a chance?

Just a year later, Hope would emcee the fiftieth Academy Awards presentation at the Dorothy Chandler Pavilion (on which we got writing credit). Standing beside Fred Astaire, Jack Nicholson, Natalie Wood, Kirk Douglas, Greer Garson, Joan Fontaine, Barbara Stanwyck and William Holden, Hope delivered this opening line:

"Welcome to the *real* Star Wars."

* * * *

Perry Como hosted *The Kraft Music Hall* from 1959 to 1967 and had posted some high chart stats with hits like "Catch a Falling Star," "Papa

Loves Mambo," "Don't Let the Stars Get in Your Eyes" and "It's Impossible." Perry was a laid-back former barber, who like Dean Martin, spent most of his time on the golf course.

Also like Dean, he loved singing but didn't care to get overly involved with other elements of his show— like rehearsing. (Dean actually preferred to study a tape of Greg Garrison, his producer, rehearsing in his place!)

Perry's musical director, Ray Charles (who was nicknamed "the Sighted One") told me that Perry was loath to rehearse the comedy bits on his show and would wing it, just reading his lines so he could get back on the tenth tee. But, said Charles, it never seemed to matter. Perry would read his lines straight and became adept in sketches since that's just the delivery they require.

I learned what Ray meant while working with Perry on our *Scar Wars* sketch. During dress rehearsal, he drifted over to me, impressive in his Luke Sleepwalker costume and holding his light saber which he was about to use to try to decapitate Barf Vader. He whispered as though a little embarrassed, "Bob, can I ask you a question?"

I said "Sure, Perry," thinking he was having a problem with a line — although he had seemed confident reading Barney's cards.

Sheepishly, he said, "I've been out on the course a lot lately and may have missed something. Is this sketch based on a *movie?*"

Later, in his standup spot with Hope, he would give us this classic outtake for our blooper special:

HOPE: And now it's my pleasure to introduce a real novelty —
            an Italian who sings. Ladies and gentlemen, Perry Como!
            (Music: "Come Along With Me")

PERRY: Thank you, Robert. But for your information, all Italians
            don't sing, you know.

HOPE: Really?

PERRY: How about a guy like — no — (starts over) All Italians
            don't sing, you know — how about Sophia Loren?

Guests John Forsythe and Morgan Fairchild join Hope backstage while taping a
Christmas special in the mid-eighties. John, who was best known at the time as
"Charlie" on *Charlie's Angels*, was a regular. Once, when Hope repeatedly forgot
the melody while singing a number with him, Brooke Shields and Catherine
Boch, John said, "Why don't we sing 'Thanks for the Memory?'"

HOPE: You doing a monologue? I thought I had a line in there
               someplace. (Perry laughs) And you did it *twice*. You do
               your own retakes, or what?

By this point, Perry was laughing so hard, he was holding on to Hope for
support. The clip made it onto our blooper reel and has replayed on the
air several times. Perry was a kind, gentle, sweet man.

Clattering Antlers

Our major challenge each year was coming up with fresh ideas for
sketches that wouldn't recall chestnuts from the past. Of course, Santa
sketches were always sure bets, but before sticking a red suit and beard on
Hope, we had to make sure we had a new spin as in this 1985 outing in

Bob Hope with Seaman "Si" Jacobs, a talented speaker who once brought down
the house at a Pacific Pioneer Broadcaster's roast of Art Gilmore who had been
Red Skelton's announcer when he was on the show. When his turn came, Si
stood up and said, "What can you say about Art Gilmore? I can't say
anything. I never *met* the man." And sat down.

which Angie Dickinson — in her role as *Police Woman* — arrests him on
suspicion of burglary:

HOPE: (spotting plate near tree): Ummm, my favorite —
            prune-flavored Ding Dongs.

ANGIE: (surprising him, with gun): Okay, fat boy, drop your
            Ding Dong!

And don't think Hope didn't have to dance around the Yule Log with
the censors to save that one. For our 1980 show, we dipped him in
plastic and cast him as a department store mannequin opposite former
M*A*S*H nurse, Loretta Swit. The store has closed at day's end, and they
realize they're alone:

LORETTA: Have you ever been married?

HOPE: Almost. Once. We were modeling in bathroom supplies. She was the Liquid Plumber Girl, and I was the Tidy Bowl Man. We were meant for each other.

LORETTA: What happened?

HOPE: I guess it all went down the drain.

In 1983, we stuffed Hope with excelsior and cast him as a Cabbage Patch doll who had been kidnapped by a pair of desperadoes played by John Forsythe and Catherine Bach:

CATHERINE: (examining Hope): This one looks like they ran out of parts and had to fake it.

JOHN: I almost missed him. He was rolled up in a little ball in the bottom of the reject bin.

CATHERINE: That explains all those wrinkles.

Yule Chimes

Hope had introduced the classic "Silver Bells," the Jay Livingston and Ray Evans classic, in the movie *The Lemon Drop Kid* and he sang it on every Christmas special — in a different setting — with duet mates ranging from Olivia Newton-John, Katherine Crosby, Loretta Swit, Bonnie Franklin and Melissa Manchester to Winona Judd, Reba McEntire, Dolly Parton, Marie Osmond and — whenever the featured female guest was tone deaf — his wife, Dolores.

This holiday format held Hope in good stead for over forty years, and, despite the onset of his declining health in the early nineties, NBC continued airing some sort of Hope Christmas special until 1994 when he took down the holly and the mistletoe for the final time, leaving no doubt that he had become an integral part of Christmas for millions of Americans.

CHAPTER 4

Nancy Uses Caviar Helper

On the eighty-five specials between 1977 and 1992, the occupant of the Oval Office enjoyed more monologue exposure than any other single topic, save maybe celebrity scandals or taxes. Scarcely a one was delivered without several references — more commonly four or five — to the chief executive, his family, his trips, his state visitors, and his ongoing hand-to-hand combat with Congress. As in this line referring to a congressman's affair with an underqualified secretary:

> *President Carter hasn't been able to get anything past Congress, but it's not his fault. They've been so ornery over there ever since their secretaries had to learn to type.*

The Carter Years (1976–80)

When I joined the writing staff, Jimmy Carter had been holding the lease on 1600 Pennsylvania Avenue for a little over a year, and while he had managed to defuse hot spots in the Middle East, he was saddled with his very own domestic time-bomb that ticked throughout his term and threatened to go off at any time — most often without notice. Brother Billy was a nightmare for a president, but a dream-come-true for comedy writers.

*The biggest problem at the White House right now is Billy's
mouth, and they're really getting desperate. Yesterday, they
hired Mr. Whipple to come in and stuff it with Charmin.*

Billy owned a small garage and gas station in Plains, Georgia — the Carters' home town — that for a short time doubled as headquarters for his
first and only plunge into the distilled spirits business.

*How about brother Billy starting his own beer company? He
did his brother one better. He figured out a way to spread gas
without going into politics.*

Later, as soon as it was reported that Billy was being treated for alcohol-
ism, Hope put a hold on the Billy jokes and never delivered one again. It
was a dream topic while it lasted.

Early in 1978, the Carters journeyed to Europe, India and the Middle East on a whirlwind, week-long tour.

*They're really trying to make Mr. Carter feel at home. In
Poland, they served him grits and Keilbasa. In India, he got
curried grits. In France, it was grits a l'orange. And in Iran, he
was served grits in oil — 30 weight.*

You could be sure Hope never ordered entrees like these. His "meat and
potatoes" preferences ran toward grilled lamb chops, string beans and
apple pie a la mode. His favorite restaurant was North Hollywood's In-
N-Out Burger.

Later that year, Jimmy Carter the captured world headlines by ar-
ranging, hosting and acting as official referee at a summit meeting between Egypt's Anwar Sadat and Israel's Menachem Begin at the presidential retreat, Camp David.

*Mr. Carter actually got Sadat and Begin to sit down together
at Camp David. In fact, the meeting was so successful, now
he's thinking of sending Congress to camp.*

Unfortunately, the resulting peace treaty was short-lived when the parties realized that the devil was in the details.

> Mr. Carter is in Egypt trying to keep Sadat and Begin from hitting each other with their Nobel Peace Prizes.

A longer-lasting presidential accomplishment was Carter's formal recognition of Peking and the millions of Chinese we had been pretending weren't there.

> Premier Teng told Carter that during his visit, he'd like to see our Great Wall, and Carter said, "Fine. Congress just went back into session."

Christmas in the Carter household unfailingly provided us plenty of colorful and unique Yuletide references.

> Brother Billy will play Santa again this year, and I hope he gets it right this time. Last year, he climbed down the chimney and hid eggs in the White House lawn.

Nineteen seventy-nine had barely gotten underway when the Russians decided to turn Afghanistan into their own version of Vietnam, again giving Hope's writers some battlefield experience.

> When the president called Brezhnev on the hotline for an explanation, Brezhnev said, "You'll have to speak louder— I'm in a tank!"

U.S.-Soviet relations were strained even further when Carter decided to boycott the 1980 Olympic games being held in Moscow.

> Boy, that took a lot of guts. Without the Olympic Games, this country will have to face the future without Wheaties.

Back home, domestic problems continued to dog the Carter administration with a burgeoning national debt becoming more unwieldy by the minute.

*Mr. Carter predicts a year of economic misery ahead. I told
my wife, Dolores, we'd have to tighten our belts and she said,
"Good. Tomorrow I'll go down to Gucci and buy one."*

As it turned out, Carter's biggest problem was the threat of unemploy-
ment — *his*. The November election loomed large on the political ho-
rizon, and for awhile he hid out, conserving his political strength, but
ultimately he had to mix it up with the Gipper.

*Hey, did you watch the debate between Carter and Reagan or,
as it was otherwise known, Ultrabrite versus Brylcreme?*

But the election's outcome was never in doubt. The voters were ready for
"Morning in America."

*Talk about Santa arriving early. Ronald Reagan woke up one
morning and found the whole country stuffed in his stocking.*

The Reagan Years (1980–88)

In January, Hope would journey to the capital with a contingent of right-
leaning Tinseltowners (including Tom Selleck, Charlton Heston, Linda
Carter and Jimmy Stewart) to celebrate Ronnie's overwhelming victory.

*Why not an actor in the White House? LBJ was a rancher,
Jimmy Carter was a farmer. I think it'll be refreshing to have
someone in the Oval Office who's not handy with fertilizer.*

But the Reagans barely had time to unpack when the former 20-mule
team cowpoke caught John Hinckley's real-life bullet. As soon as it was
certain that he was out of danger, we demonstrated that it's possible to
put a fun spin on a deadly serious topic.

*Can you believe all the jokes Reagan's been cracking since the
shooting? The latest theory is that the bullet passed through
Henny Youngman.*

While Jimmy Carter had recognized Red China, Nancy Reagan knew chipped, out-of-style china when she saw it.

> *Nancy paid a thousand dollars a setting for new dinnerware. She had to. It hadn't been replaced since Ike, and it was getting embarrassing serving state dinners in mess kits.*

Maybe it fell somewhat short of Milan, but fashion was back in the capital.

> *Nancy has expensive tastes, but I think it was her parents' fault. When she was a baby, they'd tickle her on the chin and say "Gucci, Gucci, Gucci."*

I wish I had the advertising revenue our free plugs were worth to *Gucci, Neiman Marcus, Bloomingdale's, Oscar de la Renta, Halston, Yves Saint Laurent, Chanel, Tiffany* and *Cartier* during Nancy's reign as first lady. Think the FCC would grant me an exemption?

During his film career, Ronnie had seen many a film's budget skyrocket, so he had to be used to the grim predictions emanating from the office of his budget director, David Stockman.

> *Reagan gave away lots of money during his visit to Latin America. He told the leaders down there, "Here, fix your economy and if it works — let me know what you did."*

Then Stockman turned on his master and, in a speech, revealed the flaws in Reagan's so-called "Trickle-Down Theory," an economic blueprint he had helped to formulate.

> *I don't know what the Reagans will be having for Thanksgiving this year, but after David Stockman's speech, I know one thing he'd rather stuff than a turkey.*

But Reagan had yet another panacea for the nation's growing financial woes.

> *Reagan's New Federalism is his way of saying to the states, "I'm going to the men's room. If the check comes while I'm gone — pay it."*

All this while waging an ongoing war with a Democratic-controlled House of Representatives.

> *Mr. Reagan sent in his tax return this year, and it came back*
> *with corrections in Tip O'Neill's handwriting.*

A spring visit to the colonies by Britain's Queen Elizabeth provided the Reagans their first opportunity to show off a film couple's version of Hollywood-style pomp and circumstance.

> *Queen Elizabeth stopped by the Reagans' ranch during her*
> *visit, and there was some confusion about bowing, which I*
> *thought was ridiculous. I know Nancy, and she doesn't care if*
> *the Queen bows or not.*

Hope was fascinated by the royal practice of bowing and ring-kissing. He once admitted to kissing Danny Thomas's ring — and added, "I just wish he didn't carry it in his back pocket."

Rising costs, lower wages and general economic chaos were not unknown in the corridors of the White House — or so the First Family would have had us believe.

> *Reagan's cutting back to give a good example to the nation.*
> *This morning, he left for Camp David on Greyhound One.*
>
> *And at the next state dinner, Nancy is using Caviar Helper."*

Reagan's age wasn't the issue it would become sixteen years later for Bob Dole, and later yet for John McCain. But Reagan did turn seventy-two while in office.

> *The president has finally been outfitted with a hearing aid. I*
> *was relieved. When I first saw it, I thought he was bugged.*

Like Reagan, Hope was both hard-of-hearing and his eyesight was failing. But that's where the comparison ceased. Hope believed that hearing aids and eyeglasses were sure signs of aging. Barney McNulty pleaded with him to wear glasses so he could print smaller and use fewer cue cards, but Hope would have none of it. I said to him one time, trying to convince him that age had nothing to do with it, "I've been wearing glasses since I was sixteen."

He looked at me in my glasses and said, "I rest my case."

But with his new hearing aid, Reagan had a volume control he could use to turn down the din coming from Fritz Mondale, Gary Hart and Jesse Jackson as he prepared to face his bid for reelection in 1984.

> *Reagan says if he's not reelected, he'll return to acting. Boy, if that's not a surefire way to get votes, what is?*

Following a U.S.-Soviet Union summit meeting in Reykjavik, Iceland, Reagan stopped off in Anchorage, Alaska and ran into an old pal at the airport. The pope didn't have to worry about getting re-elected, but Reagan did.

> *The two leaders exchanged gifts. The pontiff gave Reagan a holy card with a picture of Mother Teresa, and Reagan gave him an absentee ballot.*

Exchanging gifts was a favorite Hope topic whenever world leaders met. When Gerald Ford met with the pope, "The pope gave him a holy card with a picture of Mother Teresa, and he gave the pope a win button." The joke worked for coins, too. In Australia, he said, "I gave the cabbie three pence, a farthing and a haypenny; and for change he gave me two shillings, a cap from a bottle of Swan Lager and a photo of Phyllis Diller in a bikini."

Fritz Mondale and running-mate Geraldine Ferraro spent most of the campaign looking for the beef; and on Election Day, the votes seemed to be missing, too. With no help from the William Morris Agency, Reagan's option was picked up for another four years of foreign policy headaches and Pennsylvania Avenue Christmases.

> *The Reagans have a beautiful Christmas display on the White House lawn designed by Justice Sandra Day O'Conner. It's their first Nativity scene with three wise women.*

Doug Gamble (the one on the right), a political speech writer as well as a freelance Hope gag man, wrote Reagan's line referring to Fritz Mondale: "I refuse to make age an issue in this campaign by pointing out my opponent's youth and inexperience." The line was credited with helping Ronnie win the election. Later, working for Bush I, he wrote "Read my lips" which may have cost Bush a second term. But all things considered, .500 is a pretty good batting average for any gag writer.

Not until he was out of office would Reagan command million-dollar speaker's fees, but early in his second term he was making solid financial arrangements for his retirement.

> *When he was told that Jimmy Carter got only a million dollars for his memoirs, Reagan said, "Hey, if he wants to work for peanuts, that's his problem."*

By this time, Ronnie had developed a close relationship with conservative British Prime Minister Margaret Thatcher that would last well after both were turned out to pasture.

> *They have a lot in common. They're both conservatives, she still refers to the U.S. as "'The Colonies," and he still remembers when they were.*

The Reagans were about to spend their first Christmas with a cover-up scandal that pointed due north—-directly toward Ollie.

> *Ronnie and Nancy looked out the window this morning and thought they spotted the three Wise Men, but it just turned out to be another Iran-Contra investigating committee.*

The scandal deepened daily, accompanied by repeated denials, and after a long campaign reportedly engineered by the first lady, White House Chief-of-Staff Donald Regan was given the presidential heave-ho.

> *This Easter, the kids found all the eggs in about five minutes because the White House gardener had cut the grass too short. But that's understandable. Don Regan has only had the job for a few weeks.*

Meanwhile, in the Soviet Union, Mikhail Gorbachev was emerging as a new style Communist-Bloc leader — handsome, well-dressed and possessed of a Kremlin first — a wife who could hold her own in *Vogue Magazine*. Naturally, the Reagans were captivated by the Iron Curtain's mirror image of themselves, and before long, Ronnie and Gorby were exchanging nuke intel between toasts.

*Gorby asked Reagan how Star Wars was coming along, and
Reagan said "I think the Joan Collins divorce is almost final."*

During the Ford administration, the president along with his press secretary, Ron Nessen, had appeared on *Saturday Night Live* to mixed reviews, some political analysts claiming that Chevy Chase's depiction of Ford as a clumsy oaf tripping over his own feet did nothing to enhance Ford's image with the voters. But in politics, memories are short, so the practice of picking up a little free exposure on prime time was back in style.

Vice-President Bush chose to appear on Miami Vice *because
he heard that the actors get to attend wild parties and date
beautiful women. You really can't blame him. It's been years
since he's been in Congress.*

All across the nation, the problem of drug abuse was beginning to exact a heavy toll, and Nancy latched onto the issue as the customary "first-lady good cause." She dubbed her campaign "Just Say No," and Ronnie was one of the first volunteers to be tested.

*I won't say where the president left his sample, but he had to
finish up the jelly beans first.*

Reagan found himself with an empty seat on the Supreme Court, but was having as much trouble filling it as George Bush would four years later when he'd try to convince Congress that Clarence Thomas was a Thurgood Marshall clone.

Reagan's first failed nominee was Robert Bork, a Draconian federal judge whose conservative legal arguments made Torquemada look like Clarence Darrow.

His next attempt fared no better. David Ginsberg came up "tilt!" after Senate investigators discovered that in college, he'd sampled some happy weed and *had* inhaled. All of this prompted Hope to open his 1987 Christmas show with this couplet:

Reagan hopes his Christmas wish

Will come true any minute
He wants his empty Supreme Court seat
To have a fanny in it

Soon thereafter, Santa delivered Anthony Kennedy, a judge whose squeaky-clean credentials made Tiny Tim look like the Son of Sam.

Reagan has nominated Anthony Kennedy to the Supreme Court. Did you ever think you'd hear Reagan saying nice things about a Kennedy?

But Reagan's eight-year run of top billing at the Oval Office was drawing to a close, and his hand-picked successor, George H. W. Bush, was anxious to take over for the star. Actually, one has to wonder how firmly during his final term Reagan's hand was guiding the ship of state.

Jack Lemmon told us a story. While visiting Washington, he received a personal invitation from Reagan to have lunch in the family quarters. Jack was astounded since he and his wife, Felicia, were well known as card-carrying Democrats. Nonetheless, they spent the better part an afternoon with the Reagans, and Jack noticed that not once was the commander-in-chief approached or interrupted by any member of his staff — no phone calls or emergency messages.

As the four reminisced about the golden days of Hollywood, Jack described the experience as slightly surreal, not to mention unsettling. It was as though the world's problems had suddenly ceased to exist. "It made us wonder," said Jack, "who was running the country."

The only obstacle standing between Bush and the Oval Office was a diminutive former Massachusetts governor of Greek descent with a penchant for piloting tanks.

So far, Bush is having problems figuring out Dukakis's campaign strategy. He said, "It's all Greek to me."

Along with Dukakis, Bush was also fighting a wimpy image he had acquired as Reagan's gofer-in-waiting. A more macho spin on his Eastern seaboard privileged youth as the son of Ambassador Prescott Bush was needed.

> *Bush is trying to sound more like one of the guys. He just hired a New York cab driver as a diction coach.*

Bush's choice of a running-mate didn't help much, either. Dan Quayle, an obscure senator from Indiana whose privileged background matched Bush's, had the look of a Boy Scout still collecting merit badges.

> *He's only forty-one. I have golf balls older than that. I don't know where he's been, but last month, more people spotted Elvis.*

The Bush Years (1988–92)

The Bush-Quayle ticket proved victorious on Election Day with a little help from Willie Horton, a convicted murderer whom Bush accused Dukakis of furloughing from prison, allowing Horton to rape and commit armed robbery again. The controversial campaign commercial was the brainchild of Roger Ailes who would later inflict Fox News on the TV-viewing public.

We would miss the Reagans who seldom let us down when it came to producing joke fodder, but we would get to take one parting shot.

> *Following Bush's inaugural ball, the Reagans headed for California. At least that's what it said on the side of their U-Haul trailer.*

From day one, Bush proved to be a whirlwind of activity. When not flying to meet with foreign leaders (he'd later regurgitate on the Japanese prime minister), he could be found working up a sweat playing horseshoes, getting in a round of speed golf (18 holes in an hour and a half) or terrorizing the staid Kennebunkporters in his ocean-going speedboat.

> *Did you see that picture of Bush in the paper piloting his speedboat? I didn't know Barbara could row that fast.*

Having witnessed Reagan's two Supreme Court misfires, George was determined that his first nominee would be so bland and colorless, people would think he wasn't there. Judge David Souter, a lifelong bachelor who lived with his mother and read a lot, fit the requirements to tee.

> *David Souter was so proud to be nominated, he told reporters he felt five feet tall.*

> *Of course, the FBI has been investigating his past life, and, so far, they haven't turned up any evidence that he had one.*

Souter was confirmed without objection, but the following year, Bush would nominate a federal judge with a somewhat less than stellar legal record — he was rated "unqualified" by the American Bar Association — Clarence Thomas, whose confirmation hearing would have Americans glued to their TV sets.

The term "sexual harassment" crept into the national consciousness as Thomas's former law clerk, Anita Hill, tried to block the nomination of the sharecropper's son from Pinpoint, Georgia, but failed by a hair's breath.

Republican Sen. Arlen Spector would later admit that he'd been duped into approving Thomas, which he termed "the biggest mistake" of his political career. As of this printing, Clarence has yet to *speak* from the bench during oral arguments. Maybe that's not part of the job description.

But despite his nomination woes, things looked rosy for Bush. For a while, it seemed as if "Operation Desert Storm" would mean "Operation Second Term."

> *Every time one of Saddam Hussein's Scuds went up in flames, George Bush went up in the polls.*

Ironically, the exact *opposite* would be the fate of George's son some sixteen years later. Who would have guessed?

But somewhere between the sand dunes and the voting booth, Americans became distracted by an ex-governor of Arkansas who didn't know "Stormin' Norman" from a Florida hurricane, and the Bushes would spend their final Christmas surrounded by thirty grandchildren.

> *At the White House Christmas party, there's never been so much pushing, shoving and screaming to meet Santa. Barbara Bush finally had to step in and tell Dan Quayle he'd have to wait in line like everyone else.*

Thus ended Hope's parade of presidents. He would refer to the Clintons on several of his farewell specials, but his Oval Office barbs had dulled, and the jokes had lost their bite.

Hope's presidential jousting had begun with F.D.R. (*The only thing we have to fear... is your act.*) and spanned an incredible nine administrations, a remarkable achievement by any standard. Since the founding of the republic, no humorist had mined so much laughter from the foibles of her leaders over such an extensive chunk of her history. It's a record that Hope could rest assured would never be broken.

CHAPTER 5

Put Another Shrimp on the Barbie, Mate!

Though one immediately identifies Hope with a packed suitcase, aside from his overseas USO Christmas tours, until 1977 he had taped specials in foreign settings only three times — in London in 1951, Moscow in 1958 and Montreal in 1976.

You couldn't blame him for preferring the convenience of producing his TV specials close to home. He lived only a stone's throw from the studio he had designed when NBC moved from Vine Street in Hollywood to the sprawling Burbank complex in the early fifties. He'd been living in nearby Toluca Lake since 1947 when he bought a two-story Tudor, at the time one of only a few exclusive homes nestled among acres of orange and walnut groves. Today, a forest of high-rises that includes the Disney headquarters, MCA and Universal dwarfs the estate on Moorpark Street.

So convenient was the arrangement, Hope never had to use the NBC commissary — a major health benefit right there — commute to the studio or even visit NBC's makeup department. On tape days, his longtime makeup man, Don Marando, would apply the powder and pancake in a small dressing-room beside Hope's second-floor bedroom.

A common sight in those days was the freshly made-up Hope pulling into the parking lot at NBC in his gold Chrysler New Yorker — his sponsor at the time gifted him with a new one every three years or so —

with sheets of Kleenex waving in the breeze above his collar as he rushed to the soundstage. Not until well into his eighties when he was unable to persuade the DMV to renew his driver's license, did he employ a chauffeur. Most of his life, he drove himself everywhere.

The convenience factor meant a lot to him. He was gone most of the time on his personal appearance tours, and a show produced in Burbank allowed him to oversee production by phone with a trusted group of NBC staffers and tech people he had carefully assembled over the years. For the writers, meetings with Hope were few, and when they did occur, were on-the-run affairs somehow sandwiched into his schedule. Taping dates had to be set with great care to insure that he'd be in town at the assigned times.

Also important to Hope, studio-emanating shows were cheaper to produce and more profitable when licensed to NBC. (NBC never owned Hope's specials but purchased a license to air them on a specified date. And, once the show aired, he rarely allowed reruns.)

Eventually, however, shows produced in the same studio acquire a certain cookie-cutter look that no amount of creative set designing can disguise. For a weekly variety series, this sense of familiarity could be an advantage as it was for the entire run of *The Ed Sullivan Show* and Milton Berle's *Texaco Star Theater*.

But Hope specials had been airing regularly, averaging eight-to-twelve hours per year, for close to a quarter-century, and they had become, not surprisingly, not very special anymore. So at the behest of Texaco, with whom he had signed a new three-year contract, he agreed to take the show on the road, warming up with a journey to London for 1977's *America Salutes the Queen*.

Returning home with symptoms of travel bug-itis, he immediately laid plans to take the show to the land Down Under — Australia. He put the two-hour special in the hands of an experienced, Australian-born producer named Chris Bearde — again, bowing to his sponsor, Texaco, who preferred he hire separate producers for each special.

The critically acclaimed tour which included stops in Auckland, New

Zealand; Sydney; Adelaide; Brisbane; Melbourne and Perth would prove to be a major turning point for the *Bob Hope Show*, which suddenly acquired wings and could turn up at just about any spot on the globe.

Over the next decade, we kept our passports current for trips to England for *Bob Hope at the Palladium: A Lifetime of Laughter* in 1979, and for 1985's *Bob Hope's Happy Birthday Homecoming: A Royal London Gala*. Then we were off to Stockholm in 1986 for *Bob Hope's Royal Command Performance from Sweden, Bob Hope's Tropical Comedy Special from Tahiti* in 1987, *Bob Hope's Christmas Show from the Persian Gulf* in 1988, *Bob Hope's Easter Vacation in the Bahamas* in 1989, *Bob Hope's Road to the Berlin Wall & Moscow* in 1990, *Bob Hope's 1990 Christmas Show from Bermuda*, and 1991's *Bob Hope's Christmas Cheer from Saudi Arabia*.

Stateside remotes would include *Bob Hope Salutes the Ohio Jubilee in Columbus* in 1978; *Bob Hope on Campus* which took us to colleges all across the country in 1979; *Bob Hope's Birthday Party at the Air Force Academy* in 1980 from Colorado Springs; 1981's *Bob Hope's Celebration Opening the Gerald R. Ford Museum & Library* from Grand Rapids, Michigan; *Bob Hope's All-Star Birthday Party at West Point* also in 1981; *Bob Hope's Stars Over Texas* from Austin in 1982; and *All Hands on Deck: Bob Hope's Birthday Party at Annapolis* that same year.

In 1983, yet another college tour took us back to the campus for *Bob Hope Goes to College*. 1984's *Bob Hope's Christmas in Beirut* had us packing the fatigues. Then it was off to Honolulu for *Bob Hope's Wicki-Wacky Special from Waikiki* later in 1984, and again in that same year, *Bob Hope's Super Birthday: A World's Fair Salute* from New Orleans. *Bob Hope's Salute to General Doolittle* took us to San Diego in 1986.

In 1988, we packed our bags for *Bob Hope's Christmas Show: A Snow Job in Florida* from Ft. Lauderdale and kept them packed for *Bob Hope's Christmas Show From Waikoloa, Hawaii* in 1989, dusting off our sombreros for *Ole! Bob Hope's Spring Fling of Comedy and Music from Acapulco* in 1990.

And, as difficult as this is to believe today, I was never the victim of lost luggage!

But as important as Australia was, it was only a warm-up for Hope's most ambitious — and expensive — with production costs of $1.7 million — tour of the People's Republic of China the following year.

Waltzing Matilda

At our production meeting with Chris Bearde, we decided to attack the land of the boomerang on two fronts — the main portion of the show would be taped at the just-completed, 8,300-seat Perth Entertainment Center on the far western coast of the continent. On his way there, Hope would detour to perform monologues at each satellite city along the way.

Using the same process he had successfully developed for the overseas Christmas tours, Hope made sure that the writers were well-provided with background information on each city he would visit. Gig, Charlie

Here's Chris Bearde with Barbara Eden minutes after we touched down in Perth. Chris had flown to Australia a week before to set up our production facilities and coordinate with our Aussie tech crew. As Writers Guild members, Gig and I had to apply for a waiver from the Australian Writers Guild. Whenever we worked in a foreign country, we complied with local guild rules — except, of course, in China.

Florence Henderson had come a long way since being discovered by Jack Paar who had her on frequently when he hosted *The Tonight Show*. And if you have to spend twenty-three hours on a 747, you can't wish for a better seatmate than Florence.

and I would share writing chores with Bearde and a friend he'd worked with on a few previous shows, David Letterman. Dave was and still is a member of the Writers Guild of America (he paid his writers during the Guild strike in 2007), and that year needed a writing assignment to keep his Guild health insurance current. Having Dave onboard wasn't unusual. Our regular crew was often joined by writers who were brought in by the producers.

Our flight from Los Angeles to Perth would take twenty-three hours, and on board our Quantas 747 were guest stars Barbara Eden, Florence Henderson and Charo as well as twenty Hope staffers that included Les Brown's musical arranger, Bob Alberti , makeup man Don Marando and Hope's longtime cue card wizard, Barney McNulty. Eighteen hours after lifting off at LAX, we touched down in Sydney for a two-hour refueling stop before completing the five-hour hop to Perth.

The Aussies' welcome was as warm as the water of the half-mile wide Swan River that flows through the pristine city's center. *I Dream of Jeannie* and *The Brady Bunch* were still in their first runs on Australian TV, so

Barbara and I are in front of the Parmelia Hotel which sits on a hill overlooking the city. Their typical Aussie hospitality would make our two-week stay truly memorable. Perth is a favorite city among Australia's wealthy retirees, and it's easy to see why. Barbara, by the way, lived in a bottle only on her show.

from the moment they stepped off the plane, Barbara and Florence were stalked by screaming, autograph-seeking fans.

A Shark in Jockey Shorts

Armed with one of the longest monologues he'd ever deliver, and with 8,300 Aussie fans cheering wildly, Hope strode on stage dressed in a crisp, beige linen suit.

> *I can't tell you how happy I am to be here in Perth, the most isolated city on earth. Now I know why you didn't send a man to the moon — you're on it.*

With the city barely visible through the morning mist — Perth was smog-free in 1978 —
Florence Henderson models her "Bob Hope in Australia" T-shirt. The Brady mom was
as popular Down Under as she was back home. *The Brady Bunch* was still in its first run.

Perth is strategically located — between nowhere and nothing.

Even for a seasoned air traveler, the flight to Perth had been tedious.

*It's such a long flight from Los Angeles, by the time we got here,
I was starting to look like my passport picture.*

*I love to fly, but I have a terrible fear of being hijacked to a
country where they never heard of me.*

That line was strangely prophetic. A little over a year later, along with
his wife, Dolores, Gig and me, Hope would carry his own luggage from
a China Airlines 707 that had just touched down at the Peking Airport.

Thanks to a welcoming committee that had been delayed, one of the most recognizable faces in the world would belong to just another visiting American.

> *And Perth has to be the friendliest city in the world. Yesterday,*
> *I saw two lobsters propositioning a kangaroo.*

Perched on the far western edge of Australia's vast Outback, the city is a demarcation point between that dusty red desert and the Indian Ocean and supports enough indigenous wildlife to keep Crocodile Dundee in business indefinitely.

> *And you have such clean air here. My lungs aren't used to it.*
> *This morning, they got up two hours before I did.*

Chuck Gouert (left) was an account executive with Benton & Bowles, the ad agency representing Texaco. Here, he's reviewing the script with Hope and Chris during dress rehearsal. Texaco's guidance and influence in the production of Hope's specials improved their quality for the remainder of his career on television.

The water here is so clear, I hear the shark from Jaws *has to swim all the way to New Guinea just to change his shorts. Is that right?*

Great Whites call the Indian Ocean home, so any reference to Peter Benchley's heart-stopping classic was sure to draw a tremendous reaction.

And there's no air or water pollution in Perth. Where have you gone wrong?

Considered one of the most desirable areas in Australia, the city of Perth looks like what one imagines — someone my age anyway — Los Angeles must have been like in the twenties.

I can't tell you how happy I am to be standing here on the stage of the biggest theater in the world, with eighty-three-hundred seats. The last twelve rows are in Indonesia.

Though maybe not as far away as Jakarta, the uppermost rows were a good 300 feet from the stage which meant that, for our sketches to be seen and understood by the entire audience, we'd have to use simple sets and readily identifiable props.

These audiences are great, but Australians drink so much beer, you're talking to more people in the aisles than in the seats.

No, I love the beer here. One sip and you don't feel old anymore. Two sips and you don't feel anything anymore.

These were not exaggerations. Down under, beer is the oil of industry. Our rooms at the posh Parmelia Hotel were equipped with small refrigerators in which daily appeared two complimentary quarts of Swan Lager, an Aussie favorite. Like clockwork, at around nine, in would pop a jaunty bellman who'd grab a bottle and ask, "Can I uncork one for you, mate?" To decline would have been ungracious toward our hosts. Wouldn't it?

I've never seen so many beautiful girls. Perth wasn't only the first city the astronauts saw from space — it was the first one they looked for.

And the beaches here are so safe. The life guards give every girl mouth-to-mouth resuscitation — whether she needs it or not.

Aside from its gorgeous women, Australia boasts the best-trained life-guards in the world. While shooting segments for the show on the beach, crack teams of them could be seen drilling nearby, racing through the surf in longboats. Matching the Aussies' love of the water is a great respect for its power.

Of course, Hope wasn't about to spend two weeks in a foreign land without his sticks.

I love your golf courses. Yesterday, I had a great caddie. He was carrying my clubs in a pouch.

On the third hole, my ball was okay, but my caddie took a bad hop.

But it worked out great. He could run faster than I could hit.

Passport Photo Finish

Following the monologue, we set the stage for our obligatory customs sketch — always surefire in a foreign country — featuring Hope, Barbara and Florence as themselves confronted by an ultra-suspicious customs officer (Charo).

	(Up on busy airport lobby)
ANNOUNCER:	"Will the Bob Hope party please report to Customs?")
	(Barbara Eden and Florence enter the arrival area and move toward a long table with a sign reading: AUSTRALIAN CUSTOMS.)
BARBARA:	What's taking Bob so long? I'd sure like to get to the hotel.

FLORENCE: It takes time to organize a spontaneous demonstration.

BARBARA: I think I saw him signing autographs. It's ten dollars an autograph.

FLORENCE: He gets ten dollars an autograph?

BARBARA: Oh, no. He *pays* it.

(Hope enters dressed in an Australian safari outfit: bush jacket, shorts, long stockings and a hat with the brim turned up on one side as is the Australian custom)

HOPE: Okay, mates, billy me bloke, let's go pick up a cobber and a jackeroo and catch us a dinkem boomerang, huh!

FLORENCE: Bob, what are you saying?

HOPE: I don't know, but five stewardesses thought it was hilarious.

This is a classic gag formula that appeared in many Hope sketches. We called it the "I don't know, but... " setup. In a sketch at the Air Force Academy, Hope enters and says "Cadet Hope reporting as ordered, sir! Flaps up, wheels down, zeroes at eleven o'clock, coming in on a wing and a prayer, bombs away, A-OK, roger, over and out!"

Loni Anderson asks, "What does all that mean?"

Hope says "I have no idea, but it sure made a star out of Jimmy Stewart."

BARBARA: Are you sure it wasn't your legs?

HOPE: Owww, there's so much jealousy in this business. (bangs on table) How about some service here!

BARBARA: Oh, look, he's doing his David Niven impression.

HOPE: Now let me do the talking. I know how to handle these

Australian accents. (calls out) What say in there, cob-
bers? How about some service!

(Charo enters dressed as a customs officer: short shorts,
white blouse with the buttons unfastened. She looks gorgeous)

Charo had been discovered at age sixteen by band leader Xavier Cougat.
Her drop-dead Spanish beauty coupled with an accent that tended to
pummel the English language into submission, had insured many return
visits to *The Merv Griffin Show*, where she became well-known to viewers
— most of whom were stunned when learning for the first time that she
played classical Spanish guitar like she'd been raised by Andre Segovia.
Charo was a Hope favorite and would appear on our *World Series* special
later this same year.

CHARO: What's going on out here? (to Hope) What are you,
           a hooligan? I am Inspector Charo. I will inspect your
           bags, look in your socks, feel in your shoes, open your
           shirt...

HOPE: Keep going. I may stay at the airport.

CHARO: What is your nationality?

HOPE: I'm an American.

CHARO: You can't be American. You don't talk like me.

HOPE: Who does?

CHARO: I must fill out this form. Please indicate the province,
           state, kingdom, territory, principality or protectorate
           from which the applicant originally immigrated. (deep
           breath)

HOPE: Could you read that again?

CHARO: What's the matter, you don't understand my inflec-
           tions?

BARBARA: That's just the problem. He can't take his eyes off of them.

FLORENCE: Bob, tell her where you were born or we'll be here all day.

HOPE: I was born in England. Here's my birth certificate. (hands it to her)

CHARO: (looks at it) Wow! It's not every day you see something signed by Queen Victoria!

HOPE: Isn't that incredible? She was dead forty years at the time.

Interestingly, it was just about this time that we began using Hope's advancing years as a joke topic. Previously, he'd been sensitive on the subject, but now that he'd reached seventy-five, it seemed silly to keep pretending he was sixty. While age would never become the driving force in Hope's routines as it would for George Burns, more frequent references to it would find their way into our scripts.

CHARO: Now I must examine your passport.

HOPE: Here you are, darling. (hands it to her)

CHARO: (looks at it) This is a very good likeness.

BARBARA: It should be. It's by Michelangelo.

HOPE: Wouldn't you help a starving art student who needed the work?

CHARO: This says your occupation is comedian.

HOPE: That's right.

FLORENCE: I hope the Aussies don't have a law against falsifying official documents.

CHARO: I must examine your luggage. Please place your suitcase here on the table.

(Hope tries to lift the bag and it doesn't budge. He tries two hands with no success.)

HOPE: Some wise guy nailed it to the floor!

FLORENCE: Bob, stand aside. (She easily places the suitcase on the table)

HOPE: Sure, it's easy when you've been on all those vacations with the Brady Bunch.

There were unique problems in staging a show in such a large venue. The microphones were strung on long surf-rods so they'd be *under* the audience's line of sight and director Dick McDonough had a total of seven cameras — three is the standard studio setup — perched at strategic locations throughout the auditorium.

CHARO: (opens bag, removes jar): What's this?

HOPE: Wrinkle cream.

CHARO: (with tube): And this?

HOPE: My mascara.

CHARO: (with bottle): This?

HOPE: Grecian Formula.

FLORENCE: (to Charo): Keep going. There's more of him in there than there is out here!

HOPE: How would you like to be attacked by my "Waterpik?"

The items removed from Hope's bag were small, but they were quickly identified so they would be instantly understood by the entire audience. Otherwise, to get laughs, the objects had to be large enough to be *seen* by everyone, like these:

CHARO: (removes an orange life-preserver) This?

HOPE: Don't pull that string! (She does and it inflates. On the back is printed: HELP!)

BARBARA:	He's been carrying that with him ever since he saw *Jaws*.
CHARO:	(removes a bra with three size EEE cups)
HOPE:	(to audience) I'm warning you guys. Never date anyone in the cast of *Star Wars*!

The sketch concluded with Charo discovering a live girl hidden in Hope's steamer trunk whom he explains is his tennis instructor. As they stroll off together, Charo decides she'd better accompany them "to make sure there's no 'coochie coochie'." Aside from the all-too-obvious blackout, the sketch worked pretty well considering the obstacles we had to overcome.

The real problem would come in post-production. Remember those seven cameras? Dick McDonough was getting such good shots, he had the cameramen keep rolling even when they weren't on the air monitor, thinking the extra footage would make editing easier. But Australian television uses a different format than is standard in the U.S. — there are more lines on the screen so the picture is much sharper. All the extra footage had to be transferred at considerable expense. When told how much, Hope could be heard as far away as Fiji.

For writers who would travel with Hope in the future, the Australia show set a precedent. The first night after Hope had arrived in Perth, Gig and I were meeting with him in his suite going over material. About a quarter to ten, Hope stood up and asked, "Bob, isn't it getting close to your bedtime?" I agreed and he said, "Well, do this stuff in the morning and leave it in my box." Gig looked like he'd been struck by a Great White. We said our goodnights and headed for our quarters.

Gig still didn't believe we'd been turned loose. "What was that all about?" I explained the promise Hope had made never to keep me up past ten. He said, "You mean you just *refused* to work late?" "That was it." Then he told me that whenever writers traveled with Hope in the past, he routinely kept them up until midnight or beyond. Next day, he'd sleep through the morning while the writers had to keep normal hours. Remarkably, no one had ever complained. Gig couldn't believe that all it had taken to break Hope's habit was someone to say, "I'm going to bed."

During our month-long visit to China the following year, the new procedure would be a lifesaver. Starting with Australia, being on the road with Hope was fun — no writer would ever again have to work without enough sleep.

Baby kangaroos are called "joeys." Florence immediately adopted this one and named him "Joey Brady." I think his dad was the one who caddied for Hope. Females can choose when a joey will be born and are able to nurse three of them simultaneously — which is probably why Mrs. Brady felt a certain kinship.

Tie Me Kangaroo Down, Sport!

A few miles outside Perth, between the western border of the Outback and the Indian Ocean, there's a wildlife sanctuary devoted to the care, feeding, raising and study of the most prolific and well-known animal indigenous to Australia, the red kangaroo. Since the long-tailed, pouched marsupial had been responsible for so many laughs in Hope's monologue, we felt the least we could do was take a day off to visit some real ones.

Tiny Bubbles

We put Hope and Florence in a real rowboat on the Swan River and provided them with some comedy dialogue to go along with their duet of "Cruisin' Down the River." For numbers like this, the music is pre-recorded so the per-

Don Marando thinks he did this guy's makeup when he was an extra on *Mutual of Omaha's Wild Kingdom*. But if he's thinking of adopting, he'll need a long leash — a fully-grown kangaroo can jump twenty-five feet or more.' Roos are so prolific, anyone driving in the Outback must have a heavy metal kangaroo guard bolted on the front bumper.

Don and Florence are ready for the long flight home. The only question is: "Does Quantas allow a carry-on that carries his own carry-on?" But check-in should be a snap. Now they can jump ahead in line — but they'd better hurry before the little guy finds Mom and asks for his old room back.

formers can lip-synch the lyrics. The dialogue was on cue cards held aloft on the shore by Barney and his assistants.

The problem was that neither Florence nor Hope, both nearsighted, could make them out. Barney tried larger lettering. Still no luck. In desperation, he decided to hold the cards above his head while walking in chest-high water just out of camera range and ahead of the rope pulling the boat just below the waterline. He took three or four steps and promptly submerged more quickly than Humphrey Bogart in *The African Queen*.

The following day, Perth's morning paper featured huge, front-page photos of one of Hollywood's most experienced cue-card men going down for the third time, his cards floating aimlessly like rectangular lily pads toward the Indian Ocean. It was an incident the affable Irishman — whose sister, by the way, played Blondie in the movies under her stage name Penny Singleton — would never be allowed to forget. At least not as long as Hope was around to remind him.

The two men had a close relationship that went back thirty years. Barney had started as a teenage page at CBS in New York. One day during a rehearsal of the *Ed Wynn Show*, Ed came over to him and said, "I'm having trouble remembering my lines. Could you run over to Woolworth's and buy me some cards to print them on?" (This was a common complaint of radio veterans transplanted to television where they had no scripts to read.) Barney ran across Times Square, picked up some Bristol board, india ink and broad-tipped pens and ran back to the studio and into a career he'd spend the rest of his life pursuing.

Barney had been with Hope since World War II, and over the years, the service he named "Ad Libs," handled cue cards for scores of variety shows, sitcoms and dramas, including *Murder, She Wrote*; *M*A*S*H*; *Cheers*; *NYPD Blue*; *The Rockford Files*; and *Hart to Hart*. He worked in movies, too, including *It's a Mad, Mad, Mad, Mad World* and the *Grumpy Old Men* films with Jack Lemmon and Walter Matthau. Barney became such a fixture on the backlots of Hollywood, he was welcomed through the front gate at every studio with a wave and a smile.

Hope and Florence arrive bright and early, eager to get aboard and launch their romantic voyage. Conditions on the Swan River are ideal as they review the comedy duet they'll perform while the cameras, strategically positioned on shore, are rolling. Barney plans to hold the cue cards ahead of the boat just out of camera range.

"All ashore that's going ashore!" The passengers board and take their positions. A tow rope has been attached to the dinghy's bow that will be used to pull it forward during the number. There's a short delay when Hope decides to flip a coin to determine who rows. Florence suggests they arm wrestle. She wins.

Florence laughs when she sees Barney disappear. Hope, who can't see Barney in the water behind him, asks what she's laughing at. Not wanting to spoil the take, she says, "Something just struck me funny." Hope says, "Don't stop. You may be the only one." The photos of Barney's dive in the paper next day constituted the only time he ever pushed Hope off the front page.

Didgeridoo What You Do Do Do So Well

Before reaching the land down under, Hope made a quick pit stop in the land *under* the land down under — New Zealand. His first monologue of the tour would be delivered to a crowd of 2,000 Aucklanders.

> *I'm happy to be in New Zealand I hear has more sheep than people. I believe it. When I got off the plane, all I heard was one, loud "baaaaaa."*
>
> *I've never seen so many sheep. I feel like I'm visiting next year's Christmas sweater.*
>
> *This is the time of year all the sheep are fleeced. Back home, we call it "April 15th."*
>
> *New Zealand is the land of the Kiwi, a bird that doesn't fly and lays an egg bigger than itself. I feel a certain closeness to the Kiwi bird. I can't fly either, and I often lay an egg bigger than myself.*

His next stop was Australia's capital, Sydney, often called the New York of Australia, where he delivered his monologue at the Hordern Pavilion in the heart of downtown.

> *I was last here in 1944, and here I am again. You can't fight popular demand.*
>
> *I thought it was safe to come back. Anyone who still remembers me is too old to do anything about it.*

The Sydney Opera House, now recognizable by most everyone — it looks like five nuns' hats stuck in the ground — had just been completed.

> *Last night, we went to your wonderful new Opera House and saw the death scene from Camille. That wasn't the performance, that was just a guy trying to find a place to park.*
>
> *I think I know the architect. Wasn't he in* One Flew Over the Cuckoo's Nest?

*And I hear it went a hundred-and-twenty million dollars over
budget. Are you sure my wife had nothing to do with this?*

At the time, the Hopes were building an $8 million hilltop mansion near
Palm Springs so he knew whereof he spoke.

Adelaide's Apollo Stadium was Hope's third stop en route to Perth.
While most Aussies are of Irish extraction, the majority of Adelaide's pop-
ulation trace their ancestry to Germany. Founded in 1836, it's Australia's
key wine-producing region.

*What a reception I got at your airport! People cheering and
whistling. Then my wig fell off, and they realized I wasn't
Olivia Newton-John.*

*I never realized that Adelaide had so many German settlers
until I saw a kangaroo driving a Mercedes.*

No, I love Adelaide. I've never been to this part of Berlin before.

On Australia's far eastern-coast near the Coral Sea lies the city of Brisbane
among whose unique features are homes built on stilts to protect them
from the dangerous flash-floods that occur during the monsoon season.

*I fit right in here. With my legs, now you've got something else
on stilts.*

The region had recently gone through an endless, economy-threatening
dry spell that had defied all efforts to end it. They received world-wide
publicity when, as a last-resort, they invited religious leaders from all over
the country to take a crack at divine-intervention. They got even more
publicity when it worked.

*I just found out how you brought an end to the recent drought,
and, if you have a minute, could you pray for my monologue?*

*And your hospitality has been overwhelming. Since I arrived,
I've received thousands of phone calls and offers. That's because*

> *I'm handsome, urbane, witty, and also because I managed to smuggle in five-hundred copies of* Playboy.

Brisbane had recently enacted an ordinance that prohibited sending or receiving the magazine through the mail. In a country where nude beaches are as common as coral reefs, the Bible-thumpers somehow still make their presence felt.

Next, Hope touched down in Melbourne, a city more conservative than Fox News. Next to a Melbournian, Pat Robertson is a member of the A.C.L.U.

> *Melbourne is Australia's most conservative city. And I mean conservative. The first three times we flew over it, it was closed.*
>
> *I've heard of rolling up the sidewalks early, but last night they did it while I was standing on it.*
>
> *They have a country club here that's so exclusive, they won't even consider you for membership until you've been dead for ten years.*
>
> *Melbournians consider themselves so superior, whenever anyone dies in Melbourne, they say he defected to Sydney.*

Daddy Warbucks

In the weeks before we arrived, a five-year-old-girl from Melbourne that the press had nicknamed "Mouse" had been getting lots of play on Aussie radio singing a song called "Tell Me a Story." A disc jockey friend of Hope's in Sydney suggested she would be a cute addition to our show. Hope agreed, although he was concerned that a child that age might be overwhelmed by the size of the audience. We were assured that she'd been interviewed on the radio numerous times since her novelty record had hit big and had shown no signs of stage fright. Of course, we were making a TV program, but show business is show business, right?

So Mouse was booked. She would chat with Hope for a few minutes and then sing "Tell Me a Story." She knew the ditty by heart, but since her reading ability was limited, Barney and his cue cards wouldn't be of much help — besides, he didn't know how to print like a five-year old. But Hope had always had a nice rapport with kids whenever we used them as extras on our specials, so it didn't occur to anyone that he might have a problem with this one.

The little girl was brought to rehearsal by her parents, and Hope gently asked her a few questions that she responded to without appearing at all nervous or fearful. That was at rehearsal with no audience. When she was introduced on the show and entered to music by Bob Alberti and the boys, she still appeared self-confident. Then she looked up and saw the Entertainment Centre crowd and suddenly went mute.

She took another look and started to sob. Gently, Hope began reassuring — "Do you know how pretty you are? "These people would love to hear you sing."—"You wouldn't want to disappoint them, would you?" The Mouse-tears continued, but Hope wasn't about to let a five-year-old get the better of him. If Art Linkletter could do it, so could he.

"You know, you're so pretty, and I have an opening in my act for a girl singer. Would you like to go on the road with me?"

Mouse stopped mid-sob, looked at Hope and said, "What's the *money?*"

Hope was laughing so hard he almost couldn't introduce her song which went like this:

MOUSE: *Tell me a story, tell me a story*
           Tell me a story, and then I'll go to bed.
           You know you promised,
           You said you would,
           You said you would if I'd be good,
           Tell me a story and then I'll go to bed.

Marsupial of The Day

We couldn't visit the land of the eucalyptus groves without paying homage to their most cuddly inhabitants, the koalas. Sticking furry-ears and rubber-noses on Hope and Barbara after perching them on a tree limb seemed like a good way to start.

BARBARA: What's the matter, honey? You look like you've just been hit in the face by the Flying Doctor.

HOPE: I'm so depressed. I'd call my therapist, but his tree is unlisted.

BARBARA: (sympathetically): Aw, tell me about it. That's why I have big furry ears — to listen to my husband's problems in koala stereo.

HOPE: I found out something shocking today. We're not bears at all. We're arboreal marsupials.

BARBARA: Don't worry about it. What's in a name, anyway?

HOPE: Easy for you to say, but would Juliet have looked at Romeo twice if he had been an arboreal marsupial instead of a Capulet? It sounds like a *disease*. If word of this leaks out, we'll be the laughing stock of the sanctuary.

BARBARA: You need to see a psychiatrist. Someone who'll get you to relax and slow down.

HOPE: Slow down? Our lives are already so slow, snails use us as examples.

BARBARA: I know, and the kids are getting suspicious. We've had our bedroom door locked for six months.

They eventually decide that attending the Bob Hope television show taping would be just what the doctor ordered to cure his case of koala-funk.

HOPE: What amazes me is how Hope can think of so many funny things to say while traveling all over the world entertaining so many people.

BARBARA: That's obvious. He must have a very remarkable mind.
             In fact, he must be a genius.
HOPE: Really?
BARBARA: Yes. (glares at him) Now can I have my *passport* back?

Musical numbers by Barbara, Florence and Charo as well as performances by several Australian pop chart favorites (including a singer from India named Jamal) completed a bill of a show that set a high standard for the foreign specials Hope would produce throughout the eighties, topping a list that would be highlighted by a three-hour *tour de force* taped in the People's Republic of China just sixteen months later.

* * * *

The coming decade would see us journey to London, Papeete, Stockholm and Paris with plenty of stops in between. But, though we came close, we never made it to the Philippines. Hope would have liked to have taped a special in Manila, which he had visited on tour during World War II.

In the early eighties, he received an invitation from Imelda Marcos, whose husband, Ferdinand, had been president since 1966. She offered to finance the trip in exchange for the television rights in her country. Hope was always partial to reciprocal deals like that.

I had served in the Navy there and knew Hope was popular among the Filipinos. And I had friends in Manila, so I enthusiastically supported the proposal. But when, in February 1986, Marcos resigned in disgrace and fled the country with millions in government funds he had stolen, I knew the special was a goner. I could sense Hope was disappointed, too, but he said, "I'm glad now we didn't do a show over there." Then he paused and added, "Besides, I could never perform in a country whose first lady owns more shoes than Dolores."

Class Warfare

On this trip and all the junkets I would take with the show over the next seventeen years, I would be assigned a seat in First Class, thanks to a provision negotiated by the *Writers Guild of America* in the sixties covering all producer-signatories. The contract requires that whenever a *Guild* member is required to fly, his or her plane ticket shall match the producer's. I have to say, those *Guild* negotiators were really thinking, because the *American Federation of Musicians* has no such provision, and you can guess what's printed on their tickets.

On our flight home, I decided to have a little fun with the six Les Brown Band guys who had made the trip with us. I found them way back in the seats near the 747's tail — the ones that are one step above the luggage compartment.

So I approach and say, "Fellas, how many of you have heard of *First Class*?" They bombard me with crushed milk cartons — you know, the ones you used to get in Tourist. Then I say, "Bob says you can come up for a peek at how we live, but the 'Noah's Ark Rule' will be in effect."

They all yell, "What's the 'Noah's Ark Rule?'"

I say, "You have to arrive two-by-two and you're limited to five minutes. Don't take advantage."

Now the boys are tossing their plastic utensils at me.

The passengers seated nearby, aware that the Hope troupe was aboard, think the whole thing is a planned comedy routine, and they *applaud*!

The musicians on all our shows were great guys, and I enjoyed my good times on the road with them. I mention their travel circumstances here only because, after years of working with them, I really believe studio musicians are among the most undervalued, underappreciated and underpaid performers in show business. I wanted to give them a well-deserved plug in this book and figured this story was the most entertaining way to do it.

Besides, if I hadn't stumbled onto writing, I've always thought I would have enjoyed being a musician.

CHAPTER 6
A Head Stuck in a Porthole

Actors either like to rehearse or they don't. Hope didn't. He felt that over-rehearsing could dull the precise timing and spontaneity that comedy requires. Hope's propensity to under-rehearse no doubt prevented many guests who preferred more preparation from making return appearances.

Hope's aversion to rehearsing led to the oft-heard criticism of his television performances — his obvious reliance on cue cards. He was aware, of course, that the audience often caught him glancing off camera to pick up the words being held up by Barney McNulty and his crew positioned in as many as four locations around the set's perimeter. But for Hope, the alternative — memorizing lines — would have been impractical. As far as Hope was concerned, appearing on TV wasn't his primary occupation — appearing live on stage from one end of the country to the other was. He used television as a promotional tool — just a way of keeping the Hope brand in the public eye. As a result, the specials always took a backseat.

If Hope was stuck at an airport in Keokuk, preparations for the show simply proceeded without him. When a physical presence was required, his longtime stand-in, Alan Kalm, a former actor Hope had worked with on Broadway, performed the honors. Alan was a real character. He had also been Bing Crosby's stand-in and inherited Bing's used toupees, which Alan still wore. Viewed from behind, you'd swear he was Bing. Alan was yet another example of someone Hope helped whom he had known before he was a star. Property manager Al Borden was another; so was casting director Onnie Morrow.

Often, when Hope's schedule conflicted, the guests were compelled to rehearse without him; they were assured that he would miraculously appear by the time the little red light on the camera flickered to life.

Hope believed that allowing his guests too many rehearsals would give them more time to come up with objections to their lines. Ideally, he preferred to hand them their script just before the first read-through where the actors sit at a long table and recite their lines precisely as they appear in the script. We stood by in case new lines were needed — heaven forbid. It's at this point that our guests had the opportunity to voice any reservations about their lines, but because of Hope's "living legend" status, few ever did. A nice perk for us, to be sure.

Guest Accommodation

Occasionally, a guest would bolster the courage to speak up. On a Christmas special one year, Hope and Loretta Swit —"Hotlips"on *M*A*S*H* — were dressed as department-store mannequins discussing the job after everyone had gone home.

LORETTA: I feel so stupid standing there with hundreds of shoppers pointing at me and shouting, "I want what she's wearing! I want what she's wearing!"

HOPE: Yeah, those women can get pretty pushy.

LORETTA: What women? Those were the *men*."

As soon as she said it, the table erupted in laughter. Hope beamed. Everyone at the table liked the joke except Loretta. She had recently become active in several gay causes and found the line demeaning to homosexuals.

Ordinarily, no problem. Hope would cut the line, and we'd write her a replacement. But not now — the joke had gotten a big laugh. Its value to the show had been tested and proven. Once Hope knew a joke worked, he'd protect it like it was his idea. And it was, almost — he'd paid for it.

While empathizing with Loretta, he convinced her ever-so-gently that as a professional entertainer, she should never allow personal feelings to get in the way of audience laughter. She "owed the audience that much," he explained like a kindly grandfather. Loretta was no match for Hope's logic and gave in. The line stayed and got one of the biggest laughs on the special.

Sometimes, our notorious last-minute script deliveries backfired. We were in Honolulu for a special that featured guests Tom Selleck, Mr. T and Loni Anderson. The scripts were delivered to their suites in the Honolulu Hilton so they'd be waiting for them when they arrived.

Gene Perret and I had written a spot for Loni and Hope that centered on a recent made-for-TV movie of Loni's that had gotten high ratings. In the film, she played a high-class call girl who somehow raises a teenage daughter while concealing from her the less-than-wholesome nature of her profession. Gene and I assumed — wrongfully, as it turned out — that, since she had done the movie, she wouldn't mind having a little fun discussing its interesting — if totally implausible — premise. Our make-believe conversation contained exchanges like this:

HOPE: So tell me, how did you ever manage to have all those men sleeping over without your daughter getting suspicious?

LONI: Oh, that was easy. I just convinced her that she had a hundred-and-fifty uncles.

While unpacking, Loni reads the material, concludes that we've made light of a serious topic and decides not to do the routine. But she doesn't voice her complaints to anyone connected with the show. Instead, she calls her agent in California. (That's how things like this are often done in Hollywood.)

Loni Anderson represented, in one talented package, all the sultry screen sirens with which Hope had become so identified. She incorporated the allure of Rhonda Fleming, the intelligence of Jill St. John, the charm of Virginia Mayo — all that plus the comic timing of Phyllis Diller. Loni could act and her talent with lines helped keep the eighties sitcom *WKRP in Cincinnati* a consistent ratings winner.

sHope and Loni get a last-minute touch-up before their *Would You Like to Take a Walk?* duet while strolling along the beach at Waikiki. She would also play Princess Pukalani, the Goddess of Volcanoes, in our James Michener takeoff.

The agent then calls our producer, Carolyn Raskin, who's quickly on the phone to Hope who hangs up and dials us. We're dispatched to extinguish the artistic brush fire. We somehow convince Loni that we're paid to make light of serious topics and that call girls raising teens wasn't as yet a national scandal. Loni agrees to do the spot, and we breathe easy again.

We also decide never to write another routine about hookers.

Beach Blanket Bingo

That weekend, the fun was just beginning. We were at work in our rooms when Carolyn Raskin called to tell us Hope was at the beach, getting set to tape his closing remarks, "thank you's" and obligatory *Thanks For the*

Memory choruses. While going over the lyrics with Barney, he discovered the song was missing a line.

Back home in the studio an omission like that would have been noticed early. Under normal conditions, the producer or a production-assistant would check the copy before sending it to cue-cards. But on a remote location like Honolulu, the system that was reliable at home could falter. In the confusion of overseeing the logistics of getting a show in the can while simultaneously unpacking, ordering room service, finding out where everything is located and where everybody else is — all those minor travel inconveniences that are tolerable on vacation — magnify when you're trying to work. And all the cracks that mistakes can slip through widen accordingly.

When Gene and I arrived at the shooting site on the small strip of beach beside the hotel, the cameras, lights and speakers had already been set up, attracting tourists that now surrounded the set about four rows deep. We worked our way through the spectators and up to where Hope was standing dressed in a Hawaiian shirt, slacks and in full makeup.

This is the kind of situation a writer lives for. Production at a standstill, effectively paralyzed until we execute our magic. In fact, that in so many words is precisely what Hope said he'd like us to do. Fast. It's what we were being paid to be good at. Problem was, we had about two hundred onlookers anxious to judge the results of our efforts.

The challenge was to come up with a new line that fit the sound track, scanned correctly and — this is a *big* and — be funny. All the while — as you can see in the accompanying photo — with the crowd *and* Hope peering over our shoulders. It took about five minutes, but we managed to pull it off and, when Hope sang the new line, the crowd *applauded*.

The emergency recalled an incident during my first year. Whenever Hope was on the East Coast, because of the time difference, we always breathed a sigh of relief around six o'clock because that meant he'd be going on stage and couldn't call for more material. One night, about six-ten, I was outside barbecuing when the phone rang. Guess who — about to go onstage. And I mean *about* to go onstage.

Gene Perret and I struggle to come up with a line for a song being shot on the beach at
Waikiki. We weren't used to working in front of an audience and it shows; we look like
we're trying to translate the Dead Sea Scrolls. Despite my *Hawaii Five-0* ballcap, I don't
seem to have the cool confidence that was Steve McGarret's trademark. The line we
came up with resulted in a rare instance of gag writers getting applause.

I could hear the strains of the movie themes medley that played him on in the background — "Put It There Pal," "Buttons & Bows," "The Road to Morocco."

"Bob!" he shouted over the music, "I need an opening line. They have all the streets in town torn up, replacing gas lines or something. It's such a big deal, I've got to lead with it."

I said, "How much time do I have?" Now I can hear the emcee starting Hope's introduction.

"About twenty seconds."

I cupped my hand over the receiver, closed my eyes, concentrated and said, "I'm happy to be here. I've never been in downtown Beirut before. What's going on out there? Just between the hotel and the theater, the cabbie and I exchanged *teeth* three times!"

With the applause from the introduction now swelling in the background, he said, "That's it!" and slammed down the receiver.

I returned to my barbecue and announced to the guests, "Folks, I just earned my *entire* salary for 1978."

Goodfellas

Hope was so appreciative of our wacky Waikiki beach rescue (he never realized we could work *alfresco*) that he invited us to join him for dinner. In view of the multitudes who had been staking out the lobby of the Honolulu Hilton hoping to catch a glimpse of our stars, we assumed that room service would be involved.

But Hope had other ideas. He remembered a restaurant he had visited on a USO tour during World War II. He asked Don Marando (an expert on Hawaii since he would one day retire there), "Is Don the Beachcomber still here?"

Don assured him that it was — about five blocks from the hotel — and started to dial up the limo.

"Wait, Don." Hope said. "It's so nice out, let's walk."

We reminded him of the milling throngs outside, and he said, "Oh, they won't be a problem."

A world-renowned superstar walking down the main street of Honolulu on a Saturday night at the peak of the tourist season? Call us naive, but we could envision a problem.

Hope said, "Gene, you get on one side of me and Bob, you get on the other — you know, like bodyguards."

This got a laugh. Two out-of-shape couch spuds as bodyguards? He must be kidding.

"We walk fast. Anyone who spots me won't have time to do anything about it as long as we don't slow down."

Sounded crazy, but he assured us the technique was foolproof as long as no one on the street was *expecting* to see him. They might expect to spot him in the back of a limousine, but walking, in broad twilight?

While Don left to fetch the rental car to bring us back, we went down a service elevator, slipped out the employees entrance, and were off. Tony Soprano and a couple of the boys ducking out for a bite. It worked splendidly. As we strode along, the looks on the faces of tourists who thought they saw — naw, it couldn't be him — could it? — naw. Until we were about a block from the restaurant. Two army enlisted men came toward us engaged in a spirited conversation. As we passed like ships in the night, one of them — as casually as though he ran into Bob Hope every other day or so — gave a little wave and said, "Hi, Bob." And kept walking. No big deal. Just another visiting comedian.

Not that Hope didn't enjoy the fans. Just watching him react when among them, it was clear that he savored their unbridled adulation. He also enjoyed having some fun with them. One evening, Gene and I were sitting on the jumpseats in the limo taking show notes. Carolyn Raskin sat beside Hope. We were waiting for Marando directly in front of the Hilton's entrance, and despite the smoked glass, the tourists were gathering. As the crowd grew, Hope would stop mid- sentence, depress the "down" button, the window would lower, and he'd smile, showing them that famous "Pepsodent special" — you know the one — while flash bulbs popped like the stands at the Super Bowl. Then he'd hit the "up" button and continue speaking to us like he hadn't been interrupted. He repeated this ritual several times, much to the delight of the now-huge crowd.

Finally, he raised the window, looked at us while feigning disgust and said, "Peasants!"

Shell Game

Carolyn Raskin was partially responsible for my first job writing for television — on Dinah Shore's syndicated talk show. How that came about is one of the greatest mentor stories in the history of Hollywood. Carolyn had known Gene from their days on *Laugh-In*. Later, as Dinah's associate-producer, she recalled that he freelanced for Hope, writing monologues.

In the summer of 1975, Dinah was taking her show to Las Vegas and needed just that kind of material. So Carolyn calls Gene, who's now on the staff of *The Carol Burnett Show*. Gene tells her he's not available, but has someone *almost* as good.

Me.

I had been collaborating with Gene on Hope's material for awhile so he knew what I could do. Carolyn says, "Fine. Have him write some gambling material right away and report for work on Monday morning."

So far, so good, I thought—an ideal entry-level television writing assignment awaits. But Gene can't *find* me. My wife Shelley and I are house hunting while a real estate agent is selling our current house in Northern California. We're staying at a motel in Burbank, but don't want to bother Gene who calls our number in Los Gatos and gets the realtor. He tells him to have me "call Gene" as soon as I check in — but I don't check in.

So Gene calls Carolyn back, tells her I'll be tied up for a day or two. "*But*," he says, "I've got his first batch of Las Vegas jokes for Dinah. I'll send them over."

Then *he* writes the jokes, types my name on them and turns them in!

Second day, same routine since Gene still can't locate me. On the third day, I finally call and he screams, "Where have you been? I've got a *job* for you! Report to CBS on Monday morning."

Now my writing career is off and running. Shelley heads home to sell

No, this isn't two haoles with King Kamahamaha. Gene and I are on Hope's balcony at the Honolulu Hilton cooling down after a long day of "hanging ten" — not toes... typewriter keys. We adapted so well to the beachcomber's life, we'd return to Polynesia several years later for *Bob Hope's Tropical Comedy Special from Tahiti*. Can you believe we're getting paid for this?

the house and I check into a motel near CBS where I'll live (and walk to work) for a month, putting in ten-hour days — Dinah taped three ninety-minute shows a day to build up a backlog so she could play golf. The job turns out to be a seven-week crash-course in TV production which I soak up like a silk tie in minestrone. I'm not in the Writers Guild yet, but I learn everybody's job so when I'm hired for *The Dean Martin Roasts* the following year. I'm also now familiar with every aspect of TV production, which is invaluable in my new calling. And all because Gene had covered for me.

They just don't make mentors like that anymore.

Hey, every time I read that story, *I* can't believe it, either.

Mr. Censor Regrets

Another reason Hope disliked rehearsals was that he didn't want scripts floating around the set available to prying eyes — eyes belonging to the censors. Constantly standing guard over America's fragile morality, NBC's "Standards and Practices Department" were on constant lookout for an opportunity to hone in on any words, phrases or other unsavory references that might corrupt the nation's youth. They sniffed our latest rewrites like truffle hounds, dissecting our punchlines like dead frogs in a high-school science class.

One year, we cast Loni Anderson and Hope as astronauts on the first coed space-shuttle mission. The sketch opened in the morning as Loni arrived on the flight-deck to relieve Hope who had been standing watch all night.

LONI: Good morning, Lieutenant. Have any problems last
             night?

HOPE: None.

LONI: You didn't have trouble staying awake?

HOPE: No, ma'am. I watched my favorite program, *WKRP in
             Uranus.*

He pronounces the planet's name with a long "a," and laughter engulfs the room. Read-throughs at NBC were held in rehearsal halls that had been designed for dancers — huge, cavernous affairs with wooden floors and tall mirrors and a railing along one wall. Springing from a table in the corner, an S&P guy zeros in on Hope like a kamikaze pilot.

That pronunciation just won't be tolerated at the network. Hope responds that he's pronounced the name of the planet that way all of his considerable life and isn't about to change now. Anyone who had been with Hope for any period of time knew that his line would be delivered on the air exactly as it had been delivered here for one unassailable reason — it had gotten a big *laugh*. And that, lest we forget, was Hope's business — getting laughs — the bigger the better.

Ironically, the censors may have gotten the last laugh. Later, when Hope attempted to sign the *real* first woman in space, Commander Sally Ride declined, saying through an aide that she felt uncomfortable appearing on a comedy/variety show.

Maybe she'd seen this sketch.

Rank Intolerance

We were taping a show aboard the carrier *U.S.S. Lexington* that was docked in Pensacola, Florida, with guest stars Brooke Shields, Phylicia Rashad (*The Cosby Show*) and Barbara Mandrell. There had been a story in the news about a female Air Force officer and an enlisted airman court-martialed for a romantic dalliance.

So we wrote a sketch in which Barbara, a Navy lieutenant-commander, commits the unpardonable sin of falling in love with an enlisted man — Hope, of course. During a forbidden rendezvous in a paint locker aboard the Lex, two fellow officers played by Brooke and Felicia catch them in the act, and the following exchange takes place:

FELICIA: Commander, you're not the first officer to fall for an enlisted man, but why *him*?

BARBARA: I think I fell in love with Ferdinand that day he was cleaning my porthole and his head got stuck.

As soon as Barbara got her line out at the dress-rehearsal — with several hundred off-duty gobs looking on — laughter spread across the Lex's decks from port to starboard. In a flash, the network censor was immediately on the phone to NBC in New York — to Freddy Silverman, the then-president. He wanted permission to excise the offending bit, but it was too late — the bell on the flight deck had rung, the ship had left the dock and Hope had heard the audience laugh. Once that happened, not even a call from Billy Graham could make him delete the joke. The pope, *maybe*. But only because of Dolores.

To make matters worse, if such were possible, Hope responds to Barbara's line with this:

HOPE: It was my fault. I thought they were all six and seven-eighths.

The exchange appeared on the show exactly as written — no cuts, no changes. The plain truth was that, when it came to what appeared on his specials, Hope had the final word.

Until the late eighties — when his health and the quality of the shows (and the ratings) began slipping — he had complete freedom to choose on which date and at what hour they would air. Not even Seinfeld at his peak could do that. No performer in the history of the medium ever wielded this kind of control over a network. Hope had become so identified with the peacock, the young executives in the Olive Avenue ivory tower — from the president on down — were cowed by him.

The Tried, the True, the Trusted

Hope delegated his hard-earned power to no one. When it came to the directors he hired, only those who were willing to follow his instructions to the letter were invited back. Understandably, few directors appreciated being so completely under the thumb of the star, so Hope developed a group of favorites on whom he came to rely — directors who didn't mind working under these conditions. Over the years, they included Tim Kiley, Dick McDonough, Sid Smith, Kip Walton, Walter C. Miller and Bob Wynn, each of whom directed many specials.

Barbara Mandrell had everything Hope sought in a guest. She could sing and dance,
she had impeccable comic timing and — perhaps most important of all – she was a
good sport. She obviously held Hope in high regard but could, at times, seem almost
motherly toward him. She had been in a tragic auto accident that had killed another
occupant in her car and was a firm believer in seat belts before they became mandatory.
She would refuse to ride in a limo with Hope until he buckled up.

Hope's dominance extended to every facet of the show. When actors rehearse their movements on stage, it's called "blocking." The director — or, in the case of our show, Hope — choreographs each scene so he'll know where to locate the cameras to catch every nuance of the action. He also determines which shots he'll need — establishing shots, close-ups, medium shots, etc. — to properly interpret the material.

Hope kept a tight reign on the entire process, down to dictating how long the director should hold every shot. Tapes of each eight-minute segment (as they were completed) were delivered to him for his final okay. If he spotted something he didn't like, he'd issue specific instructions on how he wanted it corrected.

* * * *

Because Hope was so careful to double-check every detail of what would appear on the screen, he of course appreciated it whenever one of us spotted something that didn't look right.

After Gig retired, I was the only permanent staff member who had been in the military, so I became the show's "authenticity advisor" whenever we taped sketches with a military theme — a role that didn't always make me "Mr. Popularity" with the crew.

I had been elsewhere on the Lexington when the Hope-Mandrell sketch was taped. While watching it later in the control truck, I noticed that the two enlisted Shore Patrol officers who took Hope and Barbara into custody weren't wearing the "SP" armbands required aboard ship. When I pointed out the error to our production coordinator, Sil Caranchini, he said, "Forget about it. Who'll notice?"

I said, "Anyone who's been in the Navy will, and we have time to fix it."

We did, but that meant reassembling the set, repositioning the cameras and calling the cast back — all of which didn't set well with Mr. Caranchini.

"The sailors were wearing sidearms and carrying night sticks," he said. "Isn't that good enough?"

Hope didn't think so and ordered Sil to re-set the sketch.

I didn't get back into Sil's good graces until we were doing another special several months later. We were all watching Hope's golf tournament in the green room, and I noticed an NBC art card that had the word "Chrysler" misspelled. Since that was Sil's department, he made a quick call to Palm Springs that saved someone's job. The lesson here appears to be: It just depends on whose sharp eye is being gored.

Or something like that.

Not that I was always right. On one military-themed special, I wrote a closing speech in which Hope praised the many U.S. troops who serve in non-combat zones throughout the world. In his conclusion, I added a quote I thought had been delivered by Winston Churchill to the British people during the London blitz. Out of the millions of viewers who watched the show, two elementary school teachers from opposite ends of the country wrote to NBC pointing out that "They also serve who only stand and wait" was not written by Churchill, but by John Milton in his poem entitled "On My Blindness." They went on to suggest that a popular entertainer like Bob Hope should be more careful tossing erroneous quotes around; impressionable children may be watching. As soon as NBC forwarded the letters to Hope, I was I was called to the office.

As I stood before him, half expecting to lose my epaulets or at least suffer a reduction in rank, Hope handed me the letters and said, "Here, answer these ladies who have too much time on their hands. Thank them for writing and explain that you were too lazy to check the encyclopedia."

Then he smiled and said, "I'll take care of the Churchills."

✳ ✳ ✳ ✳

No phase of a show's preparation was ever left completely to others. Hope controlled the entire production from the original concept to the finished script, from the design of the set to the lighting, sound-editing, wardrobe and casting. He even kept a close watch on post-production editing and network promotion.

A Bob Hope special was just that — a show that was Bob Hope's and no one else's. So it came as no surprise that he didn't take kindly to anyone who failed to see eye-to-eye with him on their quality.

Reaching Critical Mass!

Hope worked hard on his specials, and because he was proud of them, he suffered an acute allergic reaction to television critics who might be less-than-captivated by the end results of our efforts. Now on the leeward leg of a long and inordinately successful career, he craved acceptance. He had become accustomed to being liked, and criticism of his performances, because it was rare, smarted all the more. By and large, because of his wide popularity and his near icon status, most TV critics had come to treat Hope with kid gloves.

Most, but not all.

In the early 1980s, Hope picked up what would prove to be a persistent and bothersome burr under his creative saddle. The burr's name was Gail Williams, a television reviewer employed by the entertainment industry trade paper *The Hollywood Reporter*. She had embarked on what Hope believed to be — judging from his reaction to her reviews — a one-woman crusade to destroy, special-by-special, his television career. This, despite the fact that Williams's reviews appeared *after* the shows had aired and couldn't possibly have affected their ratings. (Hope never allowed pre-screening for the critics for this very reason.)

Besides, as I'd often point out to him when he'd call in a state of near-apoplexy after reading one of Gail's broadsides, *The Hollywood Reporter* is strictly an industry publication with virtually no circulation outside of Tinseltown. That made no difference.

"I'm suing them for a million dollars!" he'd scream. After one particularly scathing review, he told me to call the entire staff and have them write anonymous letters to the paper defending him — not unlike Nixon, in the heat of Watergate passion, issuing orders to Haldeman and Erlichman that they would ignore. We did likewise.

While Hope carefully nurtured friendly relationships with most of the major newspaper TV critics across the country — he seldom turned down a request for an interview — he had no control over critics hired by the trade-papers who were not beholden to him. They were free to express their true feelings and Williams did — in spades.

What did Williams write that sent Hope's blood-pressure into the stratosphere? Here's just a sampling:

> ". . . Bob 'dirty old man' Hope's latest special was a standard vehicle for the comedian. . . As always, conversations were marred by excessive reliance on cue cards and sketches were broad, featuring Hope in silly costumes, and sophomoric humor." (*Bob Hope's Spring Fling* 1980)

> ". . . Hope delivered his monologue with his characteristic expressionless panache." (*Hope For President* 1980)

> "Everyone read their cue cards reasonably well, and [Loretta] Swit even managed to make her lines sound somewhat spontaneous at points." (Bob Hope's All-Star Comedy Christmas Special 1980)

And she was just getting warmed up. By the time the 1982 season rolled around, Williams' had found the range, and her editorial arrows were beginning to find more and more bull's eyes. Here are her impressions of that year's Christmas special:

> "Bob Ho-ho-ho-Hope's Christmas special this year was virtually indistinguishable from any other season's Hope holiday greeting. *The Merriest of the Merry — Bob Hope's Christmas Show — a Bagful of Comedy* (Hope special titles seem to grow larger in direct proportion to diminishing originality) was a hopelessly hackneyed effort, the sort of inspirationless Yuletide special that brings out the Scrooge in TV critics."

By the 1983 season, it was obvious that there would be no turning back. With her eyes wide open, Miss Williams had burned her bridges and effectively took herself out of the running for inclusion in Hope's will:

> Sometimes the cheap extremes to which Hope's specials stoop are so low, laughs are generated in spite of one's better instincts, but they are embarrassed chuckles, not hearty guffaws. (*Bob Hope's All-Star Super Bowl Party*)

And — *tah, dah* — the review of 1983's *Bob Hope's Road to Hollywood* that almost gave birth to the $1,000,000 lawsuit:

> Apparently, Bob Hope gives many viewers what they want because his specials frequently still earn high ratings. It's a mystery why the formula keeps working. Sure, we all respect Hope as an enduring American institution. But it's not just because he's a veteran who has entertained millions for many years. It's also because he acts like an institution. When he steps down from his pedestal in his specials, Hope can still be funny. But when he virtually stages tributes to himself. . . it's just a tad embarrassing. Perhaps Hope's standard bad sport Oscar jokes are more revealing than one realizes — maybe Hope fetes himself because he really does feel unrecognized. . . One only wishes that this prodigiously talented performer would stop resting on his laurels in uninspired, formula specials and take a few chances. . . At his best in films, Hope was disarming. Now that his specialty is introducing lineups of guest stars with insincere-sounding suavity — and starring in his own show's commercials — he's not nearly as much fun.

My instincts were correct. She wasn't even *mentioned* in the will.

CHAPTER 7

Locusts Wearing *Ray•Bans*

Despite Bob Hope's image as a rabid Republican in lockstep with the Nixons and Reagans of politics, I found him to be, if anything, apolitical.

This probably comes as a surprise, but during my close to two decades with him, as far as I could tell — and we had hundreds of conversations while perusing the daily headlines for joke material — his interest in politics and the stories emanating from Washington went no deeper than whether this or that congressional hearing, special investigation or emerging sex scandal would provide rich pickings for the writers. I never sensed that he leaned toward one political party over another. Besides, throughout his life, he was proud that he had never crossed a picket line.

Does that sound like a Republican to you?

It appeared to me from what he said and attitudes he expressed that he had become identified with the GOP simply because he socialized with the rich — and wealthy people tend to be conservative Republicans. It looked to me like no more than a case of political peer pressure. If he had paled around with more Democrats — and he had friends in *both* parties — he could as easily have become identified with them.

Hope just wasn't, as far as I ever observed, a political animal. I once discussed my theory with Barney McNulty (who had studied Hope close-up longer than anyone), and he agreed. In fact, over the years, I came to believe that Hope's controversial position on the war in Vietnam, which brought him so much public scorn, resulted from his close friendships with, and unswerving loyalty to, high-ranking military officers — among them Gen. William Westmoreland, commander in Vietnam, and Gen. Richard Meyer, one of the architects of the botched U.S. invasion of Iraq. (Both attended Hope's memorial in 2003.) Hear the phrase "War is the answer" often enough from people you like and respect — people whose *business* is waging war — and sooner or later you start believing it.

Not only was Hope politically un-savvy, at times he'd reveal an almost childlike naiveté when it came to complex issues. Discussing the national debt one day, he asked me in all seriousness, "If the U.S. is the richest country in the world, why don't we just *pay* it?"

Pedestrian Thespians

But the question remains, if Hope wasn't political by nature, why did he befriend so many politicians? I think what fascinated him about pols and the lives they led weren't the positions they held, but the *power* of those positions. In his mind, elected official were actors playing a role, albeit one that lasted round the clock.

He viewed his old-time political cronies as legitimate members of the show business fraternity who enjoyed a privilege he would have traded in his 12-handicap for — the power to call press conferences and get instant television coverage. Like Hope, politicians must rely on a positive public image propagated by carefully managed press relations to ensure success. The sudden sea change in the political fortunes of Newt Gingrich in 1996 or Trent Lott and Tom DeLay, John Edwards — the list goes on — are illustrative.

Though talk of Hope running for public office himself would surface now and again, he knew that the desk-bound life of a congressman, senator, city-councilman, whatever, would have been anathema to him.

Like his friend Arnold Palmer who was also mentioned as a possible candidate for Congress, (and who was as equally unqualified), Hope was flattered whenever he was urged to toss his hat in the ring. But he never seriously considered putting his name on a ballot unless it was for an Oscar. (Although we did use this topic as the basis for a 1980 special entitled *Hope For President* … He lost.)

What impressed him about public office were the *perks*. Once during Reagan's presidency, he was in Washington to receive an award and was invited to ride in a presidential motorcade. Later, recalling his visit, it was obvious that the motorcade was the high-point of the trip.

"Isn't it pretty much like any other limousine ride?" I asked.

"Oh, no," he said, "the Secret Service blocks off the on-ramps so you have the freeway all to yourself. It's really something."

Forget the nuclear button — forget the hotline — forget the presidential veto. What most impressed him about the most powerful office in the world was the Gipper's power to close down Interstate 95!

Titleist Terrorist

In the eyes of the public, Hope's ties to Reagan appeared strong, but Gerald Ford was the politician who could truthfully be termed a "pal." The former congressman, former speaker of the house, former vice-president, and former president had moved to Rancho Mirage, California with his wife, Betty, following his defeat at the hands of Jimmy Carter in 1976. They lived near the hilltop estate the Hopes had built, and the two men often shared a cart on one of the ninety-five golf courses that give the desert oasis more sand traps per capita than Iraq. Besides that, their wives were fast friends and prominent members of the social scene at the posh weekend getaway that the Hollywood film community had adopted as its own.

Hope and Ford shared a genuine rapport that was obvious when they were together — which was often. Whenever a spot on one of our specials opened up for a former president, Gerry was a shoo-in. But he had passed on the Drama Club in favor of football at the University of Michigan and recited his lines like he was reading an eye chart. But Hope believed he added class to our guest lineups so he was invited back many times.

Tuxedo Junction

When in October of 1981, it came time to dedicate his new presidential library and museum in Grand Rapids, Michigan, Ford called in all the markers he'd been collecting from Hope over the years. He asked him to host a gala to which he had invited world leaders, former Washington big-wigs, current office holders, their families and staffs. Warm and likable, Ford had accumulated a bevy of friends during his long career on the hill (especially Nixon following the pardon) — so the guest list would be top-heavy with luminaries.

To produce the NBC special, Hope hired Bill Harbach, the son of composer Otto Harbach, who'd had extensive experience with shows taped before an audience of wall-to-wall designer gowns and $3,000 tuxes. Bill tapped Tony Charmoli, similarly qualified, to direct. The guest list was as gilt-edged as they come and included the Reagans, the Bushes, the Henry Kissingers, the Tip O'Neills, the Alexander Haigs, the John Saxons (ex-actor and former Ambassador to Mexico), the Casper Weinbergers, Margaret Truman Daniels and Lady Bird Johnson. Foreign visitors included French president Valery Giscard d'Estaing, Canadian Prime Minister Pierre Elliot Trudeau, Mexico's President Lopez-Portillo, and Japanese Foreign Minister Sunao Sonoda. This had to be the largest gathering of world leaders short of a state funeral —- and we were offering *entertainment*.

The Hope troupe arrived in Grand Rapids on a Thursday — the show would tape the following Sunday — and over the next four days the town, whose former claim to fame was as the nation's furniture capital and whose biggest event up until then had been the annual Amway Convention, would be transformed into a United Nations theme park rivaling Disney World.

As the foreign visitors swept in, each with an entourage that included family members, staff and bodyguards, the Hyatt Regency would be converted into an international security nightmare that rivaled Yalta. Agents in plainclothes, wearing mirrored Ray-Bans and Bluetooth-like ear-pieces, were posted everywhere. Metal detectors stood guard at all points of entry and exit. German shepherds strained at taut leashes, sniffing elevators, broom closets and an occasional guest for explosives or other unwelcome contraband. And, remember, this was *pre*-nine-eleven.

Since most of the dignitaries were staying at the Hyatt, you never knew who you might run into. One afternoon, heading to Hope's suite from my room, I went to the elevator and pressed the "up" button. The elevators were busy and I could follow the progress of this one floor-by-floor. It was stopping at every one of them.

Finally, that little arrival bell sounded, and the doors slowly slid open. Standing there, all facing forward as though posing for a class-reunion photo were, left to right, Henry Kissinger, Lady Bird Johnson, Tip O'Neill, Margaret Truman Daniels, Pearl Bailey and Mark Russell.

I said, "I'll pass. I never take an elevator with no civilians on it."

Most of them laughed. Okay, Henry Kissinger may have just grunted. But you didn't think I'd pass up an opportunity like that, did you?

On tape day, I was awakened by the crackling of radio static in the hallway just outside my room. I peeked out and could see scores of Secret Service agents who looked to be about the same age as the troops Hope entertained dry-running their Dick Tracy wrist radios. It was early and I had to get on the job myself, but I asked one of the agents if they weren't afraid of waking up the other guests.

"Sir, there are no civilians on this floor except you."

I learned later that I wasn't *completely* alone on that floor. I had slept just a few doors from Nancy and Ron who had checked in during the night. I noticed that whenever we worked in close proximity to presidents, congressmen, or world leaders, just being a Hope writer gave you an automatic "This guy can go anywhere" security designation.

With Hope's close ties to Washington, we worked with the Secret Service many times over the years, and I can attest that they take their work very seriously. Each morning as I headed to the hotel coffee shop for breakfast, I'd pass a particularly stern-looking agent standing guard at the entrance. Just to be neighborly, I'd recite what I thought was our

Note the inscription. I think Hope advised Gerry to make nice so we'd write funny lines for him. Hope was trying out the desk in the library's Oval Office and asked, "What should I say?" I suggested "I think I'll pardon Chuck Barris." Ford laughed, and the line was on the show. Gerry was that rare politician who could laugh at himself.

best joke from the previous day's output just to get his reaction, but got nothing but cold stares. On the morning of the show, I tried one last time and failed again.

"Gee," I said, "I hope you laugh more than this when you're in the audience."

Without even a hint of a smile, he replied, "Don't worry, sir. I'm off duty tonight."

Our guests that night included Sammy Davis, Jr., Pearl Bailey, Danny Thomas, Debbie Boone, Foster Brooks, Glenn Campbell, Gordon MacRae, Tony Orlando and Mark Russell. Hope would deliver his longest monologue on a TV special. He had been given the rare opportunity to entertain an unprecedented gathering of world leaders and he would take full advantage of it. For twelve minutes, he'd kid Ford, the guests and the library.

> *Everybody who's anybody is here tonight, which is why I'm up here. I wasn't big enough to be in the audience.*

In the midst of such a glittering assemblage, Hope displayed little of the nervousness that we had often noticed when he performed for Queen Elizabeth. Apparently, statesmen were one thing, but royalty was something else again.

> *At the cocktail party earlier, I wore myself out curtsying. I figured if Nancy Reagan wasn't going to do it, somebody had to.*

This line elicited a particularly sharp reaction from a G.O.P.-dominated audience still somewhat sensitive over Nancy's new White House china and tax-free use of donated designer gowns.

> *Mr. Ford has been a congressman, a vice president, a president and now he's a hit man for the PGA.*

Over the years, Ford's slash-and-burn approach to the game provided us with literally scores of jokes like this. Between his beaning spectators with misdirected Titleists and his reputation for having played football in college without a helmet, he became our gold standard for minor injury causing ineptitude. We weren't alone. Chevy Chase had made Ford's two left feet weekly regulars on *Saturday Night Live.*

> *The Secret Service brought in dogs who spent three hours searching for bombs. I wouldn't mind, but they kept sniffing my monologue.*

We came up with that line while Secret Service dogs were actually sniffing the stack of Barney's monologue cards. References to the tight security were standard comedy fare whenever Hope appeared at an official government function. The jokes tended to remind the audience, however subtly, of what important people they were to merit such extraordinary precautions. It was but another example of what a consummate salesman Hope was.

Make Room for Gunplay

One our guests in Grand Rapids was Danny Thomas, who, in his later years, had grown paranoid about the rise in crime and general lawlessness that he believed was crippling the country. Concerned for his own safety, he wore a pistol in a holster strapped to his ankle.

We were taping a special in Burbank called *NBC Investigates Bob Hope,* a sendup on the Iran-Contra hearings on which Danny played a senator. One day, he stormed into Hope's dressing room.

"Some son-of-a-bitch just tried to run me off the road!" he said.

Hope sympathized, in an attempt to calm him down. "I hope you didn't stop, for God's sake." (There had recently been a rash of drive-by shootings.)

Danny said he not only stopped, but confronted the offending driver *on foot.*

Hope said, "Jesus, Danny, you could have been killed."

Danny said, "No, *he* could have been. I stuck this in the bastard's face." He reached down and drew the pistol as Hope dove across the couch, leaning away from the waving Derringer. Hey, I wasn't taking any chances, either, and slipped behind the door of the adjoining bathroom.

My wife, Shelley, met Betty Ford at the Hopes' Palm Springs house-warming party in 1980. Shelley had worked in Washington for the House Armed Services Committee, so she and Betty had a long conversation about life in the capital that was cut short only when her husband pulled his wife away to "... come meet Jack Lemmon." Betty was as down-to-earth as Gerry, and I think that's why the Hopes were so fond of them.

I could see Hope's face, and it was as white as milk-of-magnesia — and he was wearing *makeup*.

Hope wasn't happy with Danny. Not happy at all.

"Put that damn thing away," he said sternly. His color slowly returning, he asked, "It's not loaded, is it?"

Danny said, "Why would I pack an *empty* gun?" Danny couldn't believe that Hope didn't own a sidearm. Hope was partially deaf thanks to a prop pistol and wasn't keen on facing a real one. He made Danny unload the pistol and promise never to bring it on the set. There was a noticeable coolness between the two for the remainder of the shoot.

If Hope had to work near loaded guns, they'd better belong to Secret Service agents.

Air Pentagon

Throughout his career, Hope's friendships with high-ranking politicians paid tremendous dividends. Whenever he visited the capital, the red-carpet was promptly unrolled. He was beeper-friendly with government officials from congressmen to press aides to Pentagon generals, and for Reagan's two terms, he was only a phone call away from the Oval Office.

In May 1987, the Hope Squadron was airlifted to Pope Air Force base in Fayetteville, North Carolina aboard the personal plane of Gen. Dwayne Cassidy, the chief of the Air Force's Military Airlift Command. We would tape a 90-minute special there celebrating both Hope's eighty-fifth birthday and the seventy-fifth anniversary of the outfit that had transported him from base-to-base during his overseas Christmas tours.

Also on board sharing the general's special VIP quarters that included a kitchen (complete with chef) were Dolores Hope, Lucille Ball and her husband Gary Morton and the Hopes' toy poodle, "Toby." The pampered pooch was seldom left at home whenever the Hopes traveled. Since Hope believed that spaying constituted cruel-and-unusual punishment, the catered-to canine had left his distinctive scent on some of the most expensive hotel suite curtains in the world — including his favorites in New York's posh Waldorf Towers.

The first inkling I had that there might be trouble on our flight to Pope came as I was returning from the galley after breakfast to catch a nap in the passenger seats they had set up for us in the rear of the plane, further from the engines and a little quieter. I passed a bird colonel standing at the bottom of a seven-foot ladder with a large maintenance manual open on the ladder's shelf. He was studying it intently while handing tools to someone who, from about chest-high, was invisible. He reached for another tool and I could see stripes — he was a tech sergeant!

Colonels don't ordinarily follow a sergeant's orders. I went to find Jim Lipton, an experienced pilot himself, to see what I could find out.

"Don't tell anyone else," he whispered, as much as one can whisper on a Starlifter in flight. "The pilot may not be able to lower the flaps all the way when we land. They think it's a hydraulic problem, and they're trying to find the leak."

I said, I thought rather calmly under the circumstances, "Can we land *without* the flaps?"

We could, but, since the flaps slow the plane, it would require a longer air field — about 250 more feet than Pope has. And foam — lots of foam.

We were still about an hour-and-a-half from touchdown. Plenty of time to isolate that leak, right? No one else seemed to notice the little drama I had spotted immediately. Writers are just more observant, I guess. Sometimes, it's a curse.

After a nail-biting fifteen minutes, the sergeant smiled, replaced the sound-baffling panel he had removed to access the hydraulic lines, and climbed down the ladder. I think I saw the colonel salute *him*. We would land with the flaps fully extended after all. And that, my friends, was the closest we came to real trouble — as far as I was ever aware — during the thousands of miles I flew with the Hope show.

Pretty remarkable, no?

* * * *

Hope would meet us at Pope after flying in from a personal-appearance tour on the eastern-seaboard. Our guest stars, Glen Campbell, Barbara Mandrell, Don Johnson, Emanuel Lewis, Brooke Shields and Phylicia Rashad, were waiting to go to work. Over the next several days, we rehearsed the show that would be taped before a crowd of four thousand servicemen and their families — as well as soldiers from nearby Ft. Bragg.

The monologue would be taped with the latest military hardware in the background to remind the viewers at home just how the Defense Department was spending their taxes — payback for their picking-up a good portion of the production costs.

Twinkle, Twinkle, Little Stars

Our second night on the base, we were invited to a dinner dance at the Pope Officers' Club celebrating the Air Wing's birthday. High-ranking pilots had assembled from all over to take part in the week-long celebration, and members of Hope's inner-circle were seated with the officers and their wives, distributed so each table would have at least one or two of the Hollywood visitors. We were always honored to be invited to shindigs like this because it gave us a chance to strut our stuff a little, an opportunity we seldom got. Our duties were, by nature, solitary.

The officers and their spouses were obviously interested in what we did, how we did it, what Hope was like to work for — all the usual topics. Table mate Don Marando and I were happy to fill them in. We, in turn, were impressed by *them*. I'd been an enlisted man in the Navy and never dreamed I'd someday break bread in an officers' club — with actual officers yet.

But I was about to be even more impressed. Since they were all wearing civvies, I asked how many pilots were at the dinner.

"All of us are pilots, sir," our host said.

They all looked so *young*. I said, "So only pilots were invited?" He said, "Only pilots with at least *three stars*."

All of these fresh-faced "kids" were generals! With three twinklers at that.

I said, "You mean if a two-star showed up, he'd be turned away?"

"Yes, sir," he replied.

I still have visions of a general and his wife "making do" at the local Denny's because he didn't have the requisite number of stars on his shoulder.

In-flight Reservation

The logistics of staging a show like this one were complicated, but things had progressed smoothly and tape was ready to roll. Hope had read in the local paper that morning that Reagan was flying back to Washington after delivering the commencement address at the University of Georgia. He said to Lipton, "Call the White House. Maybe we can get Ronnie to pop over and appear on our show."

Jim gulped hard. "Nice idea, but, gee, Bob, every segment is locked-in and we start seating the audience in two hours."

Hope was not deterred. "We can always find an extra five minutes somewhere. *Call.*"

Hope was well aware of the impact a presidential visit would have on Pope and the infantry outfits. Lipton called the personal number that Hope gave him and was soon patched through to Air Force One, already airborne. The call was switched to the Winnebago in the main hanger that had been provided for Hope as a dressing room. As Gene Perret and I sat on the fold-down couch across from him, the following conversation took place:

"Ron? Bob. Hey, we're doing a little birthday thing here at Pope Air Force Base and — *Pope* — it's in North Carolina. We thought you might take a quick left turn and drop in. Be great, you know. I'll have the boys bang out something we can do together. The whole thing shouldn't take more than a half hour, tops."

There was a long pause as Hope listened to the most powerful leader in the free-world confer with his aides. Then he covered the receiver with his hand and mouthed the words: "He'll do it."

Like the comedy relief pitchers we were trained to be, Gene and I sprung into action. While Air Force One winged toward Pope, we'd bang out a page of dialogue for the two old veterans of the silver screen. After Hope okayed it, we'd call Reagan back so his secretary could type it up for him to memorize.

While Gene and I tapped away, the Secret Service was conferring with Lipton and co-producer Elliott Kozak. Reagan's Boeing 707 would land and taxi directly to the stage.

Within an hour, scores of agents descended on the area like a swarm of armed locusts in dark suits. Some of the same German shepherds that had "sanitized" Grand Rapids six years earlier sniffed their way through our production equipment. Metal detectors suddenly sprouted up everywhere to ensure that there would be no gate crashers. We were all instructed that once the president's plane touched down, we weren't to wander from our assigned areas under threat of sudden death by Uzi.

Here's how it all works. On any major flight, Air Force One is accompanied by an identical "decoy" plane carrying several hundred uniformed and plainclothes agents. Additionally, an unmarked C-130 troop carrier containing the bullet-proof presidential limo and specially armed escort vehicles complete the flotilla. As soon as the decision to detour to Pope had been made, these escort planes flew ahead to complete the last-minute security arrangements which (in this case) must have been nerve-wracking. Reagan had already been the target of a would-be assassin, and they weren't looking for a sequel.

As expected, the audience, having no inkling of the unscheduled stopover, literally erupted when the Gipper strode down that boarding ramp. He greeted Hope warmly, and the two old troupers did their one-minute exchange. Total elapsed time from touchdown to departure was exactly thirty minutes as promised. Exciting stuff, to be sure, all made possible because Hope could dial a president's number and know there would be one at the other end.

Among My Souvenirs

At his home in Toluca Lake, Hope had a display-room in the gate house where we sometimes met with him. In the display-room were glass cases chock full of memorabilia — dancing shoes that had belonged to vaudevillian Eddie Foy whom Hope had played in *The Seven Little Foys*; the NBC microphone he had used on radio covered by a sheepskin sheath;the oversized cowboy hat he'd worn in *The Paleface*; a vial of crude oil from the well in which he and Bing had invested; a silver money-clip autographed by Richard Nixon; golf scorecards signed by opponents such as Dwight Eisenhower, Sam Snead and Ben Hogan; ID cards he'd been issued by the Defense Department to tour the war zones; honorary Academy Award statuettes; Peoples Choice Awards; and myriad plaques, engraved cups and commemorative plates.

But the most interesting items were souvenirs that he'd been given by Allied forces at the end of World War II — personal property confiscated from captured Nazis that included an S.S. officer's ring with a skull-and-crossbones; a Nazi general's dress uniform hat; ID cards, insignia and medals taken from members of the Gestapo; daggers with markings of the Third Reich and assorted machine guns, rifles and Lugers. He even had stationery used by Hitler and his staff with a swastika embossed at the top. (which he'd sometimes hand out to guests as souvenirs).

But Hope kept the most valuable Nazi artifact in a walk-in vault off the secretaries' room where filing-cabinets filled with jokes and scripts dating back to radio were stored. It was a solid-gold liquor decanter caddy about the size of a small mailbox — with remnants of brandy, vodka and scotch still in the bottles — an ornate jeweled handle and hooks on which hung small glasses embossed in gold leaf. The story was that the caddy had been discovered in Hitler's bunker seconds after Allied troops overran it. Two glasses were beside the decanter, partially filled as though they had been used just before the Nazi officers escaped.

As impressive as the decanter was, it wasn't Hope's favorite wartime gift from the military. That honor went to a faded, black-and-white photograph that he kept under lock- and-key and brought out proudly for any guest getting a personal tour of the display room. It was a picture of General George Patton using the Rhine as a urinal.

Put It There, Pal

Every bit as strong as his ties to the military, Hope's loyalty to his political pals was rock solid. He stuck by Richard Nixon long after events and indisputable evidence of high crimes and misdemeanors had succeeded in tossing the disgraced president into history's dumpster. One day, I spotted a handwritten note on the "RN" letterhead lying on a desk in the office — "Dear Bob, Pat and I watched and thoroughly enjoyed your Valentine special on Sunday night..."

But in November 1991, when his ability to give politicians free plugs and air time on his television specials was behind him, Hope was given an opportunity to observe just how mutual that long-standing loyalty was. He was invited to attend the formal dedication of the Ronald Reagan Library and arrived expecting to be greeted warmly by the four GOP presidents to whom he had contributed much — Bush, Reagan, Nixon and Ford. Maybe, he thought, be given the opportunity to reminisce over their old times together — Nixon had once landed in Hope's backyard in Marine Helicopter One!

But, as he told me later that night after returning from the event, they were kept at a distance, ignoring Hope — relegated to the roped-off assemblage of lesser VIP's on the order of Hollywood agent Lew Wasserman and Disney chief, Michael Eisner. Hope's disappointment at the snub was obvious in his voice.

"To tell you the truth," he said sadly, "I don't know why they invited me."

It was one of the few times I sensed his feelings had been deeply hurt.

His experience brings to mind a similar disappointment in the early forties when the Friars' Club, an exclusive fraternity of successful actors and comedians, honored him with a roast. Though a seat on the dais was reserved for him, Bing Crosby, a Friars' board member, failed to show up. Hope's *Road* buddy later explained to a reporter: "I wasn't hungry."

Looks like Hope was right. Politics and show business *are* a lot alike.

CHAPTER 8

How Now, Chairman Mao?

In 1974, soon after Richard Nixon opened relations with the People's Republic of China, Hope began a behind-the-scenes campaign to become the first American entertainer to tape a television special there. He spent the next five years cajoling the State Department and the Department of Defense — at the start of every new season, I'd say, "We doing China this year?" and he'd say, "Any day now. Stay packed."

Leaning on a raft of influential government pals including Henry Kissinger and calling in markers he'd been collecting from the government since World War II, he finally received permission to take our show there as part of a cultural exchange program dubbed "Ping-Pong Diplomacy" by the press.

On June 16, 1979, after a four-hour flight from Narita, Japan, a Chinese Airlines 707 filled with our merry band of mirth makers eager to get their first look at this hotbed of Communism, touched down at the Peking Airport. The group included Bob and Dolores Hope, their daughter, Linda, her co-producer Jim Lipton — with whom Gig Henry and I would share writing credit — Jim's wife, Kedakai, director Bob Wynn and a support crew made up of pretty much the same gang who had earned their Hope Squadron wings on our trek to Australia the previous year.

Since Hope was the most recognizable American to set foot in China since Nixon, we'd be whisked through Customs with some of the usual formalities either waived or abbreviated — an accommodation I'd later come to regret.

Our guest stars would arrive over the next several days — Mikhail Baryshnikov, Crystal Gayle, Big Bird from Sesame Street, mimes Shields and Yarnell and a popular disco-duo, Peaches and Herb. Booking the show had not been easy since we'd be spending a full month on location — three weeks in Peking and a week in Shanghai. While many major stars would have welcomed the opportunity to see China, most are unwilling to commit that much time to any project short of a film and Hope wasn't paying movie caliber fees.

Where's The Stretch Rickshaw?

At the airport, we disembarked and discovered we were on our own. We would learn later that a delay in our arrival time had put us in conflict with a group of American mayors whose plane had touched down several minutes before ours. The junketing hizzoners included LA's Tom Bradley, whom we would meet later. The PRC officials were busy rolling out the red (no pun intended) carpet for them, so there we were, standing beside the plane — no movable ramps back then — holding our carry-on luggage.

"Well," said Hope, "looks like we'll end up tipping *ourselves.*"

We started off toward what looked like the main reception area — it had a portrait of Mao over the front door — and after a minute or two spotted a convoy of government limos speeding toward us. Out climbed several officials from the Ministry of Culture who immediately began spewing apologies that would have put Kobe Bryant to shame. Presently there was more bowing than a convention of Sumo wrestlers as they led us into the airport's reception area.

They had a long table set up in the lobby offering refreshments that the crew proceeded to devour while Hope was giving the first of his many interviews on Chinese soil.

We're at the Peking Airport in front of a statue of Chairman Mao who, though long dead, was still taking his final bows in a walk-thru mausoleum in Tienanmen Square. Later, we dropped by but were told he was being "refurbished." Most disappointed was Marando who was anxious to pick up some makeup tips. Mao's presence would be felt everywhere we went — statues and photos of the old revolutionary could pop up just about anywhere — including the huge portrait of him over the entrance to the Forbidden City.

We were soon convoyed to the twenty-five story Peking Hotel in small vans that carried about six people. (They would be available to us throughout our visit like free taxis.) During the half-hour drive, we got our first look at the hustle and bustle of life in the PRC and noticed few vehicles among the seemingly endless lines of bicycles. Bicycles were the norm — millions of them. The hotel was about six blocks from Tiananmen Square and on the main thoroughfare that leads to the Forbidden City. There, a few years later, a student protester would gain the admiration of the world by making a Chinese Army tank blink first.

We were welcomed by the starched hotel staff standing in formation on the front steps. Each smiled and bowed as we passed. This custom would be repeated when we checked out, and again in Shanghai when we checked into the hotel there three weeks later.

Gig and I were shown to our rooms on the eighth floor while the Hopes were escorted to the twenty-fifth. Immediately, there was a problem. Dolores's room was on the same floor as her husband's, but about fifty yards down the hall. She was told that was the custom among upper-class Chinese. Apparently, our hosts believed that the centuries-old norm for emperors should apply to tourists with emperor status on their home turf. Dolores would have none of it, requesting that her bed be placed in a large anteroom just inside one of the entrances to Hope's suite where it would remain for her entire stay.

Most of the company — staff, crew and talent, forty-five of us in all — were lodged in the Peking (whose marble-heavy architecture resembled a Hilton shipped in from Moscow). The Russians had supervised its design and construction, and it showed. Our rooms were basic, comfortable — a color TV was included, but for some strange reason, received only programs in Chinese — and they were never locked. The sliding doors to the balconies were double-pane glass to keep guests insulated from the street noise below. On each floor near the elevator, a concierge stood guard with the vigilance of a rock concert rent-a-cop. Strangely, we came to feel no hesitation in leaving valuable belongings in a hotel room with the door open. Maybe the penalty for petty theft in China — death — had something to do with this.

Note the manual typewriter we brought along in case the Chinese hadn't discovered electricity. My complementary Thermos of hot tea sits on the table. At night, the rooms were deathly quiet, and being alone in a country that boasted a higher execution rate than Texas, one felt somewhat adrift. My bill for collect calls home was $700, but it was cheaper than hiring a psychiatrist.]

Co-producer Linda Hope stops by to make sure the assembly line is running smoothly. Linda, the eldest of four children, is the only one who opted for a show business career. She had to work in a broad shadow and her relationship with her dad was sometimes contentious — she jokingly referred to him as "The Ayatollah." Today, she manages Hope Enterprises, overseeing the comedy empire her dad built.]

A friendly game of Texas Hold 'Em with (left to right) Gig, Ron Tom and Don
Marando with yuan that we received as *per diem*. But there was nowhere to spend
it — no bars, clubs, pool halls, bowling alleys, or fitness centers. Not even a
Starbucks, a McDonald's or a KFC. Not so today, however. When I returned to
China in 2007, I found a country as Americanized as Cleveland.

Gig and I were assigned a young, affable Chinese college student, who spoke excellent English and was spending his summer with the government, to act as our guide and interpreter and to make sure we didn't wander onto any military installations. When behind the Bamboo Curtain, one feels much safer with a plainclothes agent within earshot. Or any kind of shot.

In 1979, first-class hotels in China had yet to come equipped with gyms, spas and swimming pools, but we had the next best thing — Dale Huffstedler, Hope's masseur. Whenever we worked late, Dale would drop by, deliver a quick rub-on-the-run , and we'd soldier on, refreshed.

Each morning, there would be a large Thermos of hot tea outside the door, which was the closest we ever got to Room Service. All of our meals were served in a cavernous, high-walled dining hall with huge murals of the Yangtze's Three Gorges. It was about the size of UCLA's Pauley Pavilion and every bit as intimate. Mealtimes were posted, and if you missed them, you were out of luck. McDonald's and other fast food meccas had yet to invade the People's Republic, but going hungry was never a problem since the Chinese traditionally demonstrate their hospitality through copious gifts of calories. Important visitors rate eight-to-twelve-course banquets — almost every evening. We ended up attending more banquets than a major league manager in the off-season.

Every day, lunch was a buffet that was heavy on seafood. Piles of shrimp, scallops, clams, mussels, oysters, crab, calamari, octopus, sea snails, fresh salmon and sea bass and other undersea creatures known only to the Chinese were arranged in attractive displays along with the usual items found on most Chinese menus back home — the only noticeable difference being a subtle "gaminess" due to the duck fat used in China for frying.

Gig claimed he was allergic to seafood and had to be careful. His allergy severely limited his choices; but one day, he announced that he'd found sliced tongue that was as good as the Stage Deli's in New York. It was available daily, so he took advantage of it. Toward the end of our stay, I was in line with one of our Chinese technicians and said, "Have you tried the tongue? My partner says it's fantastic."

He said, "That's not tongue. It's *sea slug.*"
I never had the heart to tell Gig.

✳ ✳ ✳ ✳

When not out on location somewhere, Gig and I spent our days grinding out material in our rooms or working with Hope in his suite. One day, waiting for him to return, I was there with Don Marando and left to pick up something from my room. I couldn't have been gone more than two-minutes, tops. When I returned to the suite, I found the door locked — so I knocked. A voice that I *thought* belonged to Don said, "Who is it?"

Always clowning, that Don.

"Me, ass——!"

The door opened a crack, and Dolores said, "I beg your pardon." She had come back to her makeshift bedroom-alcove during the two minutes.

I said, "You're supposed to be Don."

She laughed and said, "And I thought you were a good Catholic boy." She smiled again and added, "Don said he'd meet you for dinner later."

It always helps when your employer is married to a good sport.

Dolores and I had a history of mistaken identity. One day, while I was working with Hope at his house, his phone rang. He was across the room and said, "Grab that, will you." I picked up the receiver and a voice said, "Hello, Bob?"

Instinctively, I said, "Yes?" I recognized the voice, but before I could stop her, she said, "Betty Ford called. She wants us to join them for —"

"Dolores, it's me — Bob *Mills*." I cut her just short of revealing any state secrets, but we both knew it was a close call.

Gated Community

We taped the show's opening segment which featured Hope singing "We're Off on the Road to China" – à la "The Road to Morocco" — along the walkway atop the Great Wall. There weren't many visiting tourists, and the few there were agreed to remain out of sight while we filmed.

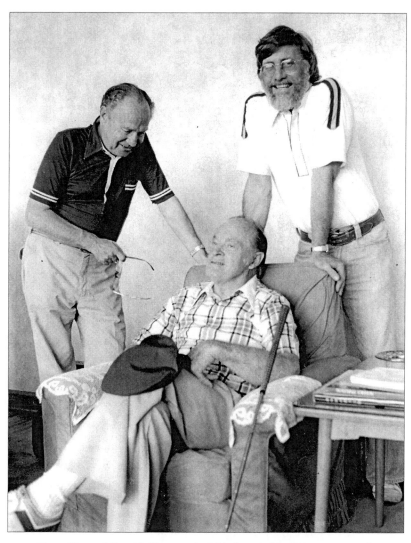

Gig and I met daily with Hope on the 25th floor, in his Chinese version of a presidential suite. Later, we taped a segment there in which Hope teaches three Chinese comedians golf and in the process shatters several *faux* Ming vases. A statue of Buddha guarded the entrance, so we gave him this line: "For weeks I admired the statue of Buddha in my vestibule — and then I realized it was a *mirror*."

Hope and I are comparing war wounds — actually, our reaction to the myriad shots we had to get before departing for the Orient. In 1979, China required inoculations against everything from chicken pox to restless leg syndrome. So we all reported to a doctor in Hollywood who gave us a group rate. I just wish he hadn't used the same needle. Today, no shots are required. I guess we've gotten healthier.

As Hope proceeded to strut down the ancient cobblestones, he lip-synched to a music track from speakers set up behind him. Only occasionally did he glance at cue cards with Jim Lipton's lyrics that Barney McNulty had taped beneath the guard rails just out of the camera's view. Using a 3-wood as a walking stick, he sang:

> *Hey, we're off on the road to China*
> *With fun and adventure in mind*
> *The seventh Wonder of the World*
> *Is here beneath our feet*
> *Compared to this the road to*
> *Mandalay is obsolete*

We're off on the road to China
Who knows what we're going to find
Like Marco Polo long ago
We enter starry-eyed
Ready to be Peking-eed
And hot to be Shanghaied

We'll meet on the road to China
If you're into foreign affairs
And since there is so much to see
From sea to shining sea
We'll sample one from column A
And one from column B

It's neat on the road to China
We've nothing to lose but our cares
We're half a world away
From old New York and London Town
We're doing pretty well for people
Standing upside down

It's time for the feast to begin
Our table's set with China
So let's all dig in

With the Great Wall spiraling into the distant sky, it was the most auspicious and visually impressive opening Hope ever performed on television. We had no doubt that it was worth the time, expense, and full day of shooting it had taken to get it on tape.

✳ ✳ ✳

Anxious to see as much of the wall as we were allowed to, and while Hope was off taping a commercial for Coca-Cola, several of us headed north — away from those sections with which the outside world is now so familiar.

About a half mile past the steepest inclines — where it's one step at a time, slowly — the rebuilt portion ends. Beyond stretches a band of rubble that extends as far as the eye can see. At this remote location, what strikes the first-time visitor is the *silence*. It's been that way for at least a century, we were told, the result of starving peasants denuding the landscape of insects, birds, small and large mammals — the entire kingdom of indigenous wildlife that once thrived there.

With no ambient sounds save for the breeze gently rustling through the undergrowth — which looks like that in northern California — the atmosphere is eerie and unearthly. It's the sound you'd imagine on the surface of the moon. It's a grim reminder of the fragility of the earth's

Here I am returning from my trek to the unrestored section of the Wall that doesn't appear in the guide books. The towers have openings in all directions so anyone attempting to sneak in would be spotted immediately. Think maybe they were designed by an ancestor of Lou Dobbs? It snows in this part of China so Great Wall sentry duty in the winter must have been the Chinese equivalent of the Russian Front.]

Here we are making sure we'd have proof to show the folks back home that we really had made history — the first American TV crew allowed in China. The only notable absence is our star himself who was elsewhere taping a commercial for Coca-Cola. Gig is missing, too — probably with Hope to help punch up the ad copy.

Front row: (l to r) Don Marando, the author, Carl Jablonski (choreographer), Marcia Lewis (associate producer), Robert Shields & Laureen Yarnell (mimes), Chinese liaison, Mrs. Hope's interpreter/guide, Barney McNulty (cue cards). Second row: A production assistant, Linda Hope (coproducer), sound and lighting crew. Standing: Chinese aides, Dale Huffstedler (masseur), Lon Stucky (lighting), Dolores Hope, Bob Keyes (Handicam), Bob Wynn (director), Chinese assistants, Kedakai Lipton, James Lipton (producer), Chinese assistants, Will Oborn (comptroller).

Right after we shot Hope's opening number, NBC photographer Ron Tom spotted a chance to take advantage of the still-empty Wall. Several of us posed with Hope for a once-in-a-lifetime opportunity to use the Great Wall of China as a backdrop.

Here Gig and I defy the law of gravity — we were on the underside of the planet after all. I'm the one leaning, Gig is standing naturally. This area is similar in topography and climate to northern California, although to get a shot like this back home would require a few hits of that Mendocino County medicinal greenery.

ecology and the irreversible carnage mankind can inflict on it. Rush Limbaugh should see it. Just once.

Moo Shu Miracle•Gro

On the bus ride to the Great Wall, we learned that in some unexpected ways, China is more like the West than any of us had imagined. We were about an hour out of Peking as the bus started its winding ascent into the hill country north of the city.

Peering out the window with that glaze the eyes get when wonder begins giving way to monotony, one of our young sound engineers spied something on the roadside that he'd seen a few times before, but never expected to see in collective-farmville. Soon everyone on board agreed that the foot-tall plants lining the roadway for about a mile were what some refer to as "happy hemp," others as "giggle weed" — mature marijuana.

Putting work before pleasure — an honored tradition among Hope staffers — it was on the return trip that the fun-loving Future Farmers of Shanghai prevailed upon the driver to pull over so they could do a little harvesting. Granted, the crop was a bit on the green side, but it was nothing that a few hours under a hair dryer couldn't — pardon the expression — cure.

Within hours, toasts were being made to the People's Republic by a few enterprising young Americans who had no idea that fifteen years later, an 18-year-old Westerner in Singapore would be caned for spraying graffiti on a Mercedes. I didn't join them, of course.

My generation had *Woodstock*.

Billboard Ban

The Communist Chinese government is divided into Ministries — a Ministry of Commerce, a Ministry of Health, a Ministry of Education and so on. From day one, the nemesis of *The Bob Hope Show* — and Hope personally — was the Ministry of Culture.

As a condition of being allowed to tape within their borders, the government insisted on approving every word of our script beforehand. This was not only unrealistic, but virtually impossible since we made script changes right up until tape began rolling. Allowing them to check each segment after it had been shot wouldn't have been a problem, but for some reason known only to Confucius, the Culture Ministers wouldn't go along.

Their insistence on a policy of *prior* approval would be major stumbling block during the entire shoot. Looking back on it, I think the Chinese officials had heard of Hope's legendary reputation for political jokes, feared they would be in his crosshairs, and decided to make sure they'd be protected from his comedic barbs. (Can't blame them there: they were correct on all counts.)

Our first run-in with the policy evolved as follows. Gig and I had written a spot that was to be taped in front of the Democracy Wall, a poster forum in downtown Peking that had recently received a lot of ink in the world press. Now that they had undergone a Cultural Revolution (so the theory went), any Chinese citizen was free not only to criticize the government, but to post his thoughts for all to read.

Our version of this newly-found right of free speech went like this:

HOPE:	(to Chinese man pasting) Sir, would you mind translating that for me?
MAN:	Not at all. I'm complaining about all the crime in the streets, traffic congestion, loud music at night and air pollution.
HOPE:	Gee, I had no idea Peking had all those problems.
MAN:	Oh, I'm not from Peking. I'm from from *Passaic, New Jersey.*

A permit to film at the wall had been requested and granted. The problem was, the actual script was completed just minutes before it was to be shot. There simply was no time to obtain an additional signature on our permit covering the changes.

News of the sketch we shot reached Culture faster than the invasion of Nanking. You'd have thought the guy was from Tibet. The officials demanded the tape right out of our camera. Bob Wynn explained that it couldn't be removed without destroying other material on the same reel. After several head-to-head meetings, Hope was issued an ultimatum: unless the Democracy Wall tape was turned over to them by day's end, no tape of our special would be allowed to leave the country. While Hope, Lipton and Wynn continued the delicate negotiations, we managed to smuggle out the offending segment hidden among footage being sent back to Los Angeles with Jess Marlow, a local newsman who was covering our trip for KNBC.

The Ministry backed down only after receiving a signed affidavit from Hope that the segment wouldn't be included in our special. It wasn't, but from that point on during our visit, even the food served at our honorary banquets seemed markedly cooler. The Democracy Wall was demolished shortly thereafter and has never been rebuilt.

Ironically, there were other segments more deserving of Chinese scrutiny than the poster wall sketch. During our three-week stay in Peking, we would tape at locations from one end of the city to the other, hoping to capture just a hint of China's mystery and fascination for the Westerner. But our Hollywood brand of *chutzpah* could kick in at any time. We actually taped disco duo Peaches and Herb doing a number on

Happy Hour at the bar/gazebo located in the garden behind the Peking Hotel. Instead of a bar, the hotel offered an ice-cream counter located just off the lobby. L to R (standing) Ron Tom (NBC photographer), Marcia Lewis (associate producer), Bob Wynn (director), me. L to R (seated) Gig Henry, March Fong (NBC executive), lighting crew member, Jess Marlow (KNBC Los Angeles).

the steps of the tiled, gold-encrusted Temple of Heaven that had provided Chinese peasants a place of worship since 1420. You could almost hear the emperors spinning in their sarcophagi.

Mike Fright

We didn't know it yet, but the Democracy Wall debacle was just round one of what would turn out to be an ongoing game of cat-and-mouse with the Culture Ministers. We would soon learn just how serious they were about enforcing their version of the rules.

An admitted sweetsaholic, Hope became a frequent flier at the hotel's ice cream bar which featured one of his favorites, chocolate mocha with sprinkles. But he had to pay a steep price when he got back home — six weeks at the Betty Ford on a non-fat yogurt drip.

Hope never refused autograph-seekers anywhere in the world. Having attained icon status, Hope wasn't treated like an ordinary megastar. He was on another level — not just a celebrity, but an American institution. Note Barney McNulty over my left shoulder.

Each morning, Gig and I met with Hope in his suite to discuss ideas for the show. Gradually, we noticed that Culture was saying "no" faster than the Parole Board on Devil's Island. It was almost as if they knew what we wanted before we submitted a formal request.

As it turned out, they did.

One day, as we arrived for our usual strategy session, Hope motioned for us to join him outside on the balcony. As we slid the door closed behind us, he pointed toward the drain at one end of the deck and invited us to join him at the other. He whispered that he had been warned by someone at the American Embassy that his suite might be bugged, confirming our own suspicions that the rooms were in need of a visit from the Orkin man.

I said "Does this mean the Dali Lama sketch is out?"

"Number One Son very observant," he nodded.

Needless to say, from then on, we tried to make sure that the only microphone Hope spoke into belonged to NBC.

We had a feeling that the Red Flag limousine assigned to Hope by the government also sported some after-market wiring. Moving from location to location on shooting days, Don Marando would have to juggle Hope's heavy aluminum makeup case on his lap because, according to the driver, the trunk was off-limits to visitors. We couldn't blame him. It's not easy to explain why a spare tire needs an antenna. Even though we were with NBC and not the CIA, it didn't seem to matter. Cold War suspicions run deep.

As a further condition of being allowed to tape in China, Hope had agreed to deliver a "hands-across-the-oceans" speech extolling the newfound friendship between the two nations. Wielding a golf club and standing near the entrance to the Forbidden City with the portrait of Chairman Mao visible over his shoulder, he said:

HOPE: Peking China — amazing, isn't it? Ten years ago, who
          would have dreamt that an American comedian would be
          standing here in Tiananmen Square saying whatever he
          pleased and photographing anything he pleased. In those

Note the flagstaffs on Hope's limo. We wanted to make some flags for him — one with
the NBC peacock and the other with the Paramount Pictures logo, but he thought
Texaco would be jealous. It was strange sitting where Chairman Mao may have jotted
down quotations. Would he approve of its being used to write *jokes?*

days, the People's Republic was the Red Menace, a stern
and implacable enemy who ridiculed our way of life and
pictured us as wallowing in decadence. But in this fast-
moving world, radical changes can occur overnight. So
here I am, and in the words of Oscar Hammerstein "getting to know you — getting to know all about you, getting
to like you, hoping that you like me." I guess that's what
this trip is all about. Getting to know each other — talking
and laughing and singing and dancing together, like good
friends should. And liking each other. The Chinese are easy
to like, ready to smile, courteous and helpful. And they
make every effort to understand us — and with a troupe of
actors, that's not easy...(points) Behind that gate is the Forbidden City, which is not forbidden to anyone anymore...

Unless, perhaps, you were Chinese and didn't toe the party line. Fifteen years later, on the very spot where Hope had stood to deliver this speech, unarmed student protestors were shot by soldiers of the Chinese Army.

* * * *

As soon as Hope learned that he'd be allowed to visit China, he made an arrangement with King Features Syndicate to send back weekly reports of his impressions of the mysterious Orient. As each deadline approached, Hope would say something like "Isn't it time I had a few more impressions?" and while he took his afternoon nap, we'd tap out the columns. Then, after he approved them, we'd run them through a teletype machine — a cast-iron monster we had to learn to use since neither of us was a teletypist. The thing looked like a church organ and had to date back to the days of gunboat diplomacy. The columns were later condensed in the October 1979 issue of *The Saturday Evening Post*.

Here's a sampling of Hope's impression of the Great Wall:

> Separating sky from jutting mountain crests as far as the
> eye can see, it snakes its way across Northern China like
> a giant ribbon on a Christmas package — a present that
> was gift-wrapped twenty-five centuries ago. They say that
> high walls make good neighbors, but as you experience the
> breathtaking grandeur of this one — stone laid upon stone,
> millions and millions of them — it's hard to believe that it
> all began centuries ago when an unemployed brick mason
> whispered into the emperor's ear, 'But what if they show up
> from the north at night wearing sneakers?'

FA LA LA LA LA AND DO RE MI

DECK THE WALL WITH BOUGHS OF HOLLY

The Hopes' 1979 Christmas card. Dolores is pictured with young Chinese students who had appeared in a segment with her singing "Do-Re-Me" from *The Sound of Music* phonetically. The clip is a favorite among my cruise ship audiences. We noticed in 1979 that only children wore brightly-colored clothing; adults wore dark pants and white shirts. That's no longer true today as fashion in China has been westernized.

CHAPTER 9

Laying 1000-Year-Old Eggs

We taped the stage-show segments of our China special on the Fourth of July at Peking's Capital Theater (one of the few things that Chairman Mao had allowed to contain the word capital) before an audience of PRC officials, foreign dignitaries, U.S. Ambassador Leonard Woodcock, his family, staff and American Embassy employees. The language breakdown was about half Chinese, half English-speaking.

Waiting backstage with Hope as the audience filed to their seats, we peered through a gap in the curtain as a dozen high-ranking Communist Party leaders were being seated in the front row. They wore gray, baggy suits with the impeccable tailoring of pajamas from Wal-Mart. They looked to be in the neighborhood of 80 — and it must have been a rough neighborhood. Their lined faces reflected years of proletariat struggle, party in-fighting, industrial revolution and chain smoking.

Watching this grim potpourri of Maoists, Hope frowned. "Look at them. Not a smile and they don't even speak English. How am I supposed to get laughs?"

"Don't worry, Bob," Gig offered soothingly. "How many peasants could they have purged? A couple of million. Three on the outside."

Hope said, "You're right. What am I worried about? I survived vaudeville."

At rehearsal that afternoon, we had to settle on the most efficient method of translating the material into Mandarin. First, we tried projecting the Chinese characters on a large screen beside the stage, but the Chinese, well-known as fast readers, would laugh before Hope could finish each joke. We decided he'd need an interpreter on stage beside him.

We called for a volunteer and we got a good one — Ying Ruo Cheng, one of China's leading actors, who a decade later, would play the disgraced Mayor of Peking in *The Last Emperor*. Cheng's sense of comic timing proved an equal of Hope's and he got as many laughs from the Chinese as Hope was getting from the Westerners. I had seldom seen Hope more delighted — two laughs for the price of one.

His opening line that night was hardly designed to divert the minds of our hosts from the Cold War:

> *I can't believe I'm really here, but this must be China. Last night, I went to a movie called "The America Syndrome."*

Starring Jack Lemmon and Jane Fonda, *The China Syndrome* was playing to big box office in the states and concerned a threatened nuclear meltdown, a somewhat touchy subject in the PRC. But we were there to get laughs, and remember, this was before the age of political correctness.

> *I've been seeing all the sights. Yesterday, I stopped by the Academy of Science and they offered me a job as an exhibit.*

> *Then I visited the Hall of Longevity. I promised my insurance man I would.*

> *And I loved the Great Wall of China. Of course, I love anything as old as I am.*

Though Hope was now seventy-seven, until recently lines like these would never have made it into the monologue. But he was beginning to take a certain pride in having arrived in Senior-Citizenland. And especially in China, where age is revered, jokes like these fell on appreciative ears.

> *Then we visited the Forbidden City. What opulence! It looks like Caesar's Palace without the slot machines.*

At this juncture, Cheng turned to Hope and asked, "What's a *Caesar's Palace*?" The Chinese may have been in the dark, but as you would expect, the line got a huge laugh from the Westerners. Hope said, "It's a little place that takes the money the IRS didn't get." That's a pretty quick ad-lib, but you ain't seen nothin' yet.

> *Yesterday, I visited your Marble Boat at the Summer Palace. A boat made entirely of marble. At first they said it wouldn't float — and then Billy Graham showed up.*

Again, Cheng interrupted his translation and asked, "Who is Billy Graham?" And in one of the quickest ad-libs I had ever heard, Hope replied "Billy Graham is an advisor at *Caesar's Palace*." The line proved yet again what a consummate ad-libber Hope was.

During rehearsal, we got word that the Ministry of Culture had cut this joke from the monologue:

> *They serve a drink over here called mao tai. One sip and your head feels like it's going through a Cultural Revolution. Two sips and it feels like a Gang-of-Four.*

We gladly complied and excised the offending material. After all, we were batting five hundred. We lost this joke, but we managed to slip *America Syndrome* by them — most likely because they didn't have a clue as to its meaning.

Kung Pao Pulpit

During our visit, we never doubted for a moment that the officials running Chairman Mao-land were serious about their Communist faith. Theirs is a godless society and in 1979, they still meant to keep it that way. This, however, wasn't about to interfere with Dolores Hope's devotion to her Catholic faith, the fervor of which made Mother Teresa's look lukewarm. To call Dolores devoutly Catholic is to call Bill Gates "PC-obsessed." The godless society that can keep her out of church hasn't been invented.

One afternoon, returning from an extended shopping expedition, she announced excitedly that she had managed to put the slip on her interpreter to search for a priest. She not only managed to find one, but he invited her to attend an underground mass the following Sunday. Asked if I wanted to join her (she was aware that I had once studied for the priesthood, but not that I had long since defected), I said, "I think I'm already in enough danger with my jokes."

Hope couldn't seem to share her excitement, either. "Don't you know that people here have been shot for that?" he said.

"Of course," she replied confidently. "But at least I'll die in the state of grace."

Today, there are an estimated three hundred million Christians in China. But back then there were about three, and Dolores managed to find the two Catholics.

Dolores traces her roots to Italy (her maiden name was DeFina) and is well known from Toluca Lake to Palm Springs for her considerable culinary skills. She had taken no chances when facing a month of nothing but Chinese food. She brought along several large suitcases packed with every non-perishable item she could gather up at Monte Carlo, Burbank's premier Italian deli which had been "By Appointment to the House of Hope" for decades. Each evening, we feasted on salami, pickles, sesame crackers, mushrooms in olive oil, garbanzo beans and other assorted delicacies that would complement our daily Happy-Hour pitcher of dry-martinis that Dolores would prepare at five o'clock sharp. Shaken, not stirred.

❋ ❋ ❋ ❋

We were allowed to shop during our visit but — officially — only at government-sponsored retail outlets for tourists called "Freedom Stores."

Here the prices were set and clearly marked. No dickering. Even so, they were reasonable, and I brought home three good-quality wool rugs which still serve admirably.

Longing for a little more adventure, one afternoon Don, Gig and I slipped away from our guide for a couple of hours. In a narrow alley about a mile from the hotel, we discovered a small antique shop, obviously not intended for tourists. The musty interior was piled high with artifacts from estate-sales — rugs, furniture, household utensils, silverware, paintings, photos, lamps, vases, family stamps called *chops* made of marble or ivory and decorated with dragons, lions, monkeys and other characters from China's ancient mythology. More items made of ivory — chopsticks, statuary, and finely-carved jewelry. Up a narrow flight of stairs was the clothing — kimonos, men's suits, jackets, caps, sandals, shoes — all in a pile that said it hadn't been disturbed in years.

Hanging on one wall of the dimly lit mezzanine, almost unnoticed, were old costumes retired from the Peking Opera — multicolored capes, pantaloons, garments weighted down with gold embroidery. Here was a treasure trove that foreigners weren't supposed to find! We felt like Sydney Greenstreet stumbling upon the Maltese Falcon. We made a few purchases and headed back to the hotel.

That night over dinner, we mentioned our find to Mikhail Baryshnikov — *Mischa* to his friends, thank you — and he went giddy with excitement. Peking Opera costumes? Authentic ones? Immediately. we had to draw him a detailed map so he could check them out next day.

A few days later, Mischa's manager asked me if I'd be willing to lend his client some money. He had run out of cash and he had arranged to buy five of the costumes for around $300 apiece. I said, "Like I'm gonna lend money to a Russian *defector* who's in show business? This is a joke, right?"

Actually, I *had* about tapped out too, but suggested he ask our production cashier, Wil Oborn — we were issued a daily *per diem* in yuan — for an advance.

I'm told the five priceless costumes are now on display in his Manhattan brownstone.

Gig and I head back to the hotel after an afternoon of shopping at the Freedom Store. That's one of the carpets that still lie on our floor in Studio City. Leaving China, you had to account for the funds you brought in, and official receipts for all purchases were strictly required.

I'm auditioning a child's mini-violin which I was about to buy when our guide cautioned me that it might be confiscated by Chinese Customs — in my hands it could be considered a deadly weapon, banned for export. Even in China, everybody's a comedian.

Nr Schools, Rm 4 Concubine

We weren't allowed to take photographs inside the Forbidden City, but we were given a guided tour of the ancient structures located just a hop, skip and fortune cookie from the hotel. Directly across from the now-infamous Tiananmen Square, in the days of the emperors it was — and remains today — real estate as hallowed as Buckingham Palace or Taj Mahal.

Forbidden indeed it was. Only royalty and senior bureaucrats were allowed through the ancient turnstile: and the loftier their title, the deeper into the low rows of buildings they were allowed to proceed. As we were escorted from one chamber to the next, each more ornate than the one before, even Hope, who had seen just about everything, was impressed.

As we arrived at the very center of the complex, the emperor's living quarters, we stood for a long time in silence, inhaling the musty smell of ten centuries and drinking in the royal opulence. Finally, Hope broke the silence. Examining the intricately carved and bejeweled throne which had cradled royal derrieres from every dynasty, he turned and whispered just out of earshot of our guide, "When does Yul Brynner show up?"

A Night at The Opera

We set aside a full day for our visit to Peking's Chinese Opera School, which can best be described as the *New York School for the Performing Arts* — with barracks. Hand-picked by the government, kids from all over China are given free room, board and training to someday take their place in the cast of the Oriental version of the Met — the Peking Opera. I take that back. Compared to the Met, this ensemble is a Green Beret unit.

With more centuries under their belt than they care to admit, the Opera combines tumbling, juggling, gymnastics, slapstick comedy, fencing, acting, dancing and singing. The entire company consists of a first-string unit as well as a number of road versions that constantly tour the provinces. Sort of AAA-Opera.

The kids, who range in age from about eight to twelve, gave us a heart-pounding demonstration of calisthenics that seemed to transform

Don Marando and I try to blend in with this group of young students at the Peking Opera School. Hand-picked from villages all over China, they will spend years training for the "big show," all on the government's tab. It's a golden opportunity for any peasant kid — providing he wants to be in China's version of vaudeville.

them into prepubescent pretzels. We would later borrow six of these talented youngsters for a musical number that Hope would perform on Peking's famous Marble Boat — the one Billy Graham managed to float in the monologue.

Near the city's edge is a lake, on the banks of which the emperors built a summer palace — for those times when the pressures of emperoring called for a little R&R. Its most famous resident was the empress dowager, who apparently handled money something like Leona Helmsley, who left her fortune to her dogs. Somehow she managed to blow hundreds of thousands of yuan that the Chinese parliament had allocated for a navy. To appease an unsatisfied admiralty, she ordered the construction of a boat made entirely of marble. The size of a small Mississippi paddle-wheeler, it forever stands immobile at the dock, a monument to the dowager's quick thinking gift-giving.

Not to take advantage of such a weighty set — and one with a fascinating history to boot — would have been unthinkable, so we dressed Hope as a Chinese admiral complete with a uniform borrowed from the Peking Opera, backed him with the six singers, and gave him "The Queen's Navy" from Gilbert and Sullivan's *HMS Pinafore* with lyrics by James Lipton:

When I was a lad I tapped my feet
For nickles and dimes on a Cleveland street
I sang at picnics to the crowd's delight
And came in second at an amateur night
I came in second so frequently
That now I am the ruler of the Queen's navy

I knew I'd never get rich that way
So I took my act on the two-a-day
After six short months in vaudeville
I worked my way to the bottom of the bill
When vaudeville died, I was all at sea
So now I am the ruler of the Queen's navy

When Broadway beckoned one lucky day
My career was launched on the Great White Way
The critics rose with a mighty roar
And heatedly announced I wasn't Barrymore
So many shows sank under me
That now I am the ruler of the Queen's navy

My next adventure was radio
At last I was captain of my very own show
It pleased my family and it paid the rent
And it also sold a tube or two of Pepsodent
I sailed the airwaves for NBC
So now I am the ruler of the Queen's navy

So here I stand in my navy blue
On a marble boat with a Chinese crew
When I give commands they stand and stare
If I say "Let's go" they reply "Go where?"
This boat hasn't moved since the Qin Dynasty
And neither has the ruler of the Queen's navy

On my return visit to China in 2007, I saw the marble boat once more, still dead-in-the-water near the Summer Palace. I could almost see Hope on her deck with the six Peking Opera dancers twenty-eight years before. I doubt she ever had a more talented captain.

Sweatin' to the Oldies

It seems almost everyone in China begins the day with fifteen or twenty minutes of an ancient series of gentle exercises known as Tai Chi. Starting around six, Chinese of all ages can be seen everywhere practicing their version of Eight-Minute Abs — called "forms" — that combine grace, balance and controlled strength. In city parks, on roadsides, or on the sidewalks in front of their homes, health-conscious Chinese have discovered a perfect alternative to Curves.

So one bright, sunny morning we jostled Hope out of bed at an hour he probably hadn't seen since vaudeville and hustled him over to Peking's Bai Hai Park. There, Bob Wynn plopped him into the center of about two-hundred Chinese factory workers gathered for their sunrise stretch session.

As Hope did his best to mimic their movements to an amplified track of Gordon MacRae's *Oh, What a Beautiful Morning*, the camera meandered through the crowd. Though Hope missed a few pirouettes and generally resembled a reject from the second unit of the Bolshoi Ballet, the segment worked because it gave him an opportunity to pay homage in a comedic way to a daily ritual obviously held in high regard by our hosts.

This close attention to local customs and attitudes paid big dividends in every country we visited — especially so among the Chinese, whose culture is so different from our own.

The Accidental Tourist

There were few countries in the world where Hope could walk down the street and not be recognized and, as we learned shortly after arriving in the Chinese capital, the PRC was one of them. Aside from the officials assigned to oversee our every activity, no one in the city had a clue as to who the elderly American comedian was. The average Chinese on the street, either on foot or pedaling a bicycle, had never seen a movie, much less one with Hope in it. (Hope was asked to bring along one of his movies for a special showing at the Peking Film School to be followed by a discussion of his career on the big screen. He chose *Monsieur Beaucaire*, convinced it was more visual than the others and would be easily understood by a non-English speaking audience.)

TV was becoming more and more accessible to the peasants, but the bill-of-fare was strictly Chinese — mostly Peking Opera clips, agricultural programs, documentaries highlighting the latest factory technology or crop yields, and a sketch oriented variety show that might have been entitled *Communist Propaganda Tonight*.

At first, Hope enjoyed the anonymity that he hadn't experienced since he'd become famous. He'd often corral Gig and me to join him on long after-dinner walks through the industrial neighborhoods near downtown where most of our taping was done. He could stroll along freely, unhindered by the curious celebrity-watchers so common back home. We'd stop and peer past dusty parking lots that looked like bicycle burial grounds into assembly plants whose machines ran twenty-four hours a day, operated by hundreds of peasants — men and women all dressed alike in white shirts, gray pants and black cloth slippers. Three shifts, around-the-clock in decrepit-looking buildings that boasted Peking's version of air-conditioning — permanently open windows. We didn't spot any Nike labels, but only because China had not yet become the land of the American basketball-shoe.

After several weeks of this nightly routine, we noticed that Hope was growing uncomfortable with his newfound anonymity. Where were the milling throngs — the adoring, autograph-seeking fans? Adrift in a sea of blank stares — glazed unknowing l eyes — he was starting to realize that all he had was *us*!

But we were still in Peking.

"When we get to Shanghai, the people there will know me," Hope would say, believing that his English birth would hold him in good stead in British-influenced Shanghai.

He was correct in one respect. Shanghai did *look* a lot more like London. Both the architecture and the rich mahogany interiors stood in stark contrast to the sterile marble so much in evidence in Russian-influenced Peking. But, alas, the good citizens of Shanghai were no more familiar with that famous profile than those in the capital had been.

One early evening, while scouting locations in Shanghai's shopping district, our small group had been walking with Hope for several blocks. It was obvious that we were noticed by hundreds of passersby, but only as visiting Westerners.

Then from around a corner materialized a group of squealing teenagers waving what appeared to be autograph books. As they ran toward us, Hope said, "You chaps go on ahead, and I'll catch-up after I take care of these —" The girls rushed past him and into a department store that looked to be having a sale on Junior Miss kimonos. They were waving *coupon* books. Watching them rush by him, Hope looked slightly embarrassed.

"Well, Bob," I said, "now you know how it feels to be a nobody." Without breaking stride, he shot back, "How do you *stand* it?"

✳ ✳ ✳ ✳

Our accommodations at Shanghai's Chi Ching Hotel were as comfortable and steeped in history as any we'd ever been assigned. Gig and I shared the entire fifth floor with two production assistants, with a private elevator that opened onto our common foyer. We had a full-sized living room (with a fireplace), a dining room and a *kitchen!* The bedrooms at either end of the floor were castle-like turrets with leaded-glass windows that opened onto a view of upscale homes on the poplar-lined streets below. My spring-less bed was cushioned with down from swans that must have been plucked during the Qin Dynasty. Before entering my large, black-and-white tiled bathroom, I'd knock to alert the cockroaches whose honorable ancestors had to have taken up residence when that mattress was delivered.

This wasn't a Roach Motel — it was the Roach Waldorf-Astoria!

But all-in-all, Gig and I were so enchanted by Shanghai that we included this description in our dispatch to King Features:

> "Shanghai — the word itself evokes visions of a China we in America have always thought typical — gray sampans slowly gliding across the evening shadows of the Yangtze, steamy back streets, narrow and pungent with all the exotic and forbidden smells of the Orient — opium dens, gambling, vice. I think I'm homesick. Former occupation by the British has left its mark everywhere. This morning, I could have sworn I was awakened by Big Ben chiming in Cantonese. Everything seems stamped with an English benchmark. It wouldn't surprise me to come around a corner here and run into a Beefeater wearing a Mao jacket."

One night, cast and crew were seated at a banquet hosted by the Chinese Army. As he did at all the formal dinners, considering it a gracious gesture toward our hosts, Hope was attempting to operate a set of chopsticks ("My instructor says I'm doing so well, next week he's letting me use *two.*") While giving it the ol' college try, he lost control of a large fried shrimp that sailed over his shoulder like an aquatic scud missile, barely missing an ancient artifact — no doubt a Ming vase — on a table nearby. He looked around to see if anyone had caught his *faux pas*. It had gone unnoticed except by Don Marando who leaned over and whispered, "Bob, why don't you take a Mulligan?" (For you non-golfers, a Mulligan is a free shot to replace an errant one.)

As important to Hope as using chopsticks, was his rule that, no matter what, he'd at the very least, sample every entree that was served to us. At one banquet, he leaned over to me and said, pointing to an item on the Lazy Susan, "What's that?"

"Fried salmon lips," I said. "Pretty good."

We're sitting in the room at Shanghai's Chi Ching Hotel where Nixon had signed the U.S.-China Trade Agreement in 1974 at the mahogany and inlaid-ivory desk behind us. Sitting at the desk, Hope joked, "Should I open trade relations with Moscow?" Hope enjoyed exploring the sites in every country we visited.

Placing several of them on his plate, he whispered, "From now on, don't tell me.

Compared to today's modern construction boom in China (office high-rises can take as little as a *week* per floor to erect), 1979 construction was rudimentary, labor intensive and slow, using methods that had been the norm for centuries. Scaffolds which could extend upwards four or five stories were made of sturdy bamboo stalks lashed together with hemp. Hard hats had not yet been introduced — workers wore large-brimmed straw coolie hats as they scrambled along bamboo platforms that looked like the raft Tom and Huck ran away on.

Heavy duty tricycles with large, wooden flat beds between the two rear wheels were used to transport building materials — everything from twenty-foot tall stacks of bricks to bags of cement to steel re-bar and girders.

One day I noticed one of these flat beds had pulled up beside us at a stop light (all stop lights came with a white-uniformed traffic control officer perched on a raised platform in the center of the intersection). The bed was empty save for a large canvas cover cinched around the edges with twine. Three sets of feet, toes upward, protruded beyond the edge of the canvas at the rear of the flat bed.

Pointing, I said to our guide, "Get a load of these guys catching forty winks on the way to the job site."

He shook his head and said, "No more work for them. They're dead." He explained that so many peasants came to Peking looking for employment, they became part of a faceless horde with no ties to local families and no means of identification. The flat bed driver was part of the city's "corpse corps," charged with picking up the deceased and taking them to a central location for disposal.

From the moment we arrived in China, I'd had a sense of how vastly different our cultures were, but that day I realized how wide the chasm really was. Though it's been twenty-nine years, I can still see those six sets of toes pointing heavenward.

Card Trick

On every overseas trip, Barney McNulty, a naval history buff, would check out the local maritime museums. During our week's stay in Shanghai, he struck a mother-lode and was spending much of his free time exploring the museum he found in that ancient seaport upon which the British had so thoroughly stamped their influence.

As would happen occasionally, on one foray, he lost the concept of time's unceasing march and was nowhere to be found when Hope and Mikhail Baryshnikov arrived for a scheduled run-through. Without the cue cards, they were helpless and, as the minutes ticked on, Hope became more and more annoyed. He was slow to anger, but cross the line and he could make the offending party wish he or she had stayed in bed or even out of show business — witness his dressing down Tony Randall in Chapter 2. Since Barney's tardiness was not that unusual, when it did happen, we'd all pitch in to protect him, making sure we'd catch him before Hope did to warn him.

Finally, Barney strolled into the hotel — forty-five minutes late — and we were able to alert him that he'd better have a solid story ready. He did and immediately began pleading his case — he'd never seen so many books on the British Navy, he was so fascinated by the ship models that lined the museum's walls, he was transported to another place, another time — a place where cue cards weren't on the top of one's list.

It was a gallant effort, but Hope was all over him like Simon Cowell on a tone-deaf *American Idol* contestant.

"This is it, Barney — the last straw! You've gone too far this time. I've let it slide in the past, but now it's too late. You're through. Done. I can't rely on you, and you're no longer of any use to me."

Barney looked genuinely crestfallen. "Sorry, boss..."

It was an apology that was all too familiar. We'd heard it before. As Barney slowly turned to leave. Hope said, "Where are you going now?"

"To find a Chinese guy who can print in English."

"Okay, as soon as we land in Burbank..."

Barney had a unique relationship with Hope because he was, while holding the cards, always up front and visible, vulnerable — the ideal flack-catching position if anything went wrong. Worse, he was almost in the audience. He was like an all-too-convenient whipping boy.

But there was a special bond between the two men that you could feel just watching them together. Maybe part of it was due to an incident that happened in Vietnam toward the end of the war. A secret itinerary for a USO Christmas special had fallen into the hands of the Viet Cong who scored a direct hit on the suite Hope was supposed to be occupying at the Brinks Hotel in Saigon. The room, and several to either side of it, was completely destroyed, and the only reason Hope wasn't in it was because Barn had failed to show up for a rehearsal.

Barney had saved Hope's life and the memory of that close call was never far from their minds.

One Mime At A Time

We found that having brought along Shields and Yarnell and Big Bird, whose acts were visual requiring no translation made producing a television special in a non-English speaking country much easier. A segment with Bob Shields and Lureen Yarnell mimicking mannequins in a Shanghai department store had no words, and needed none — the smiles of delight on the faces of the unsuspecting shoppers said it all. And *Sesame Street*'s Big Bird so totally captivated the kids, there's a whole generation over there now that's sworn off Peking duck.

Inside the Big Bird costume resides a talented puppeteer named Carroll Spinney who, thanks to a special contractual arrangement with Jim Henson Productions, operates the only Muppet character allowed to work solo. Besides the constant maintenance he requires (he loses about 350 turkey feathers per outing), the bird is no piece of cake to operate.

While providing the voice, Spinney must keep his left arm extended over his head to work the beak and simulate neck movement. All the while, he's watching a three-inch TV monitor inside the bird's chest cavity just to be able to navigate. A small fan supplies some air circulation, but Carroll usually emerged looking like he'd been in a sauna. He relies on an assistant named Kermit Love (no relation to the frog) to keep the Bird looking spiffy and his operator from falling off a stage or walking into traffic.

Of all our guests over the years, Big Bird was probably the most underpaid, considering what goes into every performance.

The Great Escape

I spent my final half hour on Chinese soil trying to decide how I wanted to depart the People's Republic — by firing squad or the gallows.

Traveling with an internationally recognized entertainment icon has to rank among the most exhilarating experiences known to man. You're chased after, fawned over, catered to and must keep reminding yourself that it's not you who's causing all the commotion. As long as the mega-celebrity who is causing it remains in the immediate vicinity, you're as safe as those pilot fish you see swimming beside a shark. My problem was that my shark had left Peking the previous day to complete a personal appearance tour of the Orient and suddenly, we were all on our own — on the other side of the world — with no superstar to protect us.

On getaway day, I reported to the airport and presented my passport and Chinese travel-papers to the authorities — a group of guys in brown khaki uniforms with a little red star on their cap. I was informed that my documents were virtually riddled with irregularities that likely would preclude my departure that day — soon — or quite possibly, ever.

Stunned, I looked at our interpreter — by now we had become pretty close pals — who explained that, in the confusion of our arrival with Hope's party a month before, someone had neglected some extremely important stamping and initialing. As more — and successively higher ranking — army guys arrived behind the counter to help determine my fate, I sensed the interpreter was pleading with them to release me.

The engines on the Chinese Airlines 707 were revving up just outside the lobby door. I could see that the folding stairs up front were still down, but the rear boarding ramp had been rolled away. Inside, secure in their seats, were the Liptons, the Spinneys, Micha, Crystal Gayle, Don, Barney and most of the staff. They were about to take off and my seat was empty!

As my panic was growing more obvious (sweat was spurting out of me like the Trevi Fountain), my young interpreter leaned over and whispered, "When I nod, walk directly to the plane, board, and whatever you do, *don't look back.*" My parting gift to him of several reams of high-quality erasable bond from the show's supply locker had paid off. (Tips are frowned on in China, but gifts are welcome, and back then paper was as scarce as gasoline is today.)

Now the bureaucratic summit meeting behind the counter was reaching fever pitch. As the soldiers motioned for their superiors, my trusted student agent nodded toward the door. I shook his hand, spun around and walked toward the plane with that same determined stride that had worked so well for Ingrid Bergman in *Casablanca.*

As instructed, I didn't look back as several young sound guys pulled me aboard the taxiing plane, yanked the stairs in after me and latched the door. I learned later that Jim Lipton, a pilot himself, had asked the Chinese pilot to delay the takeoff until I was aboard. I am forever in his debt for his rescue from a bureaucratic nightmare — and to the Bob Hope Show for ordering that extra paper.

When I finally plopped into my seat, everyone was applauding and a few shook my hand. I could tell they believed I had come *that* close to not making it out of there — but by some miracle I had and we were on our way home.

It would take me twenty-eight years to muster the courage to go back.

CHAPTER 10

Penalized for Unnecessary Dancing

In 1981, Ronald Reagan was firmly ensconced in the White House, Lady Diana had just married Prince Charles and the National Football League was celebrating its sixtieth anniversary. Hope and NBC decided that the event had all the earmarks of a highly-rated television special.

Actually, the idea had been brought to them by producer Jane Upton Bell, daughter of Bert Bell, founder of the Philadelphia Eagles, and one of the NFL's early commissioners. A former producer-director for Mike Douglas, Janie had all of the talents the show would require — production experience coupled with an intimate knowledge of the game and its stars, past and present. Plus, she brought an added bonus to the special — because of the contacts she had developed over the years, booking the show would be a stroll through the end zone. Moreover, Hope was confident that the archival footage of the league's embryonic years that she had access to were the best film clips available. As far as the NFL was concerned, she was family.

Janie set out to gather the stats and the film and turned the writers loose to come up with the appropriate huddle humor. The two-hour special would field a team of first-string guest stars that included Elizabeth Taylor, Olivia Newton-John, Barbara Mandrell, Howard Cosell, Susan Anton, Joe Namath, Don Knotts, George Gobel and Betty White. The gridiron greats included Roger Staubach, Rosie Greer, Bob Lilley, George Blanda, Dick Butkus, Garo Youpremian and O.J. Simpson (remember him?) as well as coaches Weeb Ewbank, George Allen and Hank Stramm.

After the coin toss, we turned Hope loose with enough porcine references to make Jimmy Dean jealous.

> *Tonight. we're celebrating the sixtieth anniversary of the National Football League. Sixty years. Football now commands some of the largest audiences on television. And why not? It's got sex, violence and a message — do unto others harder and quicker than they can do it unto you.*

Hope bet on games every weekend and never seemed to be happy with his returns. When we were taping, we'd usually have a game on in the green-room, and he'd stick his head in every so often, check the score, shake his head in disgust, and go back to his dressing room.

We often referred to his losing ways in our submissions. During a soft-shoe with George Burns, George handed Hope some sand to sprinkle on the floor and said, "Here's some sand. Make a few bucks."

Hope replied, "I need it. I bet on the Rams."

> *The instant-replays have gotten so good that they often embarrass the officials. Earlier today, I saw a wide receiver run into a cheerleader, and he was penalized for unnecessary roughness. I don't know if it was unnecessary or not, but on the instant-replay, both were smiling.*

> *They're all pretty good actors. Directing football players isn't difficult. All you need is a long stick and plenty of raw meat.*

> *I really believe it's the natural order of things as God intended. Athletes become actors and actors, become president.*

> *Even on the football field, Reagan showed signs of becoming a politician. He'd yell, "One...two...hut...no comment."*

And Gerald Ford played center for the University of Michigan. Later, he took up golf and forgot to keep his head down.

As a center, he was never too accurate with his snaps. In fact, he made runners out of three punters.

Even on the field, he showed an interest in politics. After a touchdown, instead of spiking the ball, he'd kiss a baby.

And there's so much money in pro-football these days. I'd like to have what they spend on tape alone. Sometimes I think that if you checked underneath all those bandages, you'd find Mickey Rooney.

And the players today are fast. That comes from running back and forth to the bank.

What salaries! When they go into a huddle, E.F. Hutton listens.

When he was in his late seventies, Hope was asked by an interviewer what his greatest regret in life was. Without the slightest pause, he said, "I could have bought the Rams." He wanted to own a team after he became close friends with the owner of the San Diego Chargers, billionaire contractor, Alex Spanos.

The two were so close, in fact, one year for Christmas, Alex gave Hope his airplane. It was a Hawker-Siddely that Hope had borrowed so many times, Alex decided to upgrade to a Learjet. But Hope didn't keep his new wings very long after he realized that, not only did he have to hangar it between flights, he had to have two pilots on call twenty-four-seven.

He told me, "I have to pay them an annual salary, and they can't even write jokes."

Coach Motel

We segued to our first sketch set in a Betty Ford-style rehab clinic designed for NFL coaches suffering the ravages of job stress. Sharing the therapy session with staff psychiatrist Betty White were Hope, Weeb Ewbank, George Allen and Hank Stramm:

> (Betty enters the day room of the "Shady Glen Rest Home for Coaches" in a crisp, white uniform and carrying a clipboard.)

BETTY: Good morning, gentlemen. I'll be conducting your therapy session today. My name is Dr. Freud Rice.

ALL: Good morning, Dr. Rice!

BETTY: Now, when you hear your name, please answer up. (checks clipboard) Coach Hank Stramm?

HANK: Here!

BETTY: Coach Weeb Ewbank?

WEEB: Here!

BETTY: Coach George Allen?

GEORGE: Here!

BETTY: Coach "Bum" Hope?

HOPE: Absent!

BETTY: I mean *physically*.

HOPE: Oh, that. Here.

Casting amateurs was always risky but the three coaches showed a sense of timing and projection that belied their lack of experience treading the boards. Each showed up knowing his lines, and when changes were made in the script, they were quick studies. They had as much poise in front of the camera as many of our more experienced guests lacked. I was so impressed by them during rehearsal, I mentioned it to Hope. He said, "They're not amateurs. They're on television more than *I* am."

Hope loved sports. He was a frequent visitor at some of America's top golf courses (he often played with Palmer and Nicholas). As a youth, he'd had three prize fights as a professional, boxing under the name "Packy

East," a career he abandoned after he realized, as he put it, "I was looking at more canvas than Van Gogh." Still, he remained an avid fight fan all his life.

We were in Pensacola doing a special one year, and a championship middleweight bout was scheduled for that weekend. Hope was looking forward to watching it in his hotel suite and was told the hotel didn't have satellite TV — back then relatively rare. Determined not to miss the fight, he told us to drive around the city until we spotted a dish — they were about twenty feet across in those days — on someone's roof and ask the owner if we could watch the fight there. His plan worked, and there's a family of four in Florida who still can't believe Bob Hope sat in their den watching boxing.

WEEB: Doctor, why do we have to stay here?

BETTY: Well, you're suffering from a rare form of neurotic para-
         noia evidenced by severe manic-depression and socio-
         pathic schizophrenia.

WEEB: Could you put that in laymen's terms?

BETTY: Certainly. You're all *cuckoo*. Tell me, what pushed you
         over the edge?

WEEB: Being in all those light-beer commercials (mimics) It's
         the taste. . . no, the calories. . . no the taste... no, the
         calories.

BETTY: Then why did you do them?

WEEB: The *money*!

Product endorsements had become a major income source for any rea-
sonably articulate athlete able to read an idiot card. Joe Namath hawked Legg's pantyhose; Jim Palmer Jockey Shorts; Johnny Bench Krylon, spray paint ("No runs, no drips, no errors"); and O.J. was sprinting through airports — this was in his pre-arthritis days — for Hertz "the Superstar of Rent-a-Car."

Betty White was one of TV's most versatile stars, equally memorable as "The Happy Homemaker," Sue Ann Nivens, on *The Mary Tyler Moore Show* and Rose Nyland on *The Golden Girls*, on which she had been offered the lead but declined, fearing she'd be typecast. She's now active in animal rights causes and is a major financial supporter of the Los Angeles Zoo, donating $100,000 in 2007 alone. She appeared on several Hope specials over the years.

It would only be a few years before Jim Brown would share a Pepsi with a kid in the players' tunnel and set a record for highest commercial ad rate during a Super Bowl halftime. (Since surpassed fivefold.)

HANK: (barks) Woof! Woof! Woof!

BETTY: Does he always do that?

HOPE: Yeah, he thinks he's a puppy. (to Hank) Hey, Fido!
            Knock it off!

BETTY: (scolding) Never ever do that! He must be treated with
            kindness, sympathy and understanding. Have you tried
            hitting him with a rolled-up newspaper?

Despite behavioral evidence to the contrary, it turns out that the boys are
still in possession of their full compliment of marbles and are nothing but
overpaid malingerers. As soon as Betty is out of sight, they continue their
round-the-clock poker game.

HOPE: She still thinks we're nuts!

GEORGE: I hope we can keep it up. This is the greatest vacation
            I've ever had.

HANK: And the best part is, the owners are paying for it!

This was, to a comedy writer, an example of a perfect resolution of a
sketch. It made sense, the audience didn't see it coming, and it showed
authority figures — the team owners — being bamboozled. Whichever
one of us came up with the idea most likely worked *backwards*. That is,
thought of a way coaches could scam their bosses and get away with it
and then built the story line around it. Song writers often work this way,
coming up with a *hook* first — often the title of the song — and then
writing the lyrics that lead up to it.

Toe Dancer

"Lonesome" George Gobel began his career as a gentle, guitar-plucking
country singer on a small radio station in Chicago. Gifted with a unique
and friendly charm and a wife he referred to as "spooky ol' Alice," he
worked his way up to his own network variety show and later captivated
a new generation of viewers as a regular on *Hollywood Squares*.

Since he was quick with an ad-lib and had an ear for comic dialog,
we figured he'd be perfect in the role of interpreter for a non-English

speaking place kicker — and one of the most accurate in NFL history —
Garo Youpremian:

HOPE: I never knew you spoke a foreign language, George. Are
            you fluent?

GEORGE: Well, a little, but I'll hold onto something and maybe no
            one will notice.

George was not averse to tossing back a distilled spirit or two before tackling an important assignment. Asked once why he felt this little ritual was necessary, he replied, "You don't think I'd go out there alone, do you?"

HOPE: Ask him why he decided to become a football player.

GEORGE: A devisa acque footbol?

            (Garo answers) He says because he always wanted to
            have big shoulders.

HOPE: Makes sense. Ask him why all the best place-kickers
            these days seem to be foreigners.

GEORGE: Jabba lad borgamo foreinski?

            (Garo answers) He says because none of them were born
            in this country.

This style of humor provided Burns and Allen with long, lucrative careers. Labeled in vaudeville a "dumb act," it requires carefully worded questions that the person answering — here Garo, a male Gracie — can interpret *literally*. Since the answers are silly, this type of writing looks easy, but it's not. Try coming up with a few yourself and you'll see.

Since I know not a word of Polish, while writing the dialog, I came up with what I thought sounded like passable phrases. George, being the consummate pro he was, didn't make up his own gibberish but *memorized* mine! That's the ultimate example of an actor's faithfulness to the written word. Would that they were all like that.

HOPE: When did he realize that he had a talented foot?

GEORGE:	Mika sen dorgondo el toesa?
	(Garo answers) As soon as he was born. When the doctor slapped him, he kicked the doctor seventy-five yards.
HOPE:	That's remarkable. (Garo responds)
GEORGE:	He says not really. The play was called back because his mother was offsides.
HOPE:	Ask him what was his longest kick.
GEORGE:	Meta linquoro keek distenso?
	(Garo answers) About an hour and a half. The ball hit the Goodyear blimp and stuck there.
HOPE:	George, tell him I thank him for being on the show.
GARO:	My pleasure, Mr. Hope. I really enjoyed doing it.
GEORGE:	He says —
HOPE:	I got it, George, I got it. Garo Youpremian, ladies and gentlemen.

With Garo as a guest, we had an added bonus. We noticed in the biographical material provided by his PR firm that he was an accomplished amateur singer, something the NFL hadn't publicized. So we followed up the comedy routine with a duet with Hope. Another example of Hope's practice of taking advantage of every performing skill a guest had to offer.

Necessary Roughness

Comic actor Don Knotts forever changed the image of law enforcement when he pinned on a badge as Andy Griffith's deputy sheriff of Mayberry. To take full advantage of Barney Fife's invaluable experience as an authority figure in over his head and attempting to hide the fact, we cast him as the NFL's chief referee, Moose Terwilliger:

> (Don enters in ref's uniform: striped shirt and white pants. He carries a whistle.)

Although my first network variety show was *The Dean Martin Celebrity Roasts*,
I never got to meet Dean. He just wasn't in the habit of dropping by the production
office in Burbank. We attended the tapings at the M.G.M. Grand in Las Vegas,
but Dean dealt only with our head writer, Harry Crane. Ten years later, when
Dean appeared on a special entitled *Bob Hope Salutes the Super Bowl*, he sang
a parody duet I had co-written on the players' strike called "Waiting in the
Wings." I finally met him! Good things come to those who wait.

HOPE: Welcome to the show, Moose.

DON: Thank you, Mr. Hope. Glad to be here. (blows whistle)

HOPE: What was that for?

DON: Gotta keep the ol' pea moist. Otherwise, she'll lock up
             on you.

Back in Mayberry, Barney was forever keeping his peace officer's equipment in apple-pie order — including the single bullet he wasn't allowed
to put into his gun without Andy's permission. In this routine, the whistle will play the role of a weapon, and Don holds it as though it were.

HOPE: Moose, what qualities would you say are essential to be-
             ing a good referee?

DON: You must be positive — definite. Well, sort of positive
             and sort of definite. You have to look like you know
             what you're doing even if you don't know what you're
             doing.

HOPE: Do you always know what you're doing?

DON: I don't even know what I'm doing *here*.

Don had begun his television career on the original *Tonight Show* as a
"man-on-the-street" who was often interviewed by Steve Allen. His eyes
bulged and his face twitched as he portrayed a mass of exposed nerve
endings. Here, Hope is playing the straight man — as Allen had — but
had great difficulty not breaking-up — as Steve often did.

Even though he knew what Don was about to say, Don's feigned gruff-
ness and counterfeit macho were hard to resist. No one ever portrayed a
nervous character on television more effectively, and I've always believed
that, in his later movie work, the screenwriters never took full advantage
of Don's talent. In films like *The Ghost and Mr. Chicken* and *The Reluc-
tant Astronaut*, he was portrayed as a fear-obsessed bungler. Bunglers are a
dime-a-dozen in films, but a case of nerves caused by *fear of being exposed
as incompetent* was Don's specialty, and no one ever did it more effectively.

HOPE: Do those big football players intimidate you?

DON: (holds up whistle) The league says I have all the author-
           ity I need right here. (blows whistle)

HOPE: A whistle?

DON: Silly isn't it? I wanted a hand-grenade, but...

HOPE: So it's just you and a whistle against all those giants.

DON: Yeah, but if they give me any trouble, I just stand my
           ground and look 'em right in the navel.

HOPE: Tell me, Moose, what's the toughest part of calling a
           penalty?

DON: Getting that little radio on my belt to work. During a
           game last week, I turned it on and got a rock 'n roll station.

HOPE: That must have been embarrassing.

DON: Sure was. Before I could shut the darned thing off, I had
           to penalize both teams for unnecessary dancing.

HOPE: Do losing teams ever blame your officiating?

DON: After one game where I made a few bad calls, they pre-
           sented me with the game ball.

HOPE: Oh. They're good sports then.

DON: Not really. It had to be surgically removed.

A consummate visual comedian, Don appeared as though he was actually
undergoing the procedure right there on stage. Then Hope momentarily
left the script and delivered this ad-lib:

HOPE: Boy, you're lucky it wasn't the Championship Trophy.

As you would imagine, hearing this response for the first time, Don gave
Hope what I characterized as not a double-take but a *quadruple* take. It
was the only real laugh line Hope had in the entire routine, and he had
given it to *himself!*

The line succeeded in doing what you hope all punchlines will do — create a clear picture in the mind of the audience that everyone sees at the same instant. They erupted into the biggest laugh in the show, and there were plenty of them. And Hope proved once again that he was one of the quickest ad-libbers ever.

HOPE: I'm sure some viewers aren't familiar with the hand signals the referee uses. Could you demonstrate a few for us?

DON: Sure. (hands on hips) Offsides... (swings leg up)... Roughing the kicker...(palm behind knee) Clipping... (hands shielding eyes) This means "Heavens to Betsy, I made a boo-boo!"

HOPE: I can't thank you enough for coming on the show and I'll bet your family is proud of you.

DON: They sure are. Especially Dad. He always said I'd end up wearing stripes.

This type of one-on-one interview format crafted to capitalize on a well established comic character provided a welcome respite from the grind of conventional one-size-fits-all sketch writing. We were able to create a variety of situations using costumes and props to enhance the comic possibilities. Hope would perform many of them with other established comic actors like Tony Randall, Don Rickles and Jonathan Winters and some non-actors who had become caricatures of themselves — like Howard Cosell.

I once asked Don Knotts about his early training as a ventriloquist. He told me he practiced so diligently, the Army put him in Special Services to appear in camp shows. During a USO visit by Edgar Bergen, his childhood hero, Don was assigned to escort him around the base. Sitting beside him during a rehearsal, Edgar, who was holding Charlie McCarthy on his lap, turned to Don and said, "I have to take a leak. Here, hold this." He dropped Charlie on Don's lap like, Don recalled, "a large beanbag." Don froze. He was holding Charlie McCarthy! But Charlie's head hung lifeless, and his arms and legs were twisted grotesquely. Then Don slowly realized that he was holding a prop that Bergan used to *create* Charlie — just a cleverly arranged pile of sawdust, carved wood and cloth — nothing more.

Don claimed he had learned a valuable show business lesson, but he still choked up a little telling this story.

Sliced Tongue

Howard Cosell was a former lawyer who, as a dutiful dad, had volunteered to describe his son's Pop Warner League game for a local radio station and saw his law career quickly replaced by a new and more lucrative one — in broadcasting.

Coming to the game late myself from the courtroom, on our first special together, I was anxious and excited to meet him. I went up, introduced myself and said, "Howard, you and I have something in common."

He said, "What's that?"

I said, "We both started out as lawyers."

He just stared at me for a moment and said, "*So?*"

That was my crash course in Howard Cosell.

Howard had been characterized by sports writers for so long as a certified curmudgeon, I think he gradually began believing it himself and felt compelled to deliver the crusty, cantankerous version of himself that he was convinced the public had come to expect. He was rehearsing a routine in Hope's dressing room and came to a line he thought could be improved upon. I happened to be standing nearby so Hope said, pointing to the joke, "See if you guys can come up with something better for Howard." I noted the line and went back to the writers room where about five of us "threw lines" — made suggestions for the others to rule on — until we had ten replacements that we all agreed filled the bill.

I hurried back to Hope's dressing room with the list. Hope was checking his makeup and motioned for me to hand the list to Cosell. He took it and, slowly looking it up-and-down, said, "Is this the *best* you could do?" I could see Hope wince. He obviously resented Howard's assessment of his writing staff, one of whom, Charlie Isaacs, dated back to Hope's radio days.

He snatched the list from Howard, quickly chose a new line and told me to get it to Barney McNulty to put on cue cards.

Despite his being difficult, Howard always added an air of authenticity to our sports specials, so he was invited back many times. Our NFL special featured this quintessential Cosell segment and showcased the popular commentator at his best:

HOPE: Do you just start talking, or do I have to light a fuse?

COSELL: Robert, your facility for the jocular riposte, and your mastery of droll repartee doesn't extract a measure of risability from me.

HOPE: Howard, either thank you...or you'll hear from my lawyer in the morning — Howard, you're such a personality, I wouldn't even know how to describe you.

COSELL: That's easy, Bob. Basically, I'm a journalistic interpreter, concentrating on the domain of athletic endeavor, a commentator who prides himself as much on his dispassionate veracity as on his eloquent and insightful reportorial aptitude.

HOPE: Would you make a needlepoint of that for me? I'll hang it in my office. You've been on *Monday Night Football* for some time now. Have you ever thought of retiring?

COSELL: Not 'til the children are raised.

HOPE: The children?

COSELL: The Giffer and Danderoo [nicknames for his fellow sportscasters Frank Gifford and "Dandy" Don Meredith].

HOPE: Howard, thanks for being with us.

COSELL: Robert, the gratification is distinctly and singularly

mine. And should any specific circumstance necessitate a
future reappearance on my part, simply voice your sup-
plication, and it shall be made manifest.

HOPE: Thank you. Now I'm going backstage to run that
through my decoder ring.

League of Her Own

While planning our special, Janie Bell had an idea for a sketch that would
involve the appointment of the National Football League's first *female*
commissioner. As a daughter of one, Janie was particularly interested in
the concept.

At the first of several writers' meetings, she approached Hope with
the idea and he liked it, too. But the big question was: Who could we
book who would be a large enough screen presence to carry it off? After
discussing several possibilities, Hope himself came up with a "someone"
we all agreed would be perfect: Elizabeth Taylor.

Come again?

Taylor didn't do television, least of all a variety show that had a ten-
dency to toss jabs at anyone or any institution within comic range.

But Hope had an ace up his sleeve and we were about to learn what
it was. He told Elliott Kozak, his co-producer, to call Elizabeth on the
phone — Hope could get ahold of anyone, it seemed, at any time, including the president. Elliott scurried off and was soon holding Liz on
the line for the boss. Hope spoke with her briefly, hung up, and announced that she had agreed to come on the show!

What had happened was reminiscent of the many times over the
years Hope had booked guests with a promise to return the favor with
a reciprocal appearance on their show. Even though Elizabeth wasn't on
television, she did have a show where Hope knew his presence would be
invaluable. Each year, she hosted a huge fund-raiser at Wolf Trap for the
benefit of AIDS research. Hope had her cornered, and he knew it.

We wrote a short sketch that wouldn't tax our guest and could be
taped in a few hours. The entire piece took place in the commissioner's

office where Liz fielded complaints from players accusing a George Steinbrenner-like team owner named Bobby Trueheart (Hope) of on-the-job harassment. They included Joe Namath, George Blanda and O.J. Simpson, whose appearance ironically gave rise to this exchange:

> (Simpson enters, jumping over several suitcases)

LIZ: And you have to be O.J. Simpson.

O.J.:   I don't have to be, but with all the money I've been making on commercials lately, I think I'll stay him a little longer.

LIZ: I don't blame you. I see you on TV morning, noon and night.

We hadn't seen nothin' yet!

＊ ＊ ＊ ＊

Anxious to book Liz for the show and aware that he was getting her for scale, Hope agreed to cover the cost of any wardrobe purchases necessary for her appearance. A few months after the show aired, he was reviewing production expenses and noticed an entry that read: "$700 for one pair of Tony Lama snakeskin boots."

Liz had remained behind her desk throughout the sketch.

Hope turned to Elliott and said, "Next time we lay out $700 for a pair of boots, make sure the writers work them into the plot."

Wrecking Crew

We took advantage of Janie's access to early NFL film footage with a sketch based on the pre-NFL company-sponsored teams that began playing games, without standardized rules, on small-town fields and vacant lots. (In 2008, George Clooney directed and starred in the movie, *Leatherheads,* which took place during this era.) Interspersing live action with the grainy, black-and-white clips, we staged a game featuring the kicking phenom, Crazy Nose Hope, playing on a team sponsored by a local laundry.

Announcer John Harlan provided the play-by-play:

HARLAN: Crazy Nose checks the wind, sets the ball — he pauses — kicks — it's a long, spiraling — no wait — that's his *shoe*!

Later, when Hope is being carried off the field following a bone-crushing collision:

HARLAN: Crazy Nose has been injured and it looks like it could be serious. As he was being carried off the field, he was gesturing wildly to his insurance man!

Hope's girlfriend Bonnie Sue (Barbara Mandrell) may have to postpone their wedding if he keeps breaking bones. On the sidelines, they sing:

BARBARA: *You've got a fracture...*

HOPE: *That's from the fullback...*

BARBARA: *You've got a broken toe...*

HOPE: *That's from the end...*

BARBARA: *The doctor said there's a slight concussion...*

HOPE: *That right tackle's not my friend.*

BARBARA: *They cracked your kneecaps...*

HOPE: *That was the left guard...*

BARBARA: *You have a dislocation in your neck...*

HOPE: *I've got mementos from all the players...*

BARBARA: *You're just an All-American wreck!*

Despite his career-ending injuries, the coach — Michael Conrad from *Hill Street Blues* — sends Hope back in after appropriate medical treatment — "Here's an aspirin."

And, of course — inspired by Bonnie Sue's unwavering loyalty, he recovers sufficiently to carry his team to victory.

The spot was another example of Hope taking advantage of his guests who could both sing *and* act.

$$* \quad * \quad * \quad *$$

With an entertaining balance of film clips, player interviews, music and comedy, this show would turn out to be our highest-rated sports-themed special of the eighties. With a 26 rating and a 34 share, it managed to register as much Neilsen hang-time as an NFL kickoff. It was almost as good as hitting the Goodyear blimp.

CHAPTER 11

The Potion in the Lotion from the Ocean

I n vaudeville, Hope had been a song and dance man before he began
delivering jokes. While radio didn't allow him to take advantage of his
musical background, television provided a perfect showcase for his vocal
and hoofing talents.

It was no surprise then that he preferred booking guests who could
sing and dance as well as hold their own in the show's sketches. With the
exception of a few female performers who were added to the billboard
solely for their physical contributions, he favored guests who had a voice
and could deliver lines convincingly.

Whenever we parodied a recognizable tune, Hope had to obtain the
consent of the song's publisher. Occasionally, an author would withhold
permission — not surprising in light of how we often butchered a classic for a quick laugh — but most went along with our parodies in the
spirit of fun. Hope loved to sing in the sketches and, since we collected
ASCAP royalties for our comedic interpretations, we tried to work music
in whenever possible.

Throughout the sixties and seventies, Steve Lawrence and Eydie
Gorme were frequent guests, favorites of Hope because he could use
them both as singers and comic actors. Steve and Eydie had met while
appearing as regulars on *The Garry Moore Show* where they learned the art
(and it's definitely an art) of sketch comedy.

In a 1978 special entitled *Bob Hope's Tribute to the Palace Theater*, we took advantage of their musical comedy talents by casting them in a sketch playing Sir Lancelot and Lady Guinevere opposite Hope's King Arthur in a parody we called *Squares at the Round Table*.

It's a typical example of the type of Hope sketch that combined jokes and song parodies and one that has the creative earmarks of the producer, Sheldon Keller.

This sketch is interesting in several other respects as well. It demonstrates the writers' obsession with popular brand-names, a joke source that dated back to Hope's radio days — a device that allowed them to take full advantage of the audience's instant recognition of the references, an essential element in all successful joke writing.

Sheldon Keller began his career on *Your Show of Shows* and wrote screenplays including *Buona Sera, Mrs. Campbell* and *Movie Movie* with Larry Gelbart. In the 1980s, he formed "The Beverly Hills Unlisted Jazz Band" with George Segal (banjo) and Conrad Janis (trombone). He played bass. Jack Lemmon would often sit in on piano and Hal Linden on clarinet. The band appeared on *The Tonight Show* and in the 1986 movie *Nothing In Common*.

Also, the sketch offers a prime example of a structural element that Hope favored and used whenever possible — the celebrity blackout. This, too, dated back to his radio show when he'd often prevail upon major stars to perform in "cameos"— brief walk-ons requiring little rehearsal. Usually, he didn't pay for these appearances, preferring instead to barter his own services by promising to appear in some show or personal appearance of theirs. No exchange of fees and thus no IRS involvement, always a "plus" where Hope was concerned.

For our sketch, we landed

a biggie to make a quickie appearance, but no fair skipping ahead to find out who it is.

Squares at the Round Table

(Trumpeters beside the entrance to the castle sound a fanfare. Eydie, in a flowing purple gown, enters strumming a small harp)

	('Greensleeves')
EYDIE:	(sings) *I'm Guinevere...*
	good King Arthur's wife...
	and I swore to be true to him...
	all my life...
	But alas and alack...
	now I love him not...
	because I'm hot to trot...
	with Sir Lancelot!

Note that in just eight lines, Eydie has set up the premise of the entire sketch. With only ten minutes to work with, we had no time to dilly-dally.

EYDIE:	(cups ear) Hark! I think I hear my handsome knight coming now!
	(Steve Lawrence enters dressed in a suit of mail and dragging a suit of armor behind him)
STEVE:	Sorry I'm, late, but I had to pick up my suit from Earl Scheib.

Whenever someone arrived in the middle of a sketch, an apology for being tardy was required. In a parody of *Happy Days*, Hope as the Fonz showed up late and explained that he was busy having his "thumbs oiled."

Note that we've managed to sneak in our first brand name. In cheesy TV commercials airing at the time, Earl promised, "I'll paint any car any color for $89.95!" He also guaranteed us a sure laugh at the mere mention of his name.

> (Steve and Eydie rush together and embrace. We hear the clank of metal,)

STEVE: (sings *Trolley Song*) *Clang, clang, clang goes my armor... Boom, boom, boom goes my lust...I would love you forever... but I think I'm beginning to rust!*

EYDIE: Oh, Lancy, I'm so antsy for you!

STEVE: (pulls away) No! I can't go on like this, dallying with my best friend's wife! I'm a knight, I'm English, I'm sworn to the code of honor. Let's do the decent thing!

EYDIE: What's that?

STEVE: Kill him!

EYDIE: You're sweet, you big lug.

Note that the audience has been quickly fed all the information they need to understand the intricacies of the plot. I kid, of course, but this is a strong setup considering the fact that we're only on the second page.

EYDIE: (cups ear) Gadzooks, I think I hear my pain-in-the-armor husband coming now!

> (Trumpeters sound fanfare. Hope enters as King Arthur. He dismounts from an armored hobby horse,)

HOPE: (to trumpeters) Thanks, Dizzy. Thanks, Miles. (to horse) Whoa, Seattle Slew. (to camera) Lose one race and look where you end up. (horse falls to floor) That's what I call Jockey Shorts. (to audience) I am the great and good King Arthur... I rule a land that is a magic spot... I even have a place to park my camel —

STEVE/EYDIE: Where?

HOPE: (sings) *A camel lot.*

This was typical of the late entrance that Hope preferred — delayed while the others set up the premise. Note that it's packed with multiple jokes, both spoken and visual. So far, he's gotten six laughs and he hasn't greeted his co-stars yet! And we've managed to slip in our second brand name.

HOPE: (to Edie) What kind of a day did you have, my Queen?

STEVE: Well, first I —

HOPE: Not you.

EYDIE: I had a lovely day and I'm planning on an even bet-
           ter night. And how was your day my Lord, my liege,
           Mylanta?

Comedy writers became enamored with brand names in radio when off-hand references to well-known products carefully woven into a script often resulted in free samples arriving unsolicited after a show aired. Long before radio disc jockeys were caught taking kickbacks to spin certain records, "payola" among radio writers and producers was not unheard of. Writers on some popular shows went so far as to post lists of desired items — sort of an on-air mail-order catalogue — so that someone in the market for a particular product could just order it. This flagrant abuse of the public airwaves, of course, occurred in the days before the FCC stepped in and snipped under-the-table supply lines that had been substantial income-enhancers for scores of script writers for decades.

HOPE: I had a great day. I slew three dragons, repelled a Saxon
           invasion, and fought a duel with a weird Viking, "Eric
           the Pink." And on the way home, I saved a damsel in
           distress.

STEVE: How did you do that?

HOPE: I changed my mind.

How times have changed. In a single speech, we managed to offend gays and rape victims. The network censors, ever-vigilant in their search for double entendres, never batted an eyelash over stuff like this. Today,

Hope would be called to task by the political correctness police, but back then, insensitivity was an integral part of every comedy writer's arsenal.

HOPE: (takes Eydie in his arms) But it's not what the day holds for me as long as I have you to come home to, my loving and faithful wife.

STEVE: (to audience) Boy, if he believes that, I've got some costume jewelry in my saddlebags he might like.

EYDIE: We'll celebrate your safe return. Let us withdraw to the round table and partake of a goblet of drinkie-poo.

HOPE: I could use a little drinkie. My poo is parched.

As funny-sounding as it is, the term "drinkie" is attributed to an unlikely source — Franklin Delano Roosevelt, who was quoted as having asked a group of guests at the White House upon the arrival of Happy Hour, "Who's ready for a little drinkee?"

HOPE: (raises goblet) Let's drink to loyalty and love.

EYDIE: Wait! Before we drink, let me demonstrate my devotion. (embraces Hope) (whispers over Hope's shoulder to Steve) While I'm showing him some devotion, you slip some potion in his lotion!

STEVE: Wait a minute. While you're showing your devotion, where do I find the lotion for his potion?

EYDIE: In the ocean!

This rhyming routine was a takeoff on a classic exchange in *The Court Jester* starring Danny Kaye. ("The pellet with the poison's in the vessel with the pestle. The chalice from the palace has the brew that is true!") Hope loved jokes that could be delivered in this form, especially when repetition was added. Abbott and Costello's "Who's on first?" routine and Jack Benny's "Si, Si, Sue" exchanges with Mel Blanc are good examples of repetition and wordplay used expertly to get laughs.

> (While Hope and Eydie kiss, Steve slips poison into
> Hope's drink which emits a billow of smoke)
>
> STEVE: A toast to Gwen and Artie — a fun couple!
>
> HOPE: (re smoke): Oh, oh. While she's giving me a hickey, he's
> slipping me a mickey. (distracts Steve) Look! It's Lady
> Godiva and she's still horsing around!
>
> (When Steve looks, Hope exchanges their goblets)

Rather than simply having Steve and Hope switch the goblets each time, we asked the NBC prop department to construct a table that would rotate like a roulette wheel. This made the routine much funnier to watch and, as the goblets were spun quickly, soon made the operation as confusing to the audience as a well-orchestrated shell game.

Unlike shows with limited budgets like the Canadian-born *SCTV* and the early seasons of *Saturday Night Live*, we enjoyed the luxury of being able to order first-class sets and props. Whatever we asked for was usually forthcoming because years before, Hope had the foresight — when his bargaining power was at its peak — to contractually bind NBC to set construction charges. In the seventies, he was still paying rates that had been established back in the fifties so "We can't afford it" was seldom a response to requests for special sets or props we felt were necessary.

In a sketch we wrote for Hope and Tony Randall called *Coroner to the Stars,* we requested, and the prop department built, a set complete with working sliding drawers for the stored corpses that we were told was more expensive looking than L.A.'s real morgue.

The irony was that NBC was eventually purchased by General Electric, as cost-conscious and by-the-book an outfit as ever existed. Hope's bargain-basement prices for skilled labor and materials must have driven the G.E. bean counters up the wall.

> STEVE: (notices smoke in his goblet) Man, oh, man! My
> Manischewitz is on fire here! (distracts Hope as he again

	spins the table) Look! It's Sir Shaky back from Rome with our pizza!
HOPE:	(notices switch) The poison Pepsi test is back! (distracts Steve) Look! It's the great Spanish warrior!
STEVE:	(looks) Who's that?
HOPE:	The Knight of the Iguana.
STEVE:	At last, we drink! (both take a sip)
HOPE:	(slumps in a chair) I think my life just got canceled! This is one heartburn even Liquid Plumber can't fix! (he expires after a long groan and final gasp)

In six lines, we managed to mention no less than four popular brand names, bringing our grand total to eight (with one more to come). Without checking, I would bet this is a record display of crass commercialism. We had some standards, though. We never plugged products we didn't like ourselves.

EYDIE:	(embracing Steve) At last we can be together!
HOPE:	(revives) But before I go, I want you both to know that I forgive you (expires again, then revives). And another thing, Guinevere, I want you to subdivide the castle into condominiums. They'll be very big someday. And municipal bonds are nice, too —
STEVE:	(shoves him back into chair) Will you *go* already!

In a Hope sketch, a character was never allowed a quick, simple demise. Every last laugh was wrung from the death-throes like the final remnants in a toothpaste tube. Whenever the script called for Hope to meet his Maker, the event would be accompanied by gasps, wailing and various unique forms of comedic caterwauling. He had a stock supply of gurgles and moans — along with his well-known "wolf growl" — that had served him well in his movies and were guaranteed to send the audience into hysterics.

STEVE:	Now we can begin our new lives together, my love.
EYDIE:	I can't wait! Monday nights, it's dinner at my mother's —
STEVE:	Your mo-mo-mother's?
EYDIE:	And on Tuesday nights, she comes here —
STEVE:	Tu-Tu-Tuesdays she comes here?
EYDIE:	Every Tuesday without fail.
STEVE:	Well at least we'll spend Wednesday nights alone.
HOPE:	(revives) On Wednesday nights, she gets a violent headache.
STEVE:	How do I get out of this?
HOPE:	(hands him his goblet) It's Miller time!
	(Steve drinks from Hope's goblet and expires next to him)
EYDIE:	I thought he'd *never* leave. (looks offstage) you can come in now, Sir Carsolot!
	(Johnny Carson in knight's garb and a blonde pageboy wig enters and takes Eydie in his arms)
JOHNNY:	(to audience) Well, there goes one of my nights off!

Prevailing upon Johnny Carson to provide our blackout was fortuitous, to say the least. We were in the midst of the dress-rehearsal late in the afternoon in a studio that adjoined Johnny's *Tonight Show* set. Hope, Steve and Eydie were having so much fun in their Camelot costumes, someone came up with the bright idea of having them walk onto Johnny's show while it was in progress. (Besides, Johnny had recently interrupted Don Rickles in an adjoining studio while he was taping *CPO Sharky*.)

So they strolled across the hall and, without even checking with Carson's iron-hand producer, Fred De Cordova, caught Johnny in the midst of a guest interview. Of course, the studio audience went wild since it was obvious that the whole thing was impromptu. In the meantime, we were hurriedly rewriting the ending of the sketch on the off chance that Carson would agree to do a walk-on — He was notoriously shy and seldom appeared as a guest on anyone's show. If Hope had asked him in advance, he'd have declined, but how could he turn down a request by the beloved Bob Hope right in front of his own audience? Hope knew he couldn't, and we had our perfect blackout.

* * * *

As unlikely as this may seem, Johnny was the *shyest* professional entertainer I ever met. Speaking with him off-stage, it was hard to believe that he actually hosted a show before an audience.

In 1980, he was signed to appear on our two-hour special entitled *Hope For President,* playing a campaign PR-man delivering Hope's life story to the media. He would read Hope's biography while displaying photographs (mostly comic scenes from his early movies) displayed on a large easel. Since I had written the jokes that matched the pictures, I was sent over to Johnny's office to rehearse the segment with him. While I had never spoken to him, he had to have seen me around since we often stood in the wings with his writers to watch his monologue. And here I was, a fellow-jokesmith working for a comedy icon, someone in the same business — someone around whom you'd imagine he'd be able to relax. Instead, he was — I clearly remember thinking at the time — as taught as a violin string.

He was stiff, erect — the exact antithesis of his idol, Jack Benny. And it wasn't because I was from another show. I was told he was that way around his *own* writers — and a bundle of nerves in any social situation including the annual *Tonight Show* Christmas party where he'd appear briefly, exchange a few nervous comments with the staff, and go home. He often admitted to interviewers that the only time he felt comfortable was onstage, in total control, delivering jokes. Johnny was a great talent, and deserving of the admiration he had earned, but somehow, I always felt sorry for him.

Branding Irons

As important as commercial products were to his writers, product asso-ciation had from his very beginnings in radio, been an indispensable part in Hope's career. The first in a long list of products with which he would be associated over the years was Pepsodent toothpaste.

Following glowing reviews in Paramount's *Big Broadcast of 1938*, the makers of Pepsodent offered Hope his own radio show to replace their sponsorship of the popular *Amos 'n' Andy Show*. Hope had wanted to get into radio ever since his first appearance on Rudy Vallee's *Fleischmann's Yeast Hour* earned him $700 for a two-minute interview.

This is my kind of business, he thought.

And prepare for it he did. Throughout the thirties, he appeared as a guest on radio shows including the Major Bowes *Capitol Family Hour,* the *RKO Theater of the Air,* the *Bromo-Seltzer Intimate Hour* and the CBS *White Flash* program sponsored by the Atlantic Oil Refining Company. The offer from Pepsodent, which came as a result of his successful appear-ances on NBC's *Woodbury Show* with Frank Parker and the Shep Fields Orchestra, was his first real opportunity to host his own program.

He was off and running.

He assembled a crack staff of veteran radio writers that included Milt Josefsberg, Norman Sullivan, and Jack Douglas, an experienced an-nouncer named Bill Goodwin, an orchestra leader, Skinnay Ennis — soon replaced by Les Brown — and a walrus-mustached, former trom-bonist named Jerry ("Greetings, Gate") Colonna. Over the next few years, the cast would be joined by Patricia (Honeychile) Wilder, the mu-sical group Six Hits and a Miss, society debutants Brenda and Cobina (Blanche Stewart and Elvia Allman), and Barbara Jo Allen as Vera Vague.

The *Pepsodent Show* debuted on September 27, 1938 and had all the earmarks of a hit. Unexpectedly, it got off to a rocky start.

"We really had no idea what we were doing," Hope admitted. He told us it took ten or twelve weeks of tinkering with the format before he was satisfied with the laughs he was getting from the studio audience, many of whom he personally corralled in the hall outside his studio as they emerged from *The Edgar Bergen and Charlie McCarthy Show.*

Radio was in its infancy. There was, as yet, no reliable method of measuring listenership. Later, the Hooper Ratings and the Crosleys, audience sampling systems similar to today's Neilsen Media Research, would be used to set advertising rates. But when Hope began, the Hoopers were still a few years away, and while he was satisfied with the reactions of his studio audiences, he wondered how he and his on-air gang were doing in the hinterlands.

Whenever he approached executives at the ad-agency that represented Pepsodent, all he seemed to get was, "Don't worry about it, Bob. You're doing fine. Just keep doing what you've been doing." Somehow, he got the feeling they weren't leveling with him.

One day, after the show had been on for almost a year, he was approached by a man on an exclusive country club golf course who had been playing in the foursome ahead of him. "Bob, I want to thank you," said the man. Hope, thinking he was a fan, thanked him.

"No," continued the man. "I want to thank you for making me a millionaire." Of course, Hope had no idea what he was talking about. It seems the golfer had owned a small cardboard-box factory that serviced many clients — including Pepsodent.

"About six months ago," he explained, "Pepsodent doubled their orders, then a week later, tripled them. Eventually, I dropped my other customers and provided boxes for your sponsor exclusively. My company became so successful, I ended up selling it for a million dollars, thanks to you."

Hope was stunned. No one at Pepsodent's ad agency had mentioned such a large increase in their product sales. Completely by accident, Hope had stumbled onto an audience gauge as accurate as the Hoopers would later become.

Hope smiled wryly as he concluded his story. We all sat mesmerized.

"Well?" one of us asked, "what did you do then?"

"Let's just say," said Bob, "when contract renewal time came along, I negotiated one of the biggest goddamned raises in the history of radio."

The persuasive power of the mass media to sell products couldn't have been driven home more forcefully, and Hope never forgot the lesson he learned from it. Over the ensuing years, he would make sure that his name became aligned with major sponsors whose products he would hawk enthusiastically in countless TV commercials — a practice that, early-on, some Hollywood stars of Hope's magnitude considered somehow degrading to their *art*. Later, of course, many of them would come around, lending their names to everything from beer to vacuum cleaners.

Along with Pepsodent, Hope's name would be linked with Chrysler and, later still, with Texaco, a relationship that culminated in 1974 in a five-year television production deal that netted Hope $4 million, a record at the time. In 1979, he filmed commercials for Coca-Cola on the Great Wall of China. In the mid-1980s, he received $3 million from Southwestern Bell Telephone for a series of TV spots for their Silver Pages that took him just three days to film. He appeared in numerous locally produced commercials for California Federal Savings & Loan, in which he was a major stockholder.

Fittingly, his final appearance on television, at age 95, was in a commercial for Kmart directed by Penny Marshall.

＊ ＊ ＊ ＊

In 1976, when the United States celebrated its bicentennial, Texaco wanted to take advantage of the event by issuing a promotional record album entitled *America Is 200 Years Old and There's Still Hope*. We wrote a script in which Hope beans himself playing golf, and, while unconscious, dreams that he was present at our nation's founding.

Next, Hope invited pals including Phyllis Diller, Karl Malden, Fred Travelena, and others to re-enact historic events such as the midnight ride of Paul Revere, the signing of the Declaration of Independence, Washington crossing the Delaware, and Betsy Ross sewing the first flag. He even hired his old sound-effects man, Ray Erlenborn, and recorded the album at the Capitol Records building in Hollywood.

At the Capitol Records recording studio in Hollywood, Karl Malden as Benjamin Franklin, Bob Hope as George Washington and Fred Travelena as Paul Revere reenact scenes of our nation's founding to commemorate the 1976 Bicentennial.

Hope would return to the microphone in the mid-eighties to record a long-play, two-record album entitled *Bob Hope and Friends*, which included clips and tributes by radio and TV stars including Amos 'n' Andy, Eddie Cantor, Fibber McGee & Molly, Georgie Jessel, Al Jolson, Jack Benny, George Burns, Jimmy Durante, Bing Crosby, Dorothy Lamour, Jimmy Stewart, and George C. Scott, among others. Because of the rare clips included on the album, it's now a sought-after collector's item that occasionally turns up on e-Bay.

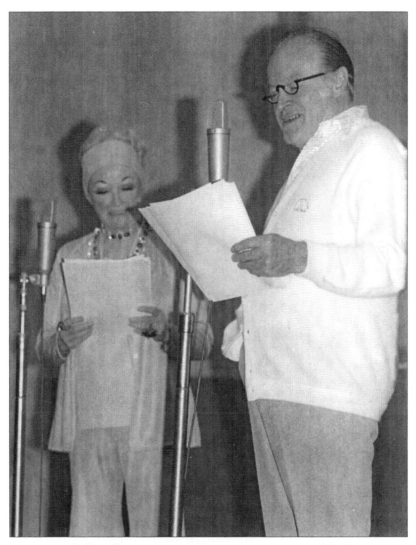

Phyllis Diller as Betsy Ross attempts to convince a color-blind
George Washington (Hope) that red, white and blue are more suitable
for a flag than puce, mauve and logenberry.

CHAPTER 12
Saluting the Clown at Jack in the Box

In his book *The Secret Life of Bob Hope* (Barricade Books, 1993), Arthur Marx quotes Steve Allen as having once said, "Bob Hope is never as popular as when there is a war going on. I don't mean that to be a wise-crack so much as a plain statement of truth."

Most likely, Hope would have agreed with him.

Throughout my years on his staff, he strove to maintain his image as "America's Entertainer to the Troops" and was on constant alert for an opportunity to fly somewhere and stage a show for the military. When operations involving U.S. troops flared up anywhere on the globe, he was on the phone to Washington, sending out feelers to the State Depart-ment, reminding them that his bags were packed and that his writers were combat ready.

Not that the government was always cooperative. He volunteered to entertain in Guantanamo, but was turned down. They also rejected his offers to visit Panama and Granada. He finally got the green light to tour Beirut and the Persian Gulf, and, in what turned out to be his last mili-tary junket, Saudi Arabia. But those tours would come late in his career.

In the meantime, during the years between Vietnam and the war in the Middle East, he decided to entertain the U.S. forces right here at home. At the start of the 1979 season, we taped a special aboard the helicopter carrier Iwo Jima docked in New York harbor. The show featured guest stars Don Knotts — as a nearsighted whirlybird jockey — a hot new disco group called The Village People, and, the then-current star of *Annie* singing "I Don't Need Anyone But You" to Hope's Daddy Warbucks, a freckled, fourteen-year-old Sarah Jessica Parker. (Occasionally, she plays the clip on *Letterman*.) The only downside of the show was a gust of wind that blew one of our $40,000 cameras off the flight deck into the Hudson River.

The military-themed show was a hit with both viewers and critics, so the following year our producer, Jim Lipton — who also produced our China special and now hosts *Inside the Actors Studio* on Bravo — proposed a trilogy of specials that would emanate from the nation's military academies.

The shows turned out to fill the bill perfectly — they offered plenty of flag waving, got Hope into uniform, and, to the great relief of the writers, involved virtually no risk to life and limb. We hoped the peace would last forever.

Winging It

In May 1980, we packed up our survival gear and trekked to the rarefied air of Colorado Springs, Colorado for our first Hope birthday special at the United States Air Force Academy. An Air Force troop-carrier swooped in low over the crowd of cadets, their families and friends assembled in the spring chill of the Academy's Mile-High Stadium.

Five stunt parachutists popped from the plane's underbelly like newborn guppies and drifted toward the infield, making lazy figure-8's against the azure blue of the cloudless sky. They trailed streams of white smoke for even greater dramatic effect. At the last moment, four of the airborne commandos peeled off, leaving a lone jumper to make a perfect two-point landing mid-field as a crowd of cadet musicians, instruments in hand, rushed onto the grass to welcome him.

The lone jumper unbuckled himself from the pile of blue silk beside him. Slowly, he removed his Snoopy goggles to reveal his true identity

Gig and I clown with Henny Youngman aboard the U.S.S. Iwo Jima. Drop-ins were common on the set. Dick Cavett visited whenever we taped on the East Coast and Art Buchwald dropped by in Peking. John Ritter and Liberace came by in New Orleans, and I once saw Andy Kaufman backstage at NBC *secretly* watching us tape. That's the Marine Band behind us playing "New York, New York."

— it was Bob Hope! Okay, so we had smuggled him out there hidden among the musicians. Still, the effect was marvelous. Acknowledging the cheers of an incredulous crowd, our seventy-six year-old Great Waldo Pepper made his way to the stage.

Though delivered to an all-volunteer cadet force, his jokes differed little from the ones he'd been offering up for years in the war zones.

Thank you, cadets. I'm so happy to be here at the Air Force Academy. . . or, as it's referred to by the other service academies... "Rocky Mountain Disneyland."

This definition joke formula was one we used often. Two years later, Annapolis would be characterized as "a federally funded yacht club."

We had a great flight in, and I wanna thank the Air Force for providing the transportation. It's the first time I've ever flown in a cruise missile.

It must have been an experimental flight. Our stewardess was a chimp.

When we arrived, the pilot landed on the football field. We made it, but next time I wish he'd try it lengthwise.

We had discovered that it's acceptable to kid pilots among an audience of future pilots as long as we made them *skillful.*

I must say, this is wild country up here. Last year, three moose graduated.

And what discipline. Last night during taps, I saw two fireflies turn each other off.

No, I've never seen so much saluting. The officers are saluted by the upperclassmen, who are saluted by the lowerclassmen, who are saluted by the clown at Jack in the Box.

Saluting was a standard topic in the military monologues. Civilians, who determine rank by the amount and cost of their material possessions, find the custom fascinating. We couldn't resist setting our comedic sights on the Academy's recently-admitted first female cadets.

I think the gals will work out fine as pilots. After all, airplanes don't have fenders.

We wouldn't welcome our first female on the staff for another six years, so the old-boys' club was still turning in jokes like that.

> *I hear you gals love flying those big jets. And why not? Where else can you stick your hand out the window and dry your nail polish in four seconds?*

It would be thirteen years before Navy Lieutenant Paula Coughlin would blow the whistle on a rowdy group of conventioneering jet jockeys in Las Vegas and ignite the afterburners on what was, until then, the biggest sexual-harassment scandal in the history of the armed forces.

And it would be almost two decades before the Army would be rocked by what could fairly be called the "Massacre at Ft. Leonard Wood," where sexual harassment was found to be rampant in the ranks. But this was 1980 when comedians could get away with such blatantly sexist jokes, and, as lovers of guaranteed laughs, we did nothing to discourage them.

Pilot Error

For our centerpiece sketch, we were lucky to book the talented character-actor Kenneth Mars who had been hilarious as the Nazi playwright in Mel Brooks's *The Producers*. We cast him as the academy commandant who discovers a cadet who has somehow fallen through the administrative cracks and has been attending classes for twenty-six years. An intelligence officer (Loni Anderson) has been sent from Washington to head off the potential scandal:

LONI: Our report says that Cadet Hope entered the academy in 1959 and didn't surface again until 1966.

KEN: That's right. When he ran for Homecoming Queen.

LONI: Homecoming Queen? That's disgusting.

KEN: It's worse than that. He won.

LONI: I guess I'll have to take care of this problem myself (winks) if you know what I mean. I assume that even after twenty-six years, he still likes girls.

KEN: We're not sure. For the last ten years, he's been sleeping
            with his parachute.

LONI: You really can't blame him. I hear it's the only nylon
            cadets ever come in contact with.

A line like this delivered by Loni Anderson — sausaged into a dress that
looked like a blister-pack — to a crowd of eighteen to twenty year-old
males with hormones in a state of higher alert than S.A.C. was as close to
a guaranteed scream as comedy writers ever get. We weren't disappointed.
Cadet Hope is summoned.

HOPE: Cadet Hope reporting as ordered, sir! Flaps up, wheels
            down, zeroes at eleven o'clock, coming in on a wing and
            a prayer, bombs away, A-OK, roger, over and out!

LONI: What does all that mean?

HOPE: I have no idea, but it sure made a star out of Jimmy
            Stewart.

After administering the standard I.Q. test in which the cadet fails to dis-
tinguish himself, Loni takes matters — and Hope — into her own hands:

LONI: (taking him in her arms) Tell me how this feels. (kisses
            him)

HOPE: Don't look now, but I think you just set off my after-
            burners.

This is vintage Hope as we took full advantage of the character he had
developed over the course of four decades in the arms of such glamour
queens as Marilyn Maxwell, Jane Russell, Diana Dors, Jayne Mansfield
and Raquel Welch — a seemingly endless line of leading ladies who were
beautiful, talented and, most important of all when it came to appearing
in sketches with Hope, good sports.

Loni was the eighties version, and we called upon her often.

Rocky Mountain Dew

Next, we slipped Loni into a pair Daisy Mae cut-off jeans that barely covered the Daisy and only part of the Mae. In our little epic, we called *Coal Miner's Son*, she's Maw Swampwater struggling to raise her guitar-strumming thirteen year old, Luke (Hope) in a Jawbone, Tennessee cabin that's so rundown "the termites are dyin' from malnutrition." Maw has just returned from her twelve-hour shift at the bottom of shaft number fourteen.

LONI: Luke, did you miss me?

HOPE: Sure did, Maw. It's gettin' dark, and your hat's the only light we got in the house.

Luke explains that he's been bitten by the music bug — more like hookworm, according to Maw — and intends to pursue a record career in Nashville. Just his luck, Colonel Tom Farkus (Andy Gibb), record company owner from that very city, happens to be conducting a hillbilly star search in the Swampwaters' zip code:

ANDY: Luke, would you like to sing for all America?

HOPE: I'm not sure. How loud would I have to sing?

ANDY: We're looking for a guitar player who can sing sad. Can you sing sad?

LONI: Sad ain't the word for it. *Pathetic* is more like it.

HOPE: (insulted) What do you mean, Maw? My gal Cindy Lou said I got a voice like a nightingale.

LONI: That ain't what she said at all. What she said was you walk like *Florence* Nightingale.

ANDY: (to Hope) Sign with my company, and you'll make a fortune with that guitar.

HOPE: Gee, I could afford to buy Maw a hairdryer, so she wouldn't have to stick her head in the stove no more.

Mere seconds before pen touches contract, Farkus comes up against a shape more important to Luke than the treble clef — his twelve-year-old paramour, Cindy Lou (Barbara Mandrell).

BARBARA: Luke, can I borrow your pucker? I got a powerful han-
            kerin' for some heavy-duty togetherness.

HOPE: (to Andy) Sparkin' is all Cindy thinks about. Would you
            believe she's on her third lip retread?

This joke, in various forms, cropped up often in sketches. In a takeoff on the early World War I film, *Wings*, Hope is asked by his girl, played by Ann Jillian, where he learned to "kiss like that." He explains that in civilian life he had a job blowing up the Goodyear blimp.

ANDY: (admiring her) Do all the gals around here look like that?

HOPE: Sad, ain't it? She was the runt of the litter.

On the spot, the Colonel decides to resign his honorary commission, marry the Widder Maw and get a real job in the mine — just in time, by the way, to act as best-man at the wedding of Luke and Cindy Lou who turn in their learner's permit for a real marriage license. Though it featured no military uniforms, this sketch had sixty-six-hundred pairs of male eyeballs at rapt attention for a full twelve minutes.

Only eight years later, Andy Gibb, brother of the *Bee Gees*, Barry, Robin and Maurice, would die at age 30, the victim of a rare heart virus.

✳ ✳ ✳ ✳

Former Supreme Diana Ross and Dolores Hope filled out the musical guest list and Olympic ice-skaters Randy Gardner and Tai Babalonia demonstrated their Gold Medal talent. Former astronaut Alan Shepard delivered a USO tribute honoring Hope. The tribute would become a permanent fixture on all subsequent birthday specials.

Here I am beside a man who hit a golf ball on the moon. I've been in a few roughs myself, but that's ridiculous. Alan Shepard had just delivered a tribute to Hope at the Air Force Academy. It would become a tradition on future birthday specials that would feature George Bush I and Al Haig delivering the kudos.

Here's a shot of my wife, Shelley, and me taken by an astronaut. I figured if Alan could hit a golf ball on the moon, he'd know how to handle a single lens reflex. Notice I'm wearing my Yves St. Laurent leather jacket that Hope said made me look like "a Hungarian Freedom Fighter."

The Long Gray Line Tour

In keeping with our tradition of dramatic entrances, at West Point, which we visited in the spring of 1981, we dressed Hope in the black cape and orange vest of the Academy's legendary "Airborne Man" and dropped him — with a little help from a stunt double — from a hovering Huey helicopter into a stadium packed to the bleachers with cheering plebes and their families.

> *Thank you, cadets. You can relax. I have a directive from the Superintendent authorizing you to laugh until further notice.*
>
> *Some of you are here because you're my fans, some are here because of our terrific guests and all of you are here because you couldn't get a three-day pass.*

He wasn't kidding. Unlike our civilian audiences, the military specials came with prepackaged, guaranteed attendance that was mandatory.

> *I've never seen so much gold braid. This looks like a direct hit on Sammy Davis's jewelry case.*
>
> *And what discipline. Yesterday, I saw a porcupine chewing out a raccoon for having his hands in his pouch.*
>
> *One cadet commander yelled, "Suck in that stomach!" and three pine trees inhaled.*
>
> *These military regulations are strictly enforced. As soon as taps sounded last night, all the lights went out, and the Hudson River stopped flowing.*

Hope was partial to jokes that involved animals, so we anthropomorphized whenever possible. Remember his kangaroo caddie in Australia?

We wanted to give the plebes the opportunity to meet a real movie-general, so we invited George C. Scott who had recently captured an Oscar nomination for his spellbinding performance as General George

Patton, the Paderewski of the pearl-handled pistols. In real life, George was a certified pussycat, about as warlike as a battalion of Quakers. Despite his well-known objections to the war in Vietnam, he had become so identified with the gruff, private-slapping Patton, when he walked across the quadrangle, the cadets would salute him — in civilian clothes yet.

A Room with a View

The Army had recently admitted its first female cadet; we had guest stars Brooke Shields and Marie Osmond in uniform faster than Shannon Faulkner would reject the Citadel's fourteen years later. The new arrivals discover that they've somehow been assigned quarters with a male.

> (Hope enters in uniform and carrying a duffle bag,)

HOPE: Howdy, fellas.

MARIE: Fellas? Can't you see that we're girls?

HOPE: Yeah, but I wasn't gonna mention it if you didn't. My name's Luke Festus, and it looks like we're roommates.

BROOKE: Are you sure you have the right room? There must be some mistake.

HOPE: I doubt it. The Army never makes mistakes.

Hope's line, of course, drew a deafening cheer. They may be future officers, but first-year plebes occupy rungs on the military ladder barely above meter maids and relish the opportunity to poke fun at their brass-laden faculty.

BROOKE: I'm sorry, Luke, but this would never work. We could walk in on one another while showering.

HOPE: I guess that's just the chance I'll have to take.

MARIE: Be reasonable. You wouldn't want to have stockings hanging all over the place to dry, would you?

HOPE: Hey, no problem. If it bothers you, I'll hang my stockings someplace else.

The fresh recruits settle in. Hope wants to change into his "jammies," but is embarrassed to disrobe in front of the girls. They offer to hold up a blanket, shielding him. With Brooke and Marie at either end of the extended blanket, he drapes articles of clothing on it. First a girdle, then a garter belt, then a pair of Madras Jockey shorts.

BROOKE: Should we look?

MARIE: Nah. It's too close to lunch.

This line gets the biggest laugh in the show, and Hope could be heard mumbling to Marie, "How did *you* get that line?" He didn't mind guests getting laughs but preferred being visible when they did.

As it turns out, Luke works on a nearby farm and has been trying to sneak into the Point for years. The cadet commander (Glen Campbell) hustles the intruder off, but not before making sure the two newcomers know where *his* quarters are.

Coed dorms had provided us fertile diggings for years, and this sketch was no exception.

Room at the Inn

During our five-day shooting schedule, most of the cast and crew were assigned rooms in the Hotel Thayer, a comfortable, old, ivy-covered building on the Academy grounds that's used primarily to house visiting family members.

It had recently received national publicity when it became the first U.S. stop for the Iranian hostages immediately following their release. It was an eerie feeling to gaze out of my fourth floor window at the historic brownstone buildings of the Point, ringed by cannon guarding the banks of the Hudson, knowing that scarcely a week before, the scene had been someone's first look at American soil after over a year in captivity. I felt so insignificant. I was merely being held hostage by a dictatorial comedian who only *acted* like the Ayatollah.

But I jest.

There was a gift shop in the lobby that offered academy-themed items. I bought a poster-sized print of an oil painting of a black, fur-plumed drum major's parade helmet. I carried it around with me all week, collecting the autographs of our guest stars. I managed to nail them all and didn't realize until later that I might have a collector's item. It's no doubt the only document in existence signed by a Bush and George C. Scott.

We often brought back souvenirs from the bases and ships we'd visited, usually gifts from the command — such as my collection of logoed caps from the Iwo Jima, the Lexington, the Saratoga, Pope Air Base, Ft. Bragg, and even one given to us by NASA when we helped celebrate their twenty-fifth anniversary. Hope appreciated the gifts, too, and whenever he received something, he'd scribble his name in some inconspicuous place as insurance that it wouldn't end up in someone else's locker. We, of course, adopted the custom.

While on a USO tour with Hope to the Persian Gulf, Gene Perret received a handsome flight jacket from a carrier fighter squadron. (Hope and a few other staffers got one, too.) So Gene quickly inscribed his name under the label in the neckband.

A few days later, after the souvenir had gone missing, he spotted one of the guests on the special wearing just such a fine jacket. "Here," he said, "... let me show you a little trick we learned from Mr. Hope." Reaching under the guy's collar, he said, "He always writes his name on everything — usually in some inconspicuous place, like right here, under the label where *my* name is."

Big Band Aids

Until the early eighties, Bob Hope specials enjoyed the occasional luxury of having the entire Les Brown Orchestra — which had been his official band since radio days — on-stage and visible to the audience throughout the show. Hope's longtime set designer, Bob Keene, would fashion the sets in four or five levels — with "home-base" — the area where sketches and talk segments were done — down front and center. The band would ring the upper level, providing a human backdrop, reminiscent of the days of

Glenn Miller and the Dorsey Brothers. For old-timers who remembered early variety shows on television, and even older ones who recalled the big bands on the stage of grand old theaters like the Golden Gate in San Francisco — a live orchestra was essential to create that unique excitement that prerecorded tracks simply don't provide. But gradually, ever-spiraling costs dictated that Hope leave the band behind whenever we went on the road. We all realized that a wonderful era had passed.

When Les Brown retired, his musical director, Bob Alberti, was drafted to conduct on- camera. I got to know Bob well during my years with Hope and traveled with him to many countries — Australia, England, Tahiti, Sweden — but *not* China. The reason Bob sent Geoff Clarkson, Hope's pianist, to work that show was because it violated his rule against visiting a non-English-speaking country.

Bob was inconsistent, though. He didn't seem to mind visiting non-English speaking *states*, willingly working on shows we taped in the South.

Just kidding. (I think.)

Bob came from a musical dynasty that could be traced back several generations in Italy. He had perfect pitch and during rehearsals could ferret out an errant note coming from any section of the band. If

Phyllis Diller was a frequent guest. She had appeared in three movies with Hope — *Boy Did I Get a Wrong Number* (1966), *Eight on the Lamb* (1967) and *The Private Navy of Sgt. O'Farrell* (1968). Among Hope's show biz pals, Phyllis was his most rabid fan and has a large oil portrait of him in the living room of her Brentwood, California mansion.

Bob Alberti on stage conducting for Phyllis Diller. Aside from his appearances at the podium on Hope specials and along with writing all the arrangements used on the shows, Bob was often seen on *The Tonight Show* subbing for Doc Severinsen's regular pianist.

he suspected a player was hitting a clunker, he'd use the mixing-board in the control booth to isolate the section from which he thought it was coming. Then, he'd stop the band and say something like "Larry, you're playing an F sharp in bar sixteen. Should be an F." Once, after doing this he said to me, "I don't know why I'm so picky. At home, they'll be listening to this on a three-inch speaker."

We were on the road one time, and Glen Campbell lost a bag that contained the arrangement of his hit "Southern Nights" that he was scheduled to sing on the special. Bob withdrew to his room and within two hours returned with a complete orchestral arrangement of the song that he had reconstructed from *memory*. Even Glen (no stranger to chromatic scales) was impressed.

Throughout the sixties and seventies, Bob was a musical fixture in Hollywood, working on shows as diverse as *The Hollywood Palace, Hee-Haw, Name That Tune,* and *The Harlem Globetrotter's Popcorn Machine* where he met his wife, Shirley, who was an assistant producer on that show and later became a production coordinator on *Barney Miller.*

Money Game

West Point is located about forty-five minutes from Broadway and that year the musical *42nd Street* was doing SRO business on the Great White Way. Wanda Richards, Leroy Reems, and thirty-five dancers filled our stage and had the Long Gray Line tapping their spit-shined shoes to the show-stopping "We're in the Money." I still recall standing near that stage watching the performance and feeling the vibration of seventy tap shoes creating what felt like a mini-earthquake.

We were lucky to get that number for our show. Jim Lipton had called the producer, David Merrick, to ask if a few members of the cast could appear since we'd be taping on a Sunday when the show was dark. Later, Merrick told us that he called for volunteers and the *entire* cast raised their hand. Since the only number in the show with the whole group was "Money," Merrick, known to be extremely protective of his hits, gave in and let us have his signature number.

It was the most stirring of any I would see in the eighty-five specials I worked on.

Freshman Orientation

To round out the comedy, we wrote a sketch with Hope, Glen Campbell and Robert Urich as West Point's first class of 1802. Commandant Mickey Rooney conducts roll call:

MICKEY: Campbell?

GLEN: Yo!

MICKEY: Urich?

ROBERT: Yo!

MICKEY: Hope?

HOPE: Yo-yo!

MICKEY: Cadet, there are no yo-yo's at West Point.

HOPE: Sorry, sir. For a minute there, I thought I was at the Naval Academy.

Hope's line got a huge laugh, as we knew it would, since rivalry among the academies is strong. But we'd allow the midshipmen at Annapolis to get even the following year.

I first met Bob Urich while on *The Dean Martin Celebrity Roasts.* The former *Vega$* star was a great guy who died much too young of a rare form of cancer. He was married to one of the Von Trapp girls in *The Sound of Music*, Heather Menzies.

ROONEY: All right, men, count off!

CAMPBELL: Count off? What's that?

ROONEY: You count off, using your number.

URICH: What number?

ROONEY: The number you were assigned. For instance, (points at Hope) he's *one.*

CAMPBELL: (looks down the line at Hope) Boy, you sure can't tell nowadays, can you?

Hey, this was another time, another era — long, long ago.

Later in the sketch, George C. Scott arrives on the scene as an Indian chief seeking the return of the land West Point stands on:

MICKEY: By the way, Chief, what did you people call this land before we arrived?

GEORGE: *Ours.*

George was a fabulous actor and a lot of fun to work with. During rehearsal, we were sitting beside each other on metal folding-chairs in the middle of the stadium. He was dressed in his full tribal regalia. I leaned over to him and said "George, would you have guessed in a million years that we'd be here getting paid to entertain future generals?" He looked at me, smiled and said, "*Marvelous*, isn't it?"

* * * *

Later, in a boxing routine, Hope took on Sugar Ray Leonard with Rooney as referee, Marie Osmond in his corner, and George delivering Hope's eulogy before the bout. Mary Martin, in her *South Pacific* sailor suit, had the cadet corps on their feet when she sang "Get a Load of Honeybun Tonight" to a mop-haired, grass-skirted Hope wearing a bra made of coconuts.

The year before we'd had a former astronaut deliver Hope's USO tribute. This year we had a vice-president, George Bush the Elder. We were coming up in the world.

Anchor Lap

For our third academy special in 1982, we set our sextant on Annapolis, Maryland and our next port-of-call, the United States Naval Academy, accompanied by an able-bodied crew that included Bernadette Peters, James Coburn, Roger Staubach, Brooke Shields and to deliver the now obligatory USO tribute, Secretary of State Alexander Haig.

This time, our dramatic entrance required Hope to descend in eight seconds from a static line a hundred and fifty feet from the top of the stadium to the infield. Over his vehement protests, we insisted that he use a stunt man. A cheering crowd of fifteen thousand applauded as he mounted the stage.

> *Thank you, ladies and gentlemen. Here we are at the Naval Academy, the nation's only federally funded yacht club.*
>
> *Annapolis. . . that's an Indian word meaning "Warden, let me out of here!"*
>
> *This place is so military. The midshipmen are required to salute anyone in uniform. And I mean anyone. Annapolis has the proudest mailman in the Postal Service.*

Remember the clown at Jack in the Box who had to salute the Air Force Academy cadets? Similar line, but that was three years earlier, and we didn't think the audience would notice. We were recycling before it became fashionable.

This morning, I had breakfast at King Hall, and I've never had to eat so fast. They give you three minutes to chew, but you swallow on your own time.

Navy food is great and there's no waste. The leftovers go into nuclear warheads.

G.I. food was a legitimate target for jokes during Hope's wartime Christmas tours, but today military cuisine, especially the Navy's, is top notch. We dropped in a food joke occasionally, but only for old-time's sake.

Avon Calling

The challenge of the academy shows was placing our guests in a military environment while simultaneously keeping the comedy level high, and using references understandable to the audience at home. In that respect, they were more difficult than the civilian specials that offer a broader base from which to generate sketches and bits.

Since Roger Staubach is considered one of Navy's legendary quarterbacks, we decided on an "at home" sketch that would cast him as a sought-after high school senior who is undecided about which college would receive the benefits of his even-then well-recognized pigskin prowess.

Leaving nothing to chance, the Navy has sent their ace recruiter, Admiral John Paul Smith (Hope), accompanied by his attractive niece, Felice (Bernadette Peters), to insure that Roger checks the right box:

BERNADETTE: You'll love military life. Women go crazy over men in uniform.

ROGER: I know. That's why Mom married Dad.

HOPE: Your father was in the Navy?

ROGER: No, he was a bus driver.

BERNADETTE: Oh, a graduate of the Air Force Academy.

Just as Hope's "yo-yo's at the Naval Academy" line had received a near standing ovation the year before, Bernadett's line rated a huge cheer from the midshipmen. The extensive background information on Annapolis contained the notation that the middies refer to Air Force cadets as *bus-drivers*. Working this factoid into a joke wasn't difficult, and we knew we had a sure-fire, built-in laugh.

It's interesting to note, though, that rivalry exists only at the academy level and not among enlisted men — jokes like this were never in scripts of Hope's overseas Christmas shows.

An Officer and a Gentlewoman

At West Point, we had Hope trying to con his way into a coed dorm. At Annapolis, we decided to promote him to a legitimate upperclassman. In our now traditional barracks sketch, we again billeted him with Brooke Shields — a year older and several inches taller — and invited Christie Brinkley to add to the glamour quotient. (A quarter-century before Christy's *unglamorous* divorce from Peter Cook.)

	(Hope has been harrassing Brooke and Christie when Bernadette Peters enters in a captain's uniform. The girls snap to attention, but Hope doesn't see her.)
BERNADETTE:	Midshipman Cruikshank!
HOPE:	(still oblivious) Pull in your bowline. I gave at the Officers Club. . . (turns around, sees her and snaps to attention) Yes, sir — I mean ma'am. . .
BERNADETTE:	Well, which is it?
HOPE:	(thinks) Spam?
BERNADETTE:	Try again.
HOPE:	(more thinking) Saran Wrap?
BERNADETTE:	(exasperated) You'll address your new commandant as "ma'am" — is that clear?
HOPE:	(salutes) Yes, sir!

Bernadette Peters epitomized the attractive songstress-sketch player that Hope favored. Her sense of comic timing was impeccable and complemented her cute-as-a-button personality that extended into her real life. Her Bob Alberti-written duet with Hope had the midshipmen on their feet during a tear-rending version of "Anchors Aweigh."

The problem of how to address the newly admitted females at Annapolis hadn't been determined at the time. Are Brooke and Christie *Midshipwomen*? So this exchange fell on sympathetic ears — at least the ones attached to the males in the audience.

More military shenanigans ensue as Bernadette puts Hope through a grueling series of knee bends and situps, finally sending him off on an eight-mile hike. This was a typical theme that ran through many of our military sketches. Hope could be placed in authority, but he'd invariably misuse it and have to pay the penalty.

Somehow, though, he never seemed as funny playing an officer as a bumbling enlisted man.

Bed ◦ Breakfast

Now eighty, Hope still enjoyed remarkable stamina, due in no small degree to an uncanny ability to nap at the drop of a yawn. Our shooting schedule at the Academy had been particularly demanding on him physically, and it was during this visit that he somehow managed to drift off to sleep mid-sentence.

He was staying at the Superintendent's quarters, an imposing three-story Cape Cod mansion with enough ship models on display in its halls to qualify as a maritime museum. The guest rooms were on the top floor, and the admiral and his family had moved into a hotel, assuming that Hope would want privacy. Only a Filipino orderly remained to prepare Hope's meals.

"I wish the family had stayed," he confided to me. "I'm all alone here." I could see what he meant. He was facing another *Night at the Museum.*

We were about to go over the script for the following day, but after we'd trudged up the two flights, he plopped down on the maple bed, a gorgeous 19th-century four-poster probably from the Merrimac, and began reading his notes. In what appeared no longer than a nanosecond, he was transported to the deepest recesses of Slumberville, his head falling back on the pillow. Jeez, why had I let him climb all those stairs?

He began snoring, and I busied myself at a small desk nearby. Fifteen minutes passed — a half hour. If anything, he's sleeping even *more* soundly. Quietly, I gathered up my papers, tiptoed down the stairs, and let myself out.

It's lonely at the top, but it can be even lonelier for a celebrity.

Our Miss Brooke

These academy junkets marked Brooke Shields' first appearances on our show. During the ten seasons that would follow, she would do thirteen more, a record. Loni Anderson was second with six or seven; we lost count.

Under the watchful eye of her quintessential stage mother, Teri, whom writer Charlie Isaacs once accused of "carrying Brooke's virginity in her purse," she arrived lugging some heavy child-star baggage that included a nude scene in a movie called *Pretty Baby* as well as another *au naturel* performance in a picture called *The Blue Lagoon*.

Hope took an immediate liking to Brooke, and she to him, showering him with the affection one would bestow on a kindly grandfather. Hope may have been a father figure, too, as her parents had been long divorced. From her first appearance, Hope took Brooke under his wing, teaching her the basics of sketch comedy — timing, delivery, entrances and exits — techniques which seem effortless, but must be learned, nonetheless.

For her part, Brooke obviously enjoyed performing on the show, was eager to learn and, as would be expected, improved as time went on playing roles ranging from Becky Thatcher opposite Hope's Tom Sawyer (at the World's Fair in New Orleans where she forgot she was wearing a remote microphone transmitter, jumped into the Olympic diving pool, and almost demonstrated GE's "We Bring Good Things to Light" slogan) to a *Showboat* singer opposite Placido Domingo's Gaylord Ravenal — "We could make believe..." to Princess Diana.

The Hope specials kept her acting career afloat during her Princeton University, pre-Andre Agassi period. She made one movie, *Brenda Starr*, that bombed.

But as often happens in Hollywood, Brooke was stricken by a sudden case of selective amnesia when, in September 1996, she told an interviewer for the *Los Angeles Times* while discussing successful guest appearances on *Friends*, that "[Comedy] is something that I've never professionally explored and I've never had the opportunity or encouragement."

There was a logical explanation for her forgetfulness. By the mid-nineties, Hope was considered passé, and generations removed from the then-current TV comedy of *Seinfeld* or *Friends*. Also, she downplayed Hope's name on her resume so as not to detract from the much-publicized debut of her soon-to-debut sitcom *Suddenly Susan*.

I wrote a letter to the *Times* — which they printed — pointing out that Brooke had been taught comedy by none other than Bob Hope over many years. My letter was never challenged.

The episode was yet another example of the sometimes ephemeral quality of Hollywood friendships and loyalties.

* * * *

Our Naval Academy show included appearances by heavyweights Jerry Cooney and Larry Holmes with walk-ons by Leslie Neilsen; Charlton Heston; Sammy Davis, Jr. and Robert Goulet in a boxing segment with Hope.

Bernadette Peters and Hope performed a sea-going medley that concluded with "Anchors Aweigh," accompanied by the Annapolis Choir that drew tears and cheers.

Cast members of Broadway's *Sophisticated Ladies* and Dolores Hope also delivered musical numbers.

Thus concluded our trilogy of academy specials, each of which received high ratings and favorable reviews and would turn out to be the last military-themed Hope specials that would approach the quality of those he produced during World War II, Korea and Vietnam.

Using recycled comedy material adapted for the purpose, Hope's military junkets to the Middle East in the early-nineties were hastily produced affairs that proved too physically demanding for an 88-year old — even one named Bob Hope. It was no surprise that they failed to recapture the excellence that had so distinguished their predecessors — shows that were the subject of a six-hour retrospective, aired on two consecutive weekends in 1980. The marathon documentary-style specials were produced by Andrew Solt and Malcolm Leo who had established themselves as the official *Ed Sullivan Show* documentarians. Of course, Solt and Leo had an advantage. It's not easy to match a special that included Bing Crosby and Bob Hope singing "Mares Eat Oats" in the war-torn South Pacific — and Bing without his toupee yet.

CHAPTER 13

Playing Your Own Birthday Cake

Whenever I'm asked what a comedy writer's job was like back when variety was king, people most often refer to the old Dick Van Dyke Show where Rob, Buddy and Sally sat in an office trying to think up funny lines for their star, Alan Brady, to deliver. While writing jokes, sketches and routines did make up the bulk of our duties, the remainder was often devoted to heading off disasters of one kind or another. Comedy, like any activity performed in public for pay, is fraught with hidden dangers.

London Derriere

London, April 1979.

It's the day before we're scheduled to tape an hour-long special, *An Evening at the Palladium,* for a black-tie audience that will include Queen Elizabeth and Prince Philip. Gig Henry and I are going over the script with Hope in his dressing room, and, as usual when he was about to perform for royalty, he's wrestling with some last-minute jitters. (*"She has the keys to the Tower of London."*) Also present are executive producers Sid Vinnage and Elliott Kozak, and a British writing team who had been hired to assist us, Dick Vosburgh and Gary Chambers.

The phone rings. Hope picks it up, and on the other end of the line is one of our guest stars, Richard Burton, whose voice fills the room even though it's not a speaker-phone. It seems that Dick's "people" — read new wife of some three weeks, one of Burton's "between Liz" marriages — don't think it's in the actor's best interest to be doing a love scene with co-star Raquel Welch in a sketch we'd prepared for them — a parody of the popular PBS series *Upstairs, Downstairs* that we had re-titled *Backstairs at Buckingham Palace*. Hope cups his hand over the mouthpiece and asks us if we can rewrite the sketch omitting the kissing. We all shake our heads "no" — if the love scenes go, there's no sketch.

Hope tells Burton he'll get back to him and hangs up. We carefully go over the sketch line-by-line just to be sure, and Hope agrees that, unless Burton has lip privileges with the downstairs chambermaid, we'll have to write a whole new sketch, and time, as they say over there, is frightfully short.

Hope gets an idea. He calls Burton back and asks him if it would help if the chambermaid were someone *other than* Raquel. Several minutes elapse while Dick again checks with his people. That would solve the problem very nicely, he tells Hope.

Goodbye, Raquel.

Vinnage starts calling his British contacts and soon locates actress Susan George who's appearing in a stage play about three hundred miles from London. Susan, an experienced performer who had recently co-starred with Dustin Hoffman in the popular American movie, *Straw Dogs*, agrees to step in for Raquel despite a case of laryngitis, finishes her matinee and arrives at the Palladium just hours before showtime. After a quick rehearsal, she bravely goes on for Raquel and ends up sharing equal-billing with Welch, Burton and Leslie Uggams. Later, Raquel explains to a group of British reporters that she had rejected the sketch because she was unhappy with her lines. This time, we were happy to take the rap.

Family Friendly

Two years earlier, we had been in London for a special entitled *America Salutes the Queen*. Aware from long experience that a happily married writer writes *funnier*, occasionally, Hope would invite our wives to accompany us on the overseas trips. So Gig, Gene and I, with our respective spouses, Frances, Joanne and Shelley, were ensconced at the Churchill, within walking distance of Hope's usual suite at Claridge's. Since this was a "wives welcome" trip, Dolores had come along, too.

One of the producers of our special, Hope pal Sir Lew Grade, hosted a party for the entire com-

Here I am with Dolores Hope in their suite at Claridge's, their HQ of choice whenever they visited the Empire. In case you didn't notice, I'm wearing my Hungarian Freedom-Fighter jacket.

pany at London's Pink Elephant on the River, an exclusive private club for showfolk on the bank of the Thames. The cigar-chomping, ex-American vaudevillian put his checkbook in overdrive for this soiree, providing *separate* limousines for each couple and a buffet-dinner dance menu that offered salmon flown from Scotland, Kobe beef, Beluga caviar, truffles, and other items my annual income couldn't pronounce. With music provided by several of Soho's top bands, we dined and danced into the night.

Three A.M. — time to settle up with the piper. Back at the Churchill, marinating in top-quality distilled spirits and anxious to capture some heavy-duty recovery slumber, we discover notes from Hope in our boxes along with a script of *The Muppet Show*. "This just arrived," his note read, "Need the rewrite by seven. Due at *Elstree* by nine. Late booking. Sorry. The King."

It was rare that he'd accept such an early call, but this *was* the Muppets, and, we learned later, he really hadn't known of the taping when he'd left the party around ten. So we sent the spouses to Zee-ville while we got to work. I took a spare blanket from the closet, spread it in the bathtub, and at least got to recline while scribbling. The rewrites were

Don Marando and my wife, Shelley, backstage at the Palladium. Our wives were always welcome on the set even when we were on active duty status, but working on a TV special on location left little time for sightseeing, so we weren't exactly vacationing.

Bryan Blackburn was Hope's man in London on whom he relied to give our British specials an authentic "Number Ten Downing Street" ambiance. Bryan would later come to the States to work on a sitcom produced by Sheldon Keller called *Hizzoner*, starring David Huddleston.

waiting in Hope's box in the morning. This was the first and *only* instance during all the years I wrote for Hope that I lost any sleep doing it.

Vikings On Vicodin

To be sure, unforeseen problems bedeviled every show to some degree, but by far the most ill-fated special Hope produced on my watch was taped at the Oscars Theater in Stockholm before Sweden's King Carl Gustav and Queen Sylvia in February, 1986. Billed as a Command Performance, Hope had agreed to emcee the black-tie gala entitled *Bob Hope's Royal Command Performance from Sweden*, the proceeds of which were to go to the king's favorite charity, the Children's International Summer Village. Hope would host the show and in return would own the American rights which he'd license to NBC. It was a potentially profitable deal since most of the production expenses would be picked up by the Swedish government.

As with our wives, Hope warmly welcomed relatives invited to watch the tapings.
Here he is charming my wife's sister, Pat, and her husband, Ned Dozier,
in from Washington, D.C. in the mid-eighties.

But even before the Scandinavian Airlines 747 had been loaded with our luggage at LAX, the hex kicked in. As Gene Perret and I sat in the executive lounge putting the finishing touches on a Viking sketch we were confident would have the Swedes in hysterics from Goteborg to Lapland, producers Elliott Kozak and Dick Arlett came in and hit us between the eyes with the news that Sweden's Prime Minister, Olaf Palme, had just been assassinated while walking his dog on a Stockholm street.

The room fell silent. Glen Campbell, who had been sitting across from us noodling a few licks, put down his guitar and stared ahead blankly. Only moments before, we had entered the lounge filled with excited anticipation of what promised to be a fun-filled and interesting journey to a land few of us had visited.

Two other troubadours who would appear on the show, Shirley Jones and Emanuel Lewis, looked on in shock as transatlantic phone calls were hurriedly made to decide if the show would be canceled. Our departure was pushed ahead an hour while we all sat biting our collective show business fingernails.

Shortly, word arrived directly from the palace — since preparations for the gala were set and invitations sent out, postponing the performance, ruled the monarch, would cause world-class headaches all around. The show, as they say, must go on. Where this old saw originated, I have no idea, but there are instances where it flies in the face of common sense, and this was, undoubtedly, one of them. Picture, if you will, taping the *Colgate Comedy Hour* just three days following the death of John Kennedy. Same problem — similar reaction. The entire Swedish nation had been plunged into mourning. On our drive from the airport, we could see people lining the street, carrying candles and placing bouquets of flowers at the spot on the frozen sidewalk where the popular prime minister had fallen. A pall hung over the capital — literally and figuratively. Ships in the harbor stood at anchor, rigid and icebound — prisoners of a climate that almost half the year chills the bones and, one suspects, is no small contributor to the highest suicide rate in all of Scandinavia.

But forget all that. The assembled glitterati applauded dutifully as the king and queen were escorted to the royal box. The show began with a rambling, largely incomprehensible introduction of Hope by Swedish actress Liv Ullman. It was obvious that she would have preferred being somewhere else, and who wouldn't?

Hope did his best to deliver his monologue, but had about as much luck getting laughs as an athiest at a Southern Baptist Convention. The evening's slate of performers — Boy George and the Culture Club, Omar Sharif , Dolf Lundgren and Scott Grimes as well as Glen, Emanuel and Shirley — carried on like the pros they are, but the project was doomed from the start. It was like watching the lounge act on the *Hindenburg*. It was a wake with entertainment.

We had written a sketch that cast Hope and Emmanuel Lewis, dressed in reindeer pelts and horned helmets, as a pair of Vikings on their annual spring plunder. As Gene Perret and I stood offstage, puzzled why our pillage jokes were drawing gasps, one of the Swedish technicians pointed out that we had named Hope's character, *Olaf.* In the confusion, no one had caught what now appeared to be an insensitive joke. During a break, we told Hope what had happened and he immediately called a halt to the proceedings and apologized to the audience.

When our Swedish fiasco finally concluded and we were winging home to a much warmer Los Angeles, I remember thinking back — I should have known from the start that the trip would turn out to be jinxed. Excited over my first junket to a Scandinavian country, I arrived at LAX *sans* passport!

A messenger from the Hope office was dispatched to deliver it, but to avoid a delayed departure, a representative from the airline soon arrived and announced that my California drivers license would do the trick! My passport would follow on the next flight — without *me.* I learned later that Sweden had waived their usual customs requirements because I was on a special assignment for the king!

Proving once again that it pays to work for someone who's close to kings.

* * * *

But even with our problems in Stockholm, I do have one a great memory of the trip.

One night, after a long day of rehearsing, we returned to the hotel around nine o'clock. It was about 40 degrees below outside, and there was a nice fire going in the lounge, so Glen Campbell asked Gene and me if we'd like to join him for a nightcap. There was a fairly good jazz quartet — piano, drums, guitars, bass — that played there every night. We had noticed them before but were always too busy to stop. We sat at the bar for a few minutes and were recalling our day in Birdseye-ville when one of the guitar players asked Glen if he'd like to sit in for a number. Usually, professional musicians hesitate to take anyone up on an offer like that since it's what they do for a living and is a little like asking

Picasso to sketch something on a bar napkin. But Glen isn't your usual pro. He loves to practice chords with his own guitar and often does — in airport lounges, television studio dressing rooms, and maybe even while showering.

Glen just *loves* the guitar. I suspect the guy in the quartet was a big fan, knew this, and also knew that Glen would have a hard time turning him down. He was right. "Okay, just one number." Glen took the instrument, fine-tuned a couple of strings and began picking the melody of "A Foggy Day" — the house musicians were British.

Now the bartender is on the phone — "You're not gonna believe this... " in Swedish, of course, but you could tell what he was saying by the excitement in his voice. Several couples who had been sitting in the lobby drifted in and took a table near the bandstand. As other guests arrived, they could see and hear that something special was occurring in the bar.

Nobody headed upstairs and nobody left. Glen, as usual, was doing some astounding riffs. I asked him once how he got so damn good, and he said that as a kid, he would *dream* guitar chords and play them as soon as he woke up. That, my friends, is genetic. Even the owner of the guitar Glen was playing couldn't believe the sounds he was getting out of it.

Glen's "one number" was soon three and then five. The crowd had grown to thirty or forty people — some sitting, some standing, all mesmerized. When he finally handed the Gibson back to its owner, the applause was enough to wake up guests in their rooms who had missed Glen's impromptu concert.

It was one of those once-in-a-lifetime moments you just never forget.

Seashell Shocked

The season following the debacle in Stockholm, it was decided we should get right back on the horse before we lost our nerve. And what more relaxing locale in which to regain our confidence than lush, tropical Tahiti?

Well, it sounded good on paper, anyway. Once again, our co-producers were Elliott Kozak and Dick Arlett — could these guys have been carrying around a voodoo curse? They had arranged what appeared to be a mutually beneficial promotional arrangement with America-Hawaii Cruises. The hour-long special would include guest stars John Denver, Howard Keel, Jonathan Winters, Morgan Brittany, and the reigning Miss America, Susan Aiken. It would be taped in and around Moorea and the island chain's capital, Papeete. Hope would perform an eight-minute monologue from the promenade deck of the cruise ship S.S. Liberte that was docked in Cook's Bay. We were in a tropical paradise known the world over for its crystal clear lagoons and azure blue beaches crawling with topless, grass-skirted beauties renowned for their warmth, charm and indigenous friendliness. What could possibly go wrong?

Well for starters, Hope, introduced from off-deck, strode out in a straw hat and multicolored Hawaiian shirt and began his monologue with this line:

> Here we are aboard the S.S. Liberte on the island of Moorea.
> S.S. Liberte. Spend a few days on a cruise liner, and you'll
> understand what the "S.S." stands for — "Swingin' Ship."

The audience, huddled together on deck chairs, stared back at Hope like they'd just been struck by an iceberg. If this bunch had ever done any swinging, it was during the Roaring Twenties. And the roar was down to a whisper. We had written a monologue for the *Love Boat,* and it was being delivered on the S.S. Geriatric. In our rush to get aboard and set up, no one had bothered to check the passenger manifest, and now the vessel was scheduled to depart within hours. It was too late to regroup, so Hope had no choice but to press on, hoping we could edit in some canned laughter back home.

> This is the Liberte which means freedom in French, and
> judging from all the cabin hopping I heard last night, it's well
> named.

Again, the audience hasn't a clue as to what he's talking about. If they had done any cabin hopping the night before, it was to borrow a cup of Metamucil from a neighbor. As Gene and I stood at the railing seriously considering a swan dive, Hope glanced over at us with a look that said, "I should have become an accountant." But Gene, ever cheerful, mouthed the words, "Keep going. You're doing great." Hope did, but he wasn't.

One guy's been so busy at night, he couldn't remember where his own compartment was. He just found out it's on another ship.

Right about now, Hope looks like he'd prefer to be on another one, too.

One gal asked the captain to perform a marriage ceremony and showed up with four guys. The captain said, "Which one's the groom?" And she said, "Don't rush me."

At last, a huge round of applause from a group of couples celebrating fiftieth wedding anniversaries. After a few more jokes, the bellman announces that it's time for another buffet, the audience files out en mass, and we hold an impromptu burial-at-sea for the monologue.

We had learned the hard way that Hope's on-deck performances worked best with audiences in uniform.

Several months later, the cruise line declared bankruptcy, and the Liberte was sold at auction, refitted, repainted and renamed. We never found out if we had contributed to its demise.

First it had been a dead prime minister, then a bankrupt cruise line. Back in 1984, the World's Fair in New Orleans had gone bust right after we taped a two-hour special there to promote it. Watch for a special on the Sci Fi Channel entitled *The Unexplained Curse of the Bob Hope Show*.

Going Native

Things began to look up when we settled into our assigned accommodations on Moorea — thatched-huts tucked among the volcanic ash and pearl-white sand of a beach that a few decades earlier had made Gauguin relocate. Each suite had its own waterfall/shower carved from coral, and at high-season rates of four-hundred dollars a day — a substantial sum for lodging back then — they were a cut above Holiday Inn.

The hotel-on-the-beach was the brainchild of three Americans —

classmates at U.S.C. — who had visited Tahiti during spring break one year and decided it would be an ideal location to erect a getaway for the rich, near-rich and people who wanted to be pampered in a spot that's so remote, it had taken four days for news of NASA's recent Challenger disaster to reach the islands. The current owner had bought out his partners, taken a Tahitian wife, produced a bunch of kids and confided to me that he didn't *mind* not getting news from the outside world for weeks-on-end. You can check out his photo in the dictionary under "laid back."

The huts at the hotel were scattered in a configuration inspired by the native villages back in Gauguin's day. A hut here, a hut there, with lush tropical plants and flowers filling the spaces in between. (Hope would sing his finale "Thanks for the Memory" verses while strolling among them.) The huts had thin walls made of bamboo stalks lashed together so sound carried.

One balmy evening, Gene and I were unwinding at the bar watching the Polynesian sun set when we heard a shriek coming from the general direction of Susan Aiken's hut.

We yelled out, "What's wrong?"

She said, "There's a huge *bug* crawling up my wall!"

Instantly responding to Miss America's cry for assistance, Gene leaped from his stool and said, "I'll go. I'm from San Marino. I know how to handle bugs!"

I said, "Hold on, Skipper, I'm from Studio City, and our bugs are *humungous.*"

We went back and forth like that until Gene said, "Let's flip for it."

While he's fishing around in his cargo shorts for a suitable coin, we heard Susan say, "Forget it, guys. I just stepped on it."

* * * *

John Denver was a newlywed, and initially he had turned down the offer to guest on the show; he reconsidered after Hope assured him that he was welcome to combine his working visit to Tahiti with a honeymoon.

John and his new bride had one of the ultra-plush huts perched on stilts over the water. To get to it, you had to traverse a thirty-foot long, narrow wooden walkway extending from the beach.

One day, while at our duty station at the open-air bar, we heard our assistant director knocking on John's door. "Half hour, John. We're almost set up." Mr. Rocky Mountain High was scheduled to tape a song while combing the beach nearby.

The assistant left but soon was back.

Knock, knock, knock. "Fifteen minutes, John." Still no John.

Ten minutes later, he reappeared, carefully threading the walkway for the third time.

Knock, knock, knock. "Five minutes, John." He pressed his ear against the bamboo door. Nothing. He shook his head and waved toward an assistant on the beach.

"The hell with it. Set up Morgan Brittany's number!"

Bali Hai∘Jinks

Each morning, Gene and I worked while trying not to notice the beach where halter tops appeared to be illegal. But we did manage to put the finishing touches on comedy bits for Jonathan as an American tourist, a Tahitian politician and a French chef as well as our *Mutiny on the Bounty* sketch. Along with our colleagues Si, Freddy, Jeff and Martha who were holding down the fort back home, we had been hammering away at the script for several weeks.

The plan was to tape the sketch aboard an exact replica of the legendary schooner that had been built by director Dino de Laurentis for his movie version of the epic tale. Actually, it was the *Bounty* from the waterline up and a luxurious yacht below with plush lounges, guest compartments, a huge kitchen and a spa. Unfortunately, our happy vessel would hit some rough seas, but not before our production would survive a preliminary bout with the weather.

On our final night in Moorea, Howard Keel was scheduled to sing "Some Enchanted Evening" at the same location Rosanno Brazzi had belted out "Bali Hai" in the movie *South Pacific*. The taping was to begin precisely at sundown so that when Howard hit the final eight bars, the golden orb would be tucking itself behind the famous mountain. Dramatic — beautiful — and technically tricky. Our director, Walter Miller, would have only one shot at it, and, if anything went wrong, he'd get no second chance — we're out of there the next day.

Just before Howard arrived to go to work, a few clouds formed in the otherwise-pristine sky. Though they blocked our view of the mountain, they looked fluffy and harmless to the crew — a form of wishful thinking common among men who depend on light for their livelihood. All at once, the sky parted and dumped enough rain on our little party to turn Death Valley into a Raging Waters theme park. The equipment was quickly covered as everyone sprinted for cover and the producers convened an emergency summit meeting to devise Plan B. It's quickly calculated that, without Howard's number, we don't have enough show. We'll just have to shoot the scene back in Burbank in front of a convincing *photo* of the mountain.

But Howard has an idea. Would the audience notice the difference between a sunset and a sunrise if they see only three-minutes of it? Couldn't we tape the number, reasons Howard, while the sun comes *up*? Howard's inventive nature earned him a four-thirty wakeup call, but the number went off in the crisp, clear post-monsoon morn without a hitch. If you ever see a rerun of the show, look carefully — the evening is so enchanted it gets *lighter* instead of darker.

Captain Blight

Now we headed to the Bounty which was anchored in a lagoon on the opposite side of the island. Our richly costumed period sketch would feature Hope as the cruel, crew-beating Captain Bligh; Howard as the ship's doctor; Susan Aiken as his nurse; Morgan Fairchild as the prim, school marm passenger; John Denver as the young, Wahini-smitten Fletcher Christian and Jonathan Winters as his tribal chief, soon-to-be father-in-law.

Even under ideal studio conditions, accommodating such a large cast on the small screen is a tall order for any director, and Walter, one of the best, had his hands full with this one. While the ship had been ideal for de Laurentis who had the time to set up multiple camera shots, it was soon apparent that it wasn't big enough to do our sketch on. People were a lot smaller in the eighteenth century, and everything was about three-quarter scale. In many of the scenes, members of the cast were sardined on her decks tighter than Cuban boat people. They looked like they were performing in a telephone booth. So much for *exact* replicas.

Walter tried setup after setup, attempting to create the illusion of size and depth. As a result, the taping ran longer than scheduled, and the entire company was supposed to depart that evening. A few crew members were sent back to our hotel-on-stilts to pack for those who had to remain to get the sketch, such as it was, in the can.

Finally, at about four in the afternoon, Walter yelled "Cut! That's a wrap!" The cameras, lighting and sound paraphernalia were stowed into dockside trucks in record time. Electronic equipment hadn't disappeared that fast since the L.A. riots. Everyone raced to the waiting busses which would convey us to the harbor where the swiftest picket boat on the island was standing by.

We arrived at the airport in Papeete with only minutes to spare, but as it turned out, our plane was grounded in New Zealand with mechanical problems and wouldn't arrive until the next day.

At this point, Howard Keel entered panic mode. He was due on the set of *Dallas* in less than forty-eight hours to film some key scenes. If he was delayed in Tahiti, it would cost the producers — and him after the lawsuit — hundreds of thousands of dollars.

A smiling Quantas representative assured him that the plane would arrive in the morning as promised. We were given our hotel assignments — a night's *free* lodging for our inconvenience. They also threw in a phone call, so we could notify our next-of-kin of the delay. "Swell," responded a tired, hungry and Bounty-weary Jonathan. "I'll call my brother. He's dead."

Our patched-up 747 arrived on schedule, and Howard made it to Culver City in a limo he had waiting with only minutes to spare. He told me later he filmed the first scene with sand in his shoes.

A sad note. Nine years later, John Denver would die after plunging his EZ Lite experimental airplane into the ocean while taking off from California's Monterey Peninsula airport. He was only 54 years old.

Cardioman

In 1978, Ohio was celebrating its Golden Jubilee, and the dedication of the newly-refurbished Ohio Theater in Columbus where Hope had performed in vaudeville. Produced by Bob Banner, our hour-long special would include a parade in which Hope would be the Grand Marshal, capped by a black-tie, invitation-only stage show.

It had been a long day for Hope, and on the evening of the performance, about a half-hour before the taping was set to begin, he was standing in the wings with Elliott Kozak. Most of the guests had already filed into their seats, and a pianist was playing a medley of Ohio-themed songs. Hope turned to Elliott and said, "Feel my pulse." Elliott did and was alarmed by what he felt. Hope's heart was racing at about two hundred beats per minute!

As Elliott led him back to his dressing room, Hope said he felt all right and had no chest pains. Regardless of the absence of heart attack symptoms, his heart was racing abnormally, so Elliott insisted he lie down.

Banner was called in from the tech truck outside the theater and after speaking with Hope, told a production assistant to go out front — and without explaining why — locate the insurance executive whose company had sponsored the charity event. Banner wanted to avoid alarming the audience with the usual announcement that was sure to do just that.

The insurance guy told the PA that a well-known cardiologist was on the guest list, but hadn't arrived yet. She got his number. Banner called him and described Hope's symptoms. The doctor told Banner to take Hope back to his hotel — just a block from the theater — where the heart specialist could examine him more thoroughly.

With Hope still protesting that he felt fine, Banner and Elliott quietly slipped him out a side door.

Meanwhile, the audience — and most members of Hope's staff — had no inkling of the emergency. Gig and I accompanied Hope to the hotel and went to our own rooms to stand by if needed.

As Hope lay on the bed waiting for the doctor to arrive, Banner had second thoughts. Maybe they were being *too* cautious in their attempts to keep the episode under wraps. After all, Hope *was* 76.

Banner dialed 911.

Within minutes, fire engines, sirens blaring, pulled up to the hotel entrance. Watching them from our balconies, Gig and I thought the unthinkable had happened. We rushed to Hope's suite where he was being examined by the cardiologist while the fire department ME's stood by in case their equipment was needed.

They were soon released by the doctor, and after they left, we learned that Hope had been diagnosed with nothing more than an episode of tachycardia — an anxiety attack. The doctor had reduced his racing heart rate by applying pressure on Hope's femoral artery. He was back to normal.

We all returned to the theater where some of our guest stars had kept the audience entertained during the hour-long delay they blamed on "technical difficulties." The taping proceeded without incident with Hope as emcee.

Over Dolores's objection, he did a few more personal appearances in the East, but when he returned home, he had a complete cardio-checkup at Burbank's St. Joseph's Hospital. His doctors declared that he was heart healthy, but he had to wear a device called a Holter monitor, which he wore for a week. Connected by phone to the hospital, it measured his heart activity in real time.

I asked him one day how he was taking to having the electronic device strapped to his belt.

"No problem," he said. "But every time I open *Playboy,* the phone rings."

Bar Exam

Sometimes, problems didn't arise until after a show had been taped which made them even more troublesome and costly.

One year, we did a Halloween special on which one of the guests was Cassandra Peterson, well-known as a Charles Addams-like character named Elvira. She appeared in a parody of the popular sitcom *Cheers* as a customer in the bar opposite Hope as the show's bartender, Coach. In our sketch, Cassandra entered the bar, looked Hope up and down, and said, "Nice job. Who's your undertaker?" The Halloween special was set to air on Sunday night but on Friday, Nick Callesandro, the actor who played "Coach" on *Cheers,* suffered a sudden heart attack at his home in Burbank and died.

Minutes after the grim news was broadcast, my phone rang. It was Hope with instructions to call the writers and have them begin working on a replacement line that could be dubbed onto the master tape, which had already been delivered to the network. In the meantime, he said, he would notify Cassandra to meet us at the sound studio for the emergency-looping session. The line we were to come up with not only had to make sense in the context of the sketch, but it also had to match as closely as possible the actress's lip movements. We tried five or six replacements until everyone settled on "Nice job. Did your makeup man quit?" The syllables matched perfectly and even on a large studio monitor, it was difficult to tell that her voice had been dubbed.

It was only a small change, but Hope had gone to the trouble and expense of fixing the line, knowing that failure to do so might make him appear crass and unfeeling to a television audience unaware that segments of so-called "live" shows are often taped well-in-advance.

When it came to protecting his image in the eyes of the public, Hope's judgment was usually sound.

Usually.

Taste Makes Waste

One day, the phone rang, and it was Hope in need of a quick joke fix. It was on a Friday afternoon about four, and he was scheduled to appear as a guest on the *Tonight Show* which in those days began taping at five-thirty. He was at home in his makeup chair with Don Marando performing his usual duties. Hope had just learned that the guest following him — he always insisted that Carson bring him on first — was comedian

Richard Pryor, making his first television appearance since his near-fatal encounter with an exploding crack pipe some nine months earlier.

Pryor had undergone extensive skin grafts on his face, neck and chest performed at the Grossman Burn Center, and his slow and painful rehabilitation had been covered extensively in the press — coverage which Hope had somehow missed, I was about to find out.

A member of the *Tonight Show* staff had called with a special request from Johnny that Hope remain for an additional segment — "move one-down on the couch" as they used to say — during Carson's interview with Pryor. Now Hope was to go on television in little over an hour. While we had already provided him with plenty of "ad-libs" to trade with Johnny, he had no lines relating to Pryor.

It was a situation in which he felt vulnerable. To him, having a few lines in his pocket was like an insurance policy. I assured him that Pryor's appearance wouldn't be packed with laughs since he'd be relating a near-death experience, hardly a fun topic. Hope disagreed. He didn't believe that Pryor's injuries had been that serious, and he wanted something witty to say when the two shook hands.

"Like what?" I asked, unable to envision anything even remotely appropriate to the moment.

"Something like this," he said. "Tell me, Richard, how did it feel playing your own birthday cake?"

I was nothing short of stunned. I knew he couldn't get away with a line like that and told him so.

"You're wrong," he insisted. "His accident wasn't that big a deal."

Even if it weren't, I pointed out, the public *perceived* it as life-threatening, and any flippant reference to it would make him appear heartless, unfeeling and worse, stupid.

I stood firm. Hope was stubborn, but you could argue with him if you were sure you were on solid ground. Actually, he appreciated staffers standing up to him if they believed it was necessary. He detested the "yes-men" who so commonly surround celebrities. Nonetheless, he continued to insist he was right about Pryor's injury.

He appealed to Don whom I could hear in the background supporting my position.

Outnumbered, he begrudgingly gave up on the idea, but continued to insist that we were both wrong.

That night I taped the *Tonight Show* and the next morning watched as Johnny finished with Hope — who managed to slip in a few of our jokes — and introduced Pryor who, slowly and obviously still in considerable pain, came through the curtain wearing a ball cap to hide his still-visible burns. Pryor appeared genuinely touched as the audience gave him a two-minute standing ovation. Hope applauded, too, as he glanced into the camera with a look that said, "What was I thinking?" He knew Don and I would be watching the show and was sending us an apology — *telepathically.*

Tent Sales

Hope's occasional lapses of judgment could get him in hot water with his writers. One such instance occurred following our return from London to tape *America Salutes the Queen* described at the beginning of this chapter (the one with the lavish party hosted by Sir Lew Grade).

Charlie Lee — who had injured his knee and passed on making the trip with us — noticed a joke in Hope's monologue that he considered anti-Semitic and at a writers meeting a few days later, told him so. Hope defended the line, assuring him that he had tested the joke among his friends, none of whom had objected to it.

"What in hell would your white-bread Republican buddies know about anti-Semitism?" Charlie never pulled any punches with the boss and had gotten away with it simply because he was a brilliant writer.

"Now, wait a minute, Charlie," Hope pleaded. "I even checked the joke with Lew Grade, and he said it was okay."

Now Charlie was livid. "Lew Grade? Lew Grade? Lew Grade hasn't been a Jew for *thirty* years!"

Chalk one up for Charlie. Not even a Bob Hope could top that.

What was the line that sent Charlie into the stratosphere? Here it is. You be the judge.

"Isn't it great to see the Arabs and the Israelis getting back together again? I mean the Arabs couldn't have gone on buying retail forever."

I sided with Charlie.

✻ ✻ ✻ ✻

Charlie was a curmudgeon of the old school — loud, opinionated, and smart, in the style of H. L. Mencken. He lived in Studio City and over the years had been banished from almost every shop and restaurant along Ventura Boulevard including Art's Deli, a San Fernando Valley landmark popular among Hollywood's film and TV crowd.

His quick wit was legendary among writers and stories about him remain a staple.

Like the day he joined Hope to collect Dolores at the Burbank Airport. As the two stood at the gate, she emerged from the plane with two nuns she had befriended, one on each arm. Charlie watched them for a moment and said, "Why can't she just buy flight insurance like everyone else? "

Hudson Hornet's Nest

Hope enjoyed trading the latest raunchy stories going around with a telephone network of cronies that at one time had included Ronald Reagan, Tip O'Neill, Dan Rostenkowski, Gen. Westmoreland, Stuart Symington, and, for a brief time in the early sixties, J.F.K. He loved a good joke from whatever source, but whenever he veered very far afield from his prepared material, the consequences could be disastrous.

In the summer of 1983, he agreed to deliver a ten-minute routine during a charity benefit aboard the Trump Princess, an elegant, converted destroyer owned by Donald Trump and anchored in New York harbor. On the vessel that night was the A-list of New York society led by Governor Hugh Carey.

During the cocktail-reception preceding dinner, Hope visited the men's room where another guest, docked at an adjoining urinal, told him a joke he'd just heard. That happens often to comedians and comedy writ-

Ward Grant handled public relations for Hope almost as long as Barney McNulty (shown here sharing a laugh) had been printing Hope's cue cards. Both exemplified Hope's long-term loyalty to faithful and trusted employees.

ers — "Hey, I thought you could use this!" Both men laughed heartily, and Hope decided that the line might, indeed, be a welcome addition to his prepared material. It was tailor-made for a New York crowd, he reasoned, since it concerned one of their proudest landmarks, the Statue of Liberty.

So, several minutes into his routine, he casually dropped in a joke that would reverberate for months and let loose something Hope was unaccustomed to — an avalanche of adverse publicity.

He said: "Hey, have you heard? The Statue of Liberty has AIDS. Nobody knows if she got it from the mouth of the Hudson or the Staten Island Ferry."

The following morning, a reporter for the *New York Post* led off with the gaff in his coverage of the event, and the worms, as they say, exited the can.

Ward Grant, Hope's faithful spinmeister quickly drafted a press-release explaining that the line had been misinterpreted, taken out-of-context, or some such excuse PR men must come up with whenever a client finds himself with a mouthful of foot. But the incident would require more than the standard damage control. Gay and lesbian groups across the country demanded a formal apology.

After the furor refused to disappear, Hope apologized and promised to be more sensitive to gay issues. He'd later do several charity benefits for AIDS at the behest of Elizabeth Taylor.

Ironically, the incident recalled the bad press that resulted back in 1971 when Hope was quoted in a *Life Magazine* cover story as having said: "The Vietnam War is a beautiful thing — we paid in a lot of gorgeous American lives, but we're not sorry for it."

Throughout his career, Hope avoided making many mistakes that would draw the public's ire, but whenever he did, they were lulus. He had learned the hard way that, as advancing age was putting him more and more out of touch with the sensitivities of his audience, he'd best stick to the script. He realized, wisely, that his days of ad-libbing a joke that hadn't been written for him were long past.

CHAPTER 14

The Beer Cans Spell Our "Bear Bryant"

From Hope's earliest tours of military bases during World War II, it was obvious that he enjoyed a unique rapport with young people. So in the fall of 1979, he made his first post-Vietnam foray into the academic world — during the Vietnam years, his stand on the war made college campuses off limits — with a carefully arranged special entitled *Bob Hope on Campus*. Co-produced by Linda (his daughter) and Frank Badami II, the ninety-minute show would take Hope from the University of Southern California to the University of Alabama to Florida's "Gator Growl" with classroom stops along the way at Indiana State University, Harvard University and Colgate.

As with the overseas military tours, weeks in advance, we were sent plenty of reference material on each school, so the jokes could be tailored to fit every audience on Hope's itinerary.

Guest stars included Vanessa Williams, Morgan Fairchild, Joe Montana, and Dionne Warwick who dropped in for a sketch or stand-up routine, but as they had in the military shows, the monologues dominated and defined the tour.

The special was such a success. Hope would re-enroll four years later for *Bob Hope Goes to College*.

Tanned and Trojan

USC was Rose Bowl-bound that year so Hope's first monologue, taped on the steps of the Student Union, not surprisingly overflowed with pigskin references.

> *USC is becoming such a football dynasty, the babies born around here are slapped on both ends so they'll know what a scrimmage feels like.*

> *And I've never seen such school spirit. It's nice to see students getting high on something you don't have to inhale.*

In the late seventies, the drug problem had yet to reach the proportions it soon would. In 1981, NBC asked Hope not to make light of illicit drugs or their widespread use. We were told to cut the pot jokes — which up until then had been a regular staple in our submissions. For the rest of his career, Hope would never again mention hard drugs on the air. Then in the mid-eighties, he participated in a network-sponsored anti-drug campaign called "Get High on Yourself" produced by Robert Evans (*Love Story, The Kid Stays in the Picture!*) as part of the community service a judge had sentenced Robert Evans to after a felony drug conviction. As it turned out, the spots were about as effective as Nancy Reagan's "Just Say No" campaign would be a few years later.

At USC, we couldn't resist taking a few swipes at Southern California's well-known reputation for seismic instability.

> *It must be tough trying to concentrate in class with all of our earthquakes. One guy enrolled at USC, took his exams at UCLA and graduated from Pepperdine.*

It would be fifteen years before the devastating 6.9 temblor would epicenter in nearby Northridge on January 19, 1994.

Poison Ivy League

Then, it was on to Cambridge, Massachusetts and the historic campus of Harvard University.

We almost qualified for advanced history degrees after poring over the voluminous background material the Crimson Triangle had been accumulating for a hundred and thirty years. The alumni list reads like "Who's Who Among the Rich and Famous and Elected on the First Ballot," so we took great delight in providing jibes for one ageless icon to toss at another.

> *Harvard was founded in 1836, and here I am standing on its stage. Who would have thought it would last that long, huh?*

We turned out numerous variations of this joke over the years. On Hope's thirtieth anniversary on television, it came out "Who would have thought NBC would last that long?"

Historically, Harvard had been acting as unofficial personnel office for Capitol Hill and the White House, and a disproportionate number of Foggy Bottom's "Smoke-Filled Room & Pork Barrel Club" members boast sheepskins with crimson edges.

> *For over a hundred and thirty years, Harvard has been producing more politicians than any other school — but they've made up for it in many other ways.*

As much as Hope admired politicians himself, he sensed that the public held them in about as much esteem as used car salesmen and took full advantage of that perception.

> *And it's one of the richest schools in the Ivy League. Of course, it's easy to collect money that has pictures of the alumni printed on it.*

Hope was performing before an audience of overindulged frat boys, a group of whom were literally perched on a ledge which ringed the second story of the library. When they heard his reference to currency used as a private version of FaceBook, several of them almost took a dive for the Crimson Tide.

> *But my favorite is that Winthrop House dorm where all the Kennedys roomed, or, as it's otherwise known, "White House North."*

Orange Crush

Winging due south, we headed for the University of Florida's annual excuse to cut loose with enough 90-proof school spirit to float Gainesville to Apalachicola. Known affectionately as the "Gator Growl," it's raucous enough to cause real alligators to seek asylum in a belt-and-wallet factory. On the eve of the homecoming game, Hope entered the Florida Stadium to the roar of fifty-six thousand screaming students and their families.

> *Wow! I took one look at this crowd and said to the dean, "Boy, I must be good." He said, "Not necessarily. They also turn out for the football games."*

This was one of those lines we hoped the home audience would pick up on even if they weren't aware that Florida was in the midst of one of its worst football seasons in recent memory.

Partying is "job one" on the resume of every Florida graduate worthy of the name — or so we were told — and we stopped just short of having Hope toss confetti while delivering lines like this:

> *I love your graduation ceremonies. Instead of mortar boards, party hats. I met a student who's majoring in Mixed Drinks. This is the only school in America whose diplomas say RSVP.*

Every campus, it seems, has a monument to the lusty pursuits of youth away from home for the first time.

> *I love that Legend of the Sentry Tower. Every time a virgin graduates, a brick is supposed to fall. They tell me that makes it the safest place on campus during an earthquake.*

The line, of course, drew a roar from every male in the audience. Throughout our tour, any passing reference to sex got the same reaction that our liberty jokes elicited from sailors. Maybe the only difference between a college dorm and a ship is a little ivy.

Here we are the University of Southern California in the fall of 1983, for the first
stop on a seven-campus tour for *Bob Hope Goes to College*. (left to right) Our entering
freshman, Gig Henry, me, NBC executive March Fong and Don Marando. Hope
would return for a graduate degree four years later for *Bob Hope on Campus*.
He just wasn't going to give up until he found a parking space.

'Bammy Whammy

Reviewing the piles of background material we received on the University
of Alabama, it was clear that we'd be limited to three topics — football,
football and, oh yes, did I mention football? We soon learned that Alabama is where the communications department has a "Joe Namath Chair
in Pantyhose" and that Bryant is a more beloved bear than Smokey.

> *We had a great flight in. This campus is easy to spot from the
> air. All the empty beer cans spell out "Bear Bryant."*

This "easy to spot from the air" setup was one of our favorites. Any time
Hope visited a college, we had the empty beer cans spell out "Beat <u>*rival*</u>."
Guaranteed cheers. Heaven.

Hope's real-life alma mater was the University of the Keith Circuit where he graduated *Summa Cum Laughter* with a graduate degree in Mirth and a *Phi Beta Kappa* key to the wardrobe trunk. He had never set foot on campus as a student, but the college kids always seemed delighted by him, which came as no surprise to anyone. He hadn't served in the military either, but the troops bonded with him in much the same way.

The tour proved such a success, we had him in robe and mortarboard four years later for yet another academic frolic entitled *Bob Hope Goes to College*.

Texas Crude

The first layover in what would turn out to be Hope's last college special was Southern Methodist University in Dallas, an oil-rich Versailles of a campus known locally as "The Harvard of the South." Coming up with jokes that would play here wasn't much of a challenge. If there's one thing Texans enjoy being kidded about besides the size of their state, it's how *rich* they are.

> *There's so much money in Dallas. Where else do you see lawn ornaments that bring in fifty-thousand barrels a day?*

Hope was not unfamiliar with "black gold." In the mid-forties, he teamed up with Bing Crosby to buy a well with some of their road picture profits. A vial of the stuff from their first gusher was still on display in Hope's Toluca Lake office.

He seemed to have a genuine affinity for Texans and the vast, petroleum-rich real estate on which they resided. His personal appearance tours took him there often, and in 1982, he hosted a television special called *Stars Over Texas* from Austin during which he delivered this line:

> *Everybody here is either in cattle or oil. Texas is the only place where you can tell what a guy does just by looking at his boots.*

This was a switch on a joke we'd written when Reagan was elected for his first term.

> *L.B.J. was a rancher and Jimmy Carter was a farmer. It'll be refreshing to have a president not that handy with fertilizer.*

Academic Indigestion

Stop number two was Clemson University where, since its founding in 1882, the student cafeteria, Harken Hall, has been the butt of more jokes than Pia Zadora's singing career. The writers wasted no time in going straight for the audience's digestive tract.

> There are four stages to a Harken Hall meal — the appetizer, the main course, the dessert and the autopsy.

Second only to the food, the most common complaint on almost every campus we visited was lack of adequate parking, and Clemson was no exception.

> I had a great trip in. Three thousand miles — and that was just driving around the campus trying to find a parking space.

Gipperville Trolley

We packed our Pepto-Bismol, crossed ourselves and headed for South Bend, Indiana, home of one of the nation's most famous schools and biggest boost for Ronald Reagan's movie career, the University of Notre Dame. The most notorious center of Catholicism this side of the Vatican wouldn't escape a barrage of ecclesiastical jibes as Hope wowed a stadium jam-packed with Fighting Irish.

> What a reception we got at the airport! Father Hesburgh blessed our plane — then sprinkled holy water on our luggage.

Father Frank Hesburgh was to Notre Dame what Father Flanagan had been to Boys Town. The Church's most famous living Jesuit (if you don't count John McLauglin), he represented the epitome of gridiron dominance that refused to take a back seat to intelligence and learning.

> They take football very seriously at Notre Dame, but unlike most other schools, here they won't award you a letter unless you can read one.

Ironically, the Fighting Irish coach at the time wasn't a Catholic and wasn't even Irish, but *Armenian*. With Ara Parsegian coaching at Notre Dame and a Polish pope in the Vatican, centuries-old Catholic tradition was crumbling fast.

One of our guests at Notre Dame was their most famous legend since the Gipper, Joe Montana. Sitting in Hope's suite one day, I asked him what he considered his greatest asset in becoming such an outstanding quarterback. With no hesitation, he said, "My eyesight." He went on to explain that his whole life he'd had uncanny *peripheral* vision. In football, this allowed him to look down field and note the positions of his eligible receivers without actually focusing on them. "The defense watches your eyes," he explained. And with Joe, the telegraph office was closed.

Not funny, but interesting, no?

Bear Necessities

Since we had visited USC on our previous college tour, we figured the UCLA Bruins deserved equal time. So, on a soggy fall Saturday, about eight hundred students and faculty unfurled their umbrellas in front of the main library. Despite the fact that the Bruins had locked up a Rose Bowl invitation, this time we decided to kid southern California's fun-in-the-sun image.

> *There's nothing like fall in southern California, watching all the blonde hair turn different shades of brown.*
>
> *Here, if you're not blonde, blue-eyed and have a perfect physique, you're allowed to use handicapped parking.*

This was one of our rare rainy days. On location shoots, we were accustomed to working out-of-doors and generally enjoyed excellent weather even in the face of dire predictions.

Aboard the helicopter carrier Iwo Jima in 1979, we were able to continue taping while rainstorms raged on three sides of us, visible mere miles across the harbor. Hope may not have been on a first-name basis with God, but he seemed to have a friend at heaven's "Weather Central."

Utah Jazzed

Final stop on the tour was the state where the buffalo and the Osmond Family roam — Utah. And since we had stopped at Notre Dame, we decided to even things up denominationally with a visit to the Mormon's pride-and-joy, Utah State University in Logan. Berkeley it's not, with the majority of students listing somewhere to the right of Ann Coulter.

Conservative campuses are in the minority, so the writers enjoyed a refreshing change of topics.

> *Utah State, where men are men and women are women, and, since the dorms aren't coed, you'll just have to take my word for it.*

> *The men live in the East high-rise and the women in the West high-rise. The most popular advice on campus is "Go West, young man."*

The subject of coed dorms — or at this school, the lack of them — which gained acceptance on most campuses during the seventies and eighties, provided us with unlimited variations on a theme — at West Point, we had the dorm room doors mysteriously blowing shut, and at Alabama, Hope lamented at the arrival of unisex bunking.

> *I think it's sad. Now a guy can go all the way through college without learning how to crawl up the back wall of a sorority house.*

Hope's final college tour ended, and when the special aired several weeks later, the audience could share Hope's obvious delight in entertaining campus after campus of bright and appreciative young people. It's no surprise that the college tours ranked among his favorite shows — and, for us, they were among the most fun to write.

CHAPTER 15

A Box Seat in front of Dolly Parton

In 1978, the World Series was celebrating its seventy-fifth anniversary, and the Los Angeles Dodgers had captured the pennant. Hope sold NBC on the idea of doing a two-hour special — back then called a "Big Event" — to showcase the Series. To produce the show, he hired the hottest young sports producer-director in the business, Don Ohlmeyer, the wunderkind-protégé of ABC's Roone Arledge, the creator of *Wide World of Sports*. An athlete himself, Don had just formed his own production company and was well qualified to oversee the compilation of World Series clips, facts and statistics for the special.

Our guest lineup was solid and included Danny Kaye as co-host. In the dugout would be Glen Campbell, Howard Cosell, Charo, Steve Martin, the Muppets, and Cheryl Tiegs as well as Dodger luminaries Tommy Davis, Don Drysdale, Sandy Koufax and on-again, off-again Yankee manager, Billy Martin. Kaye was a good choice to co-host because, aside from being a talented performer, he had an intimate knowledge of the game, was a lifelong fan and was a part owner of the then-fledgling expansion team, the Seattle Mariners. Hope, with partner Bing Crosby, had once owned a piece of the Cleveland Indians.

At our first production meeting when we met Don Ohlmeyer, he confessed that he had little experience in variety and was relying on us to come up with plenty of dugout levity. His candor was refreshing in a town where people seldom profess a weakness in anything, and right from the start, it looked like he was going to be a delight to work with. He was and must have impressed a few others along the line. He went on to become President of NBC, West Coast.

We taped the show in Burbank while the Series was in progress, so Hope had a chance to drill some of the line drives we had prepared for him.

Tonight, we're celebrating the seventy-fifth anniversary of the World Series and I love it. Of course, I love anything that's been around as long as I have.

No, I love the World Series — men who are tops in their profession vying for the big prize. At my house, it's the Academy Awards without Kleenex.

Hope had been delivering Oscar jokes for years, and so they were still referenced in his monologues even though his movie-making days were well behind him. Another favorite Academy joke that popped up from time-to-time was this one: "I love the Academy Awards, or as we call them at our house... 'Passover.'"

With the Series in L.A., there have never been so many stars in the stands. I sat in the shade. I had a box-seat right in front of Dolly Parton.

This line got a big laugh as any of Hope's references to Dolly usually did. But then he followed the setup line with this:

In the third inning, Dolly caught a pop foul and Steve Yeager is still looking for it.

The audience exploded. They laughed so hard and so long, Hope had to tell the director to stop taping until he could settle them down. Even he was surprised at the audience's reaction. He said, "Funny, every once in awhile you run into a gem, don't you?"

Years later, I played in Steve Yeager's celebrity golf tournament and asked him if he remembered the line.

"Remember it?" he said. "Lasorda kidded me about it for weeks."

Mound Sounds

For years, Danny Kaye had worn the crown as Hollywood's most talented dialectician, so we decided to showcase his keen ear for foreign-accents by casting him as a major league manager conducting pitcher's mound conferences in various countries, starting with the USA:

DANNY: (approaching the mound) What's wrong, Dizzy? You just walked six batters, gave up twenty-two hits and you just beaned the owner's mother.

HOPE: Picky. Picky. Picky.

Then, a British version:

DANNY: Hello. My name is Douglas Hume Bentley and I'm the manager. I say, old chap, have we met?

HOPE: Not formally, but I do believe I've seen you in the shower.

DANNY: How frightfully decent of you to notice me, but we seem to be twenty-eight runs behind. I'm afraid, sir, that you must be removed.

HOPE: How unfortunate. Thank God I still have my family. They'll stick by me.

DANNY: Buck up, Faversham, and take it like a man.

HOPE: I'm not Faversham. I'm Crenshaw.

DANNY: Good heavens, I've been talking to the *wrong* team.

And the Japanese entry:

DANNY: Ah, so! A thousand pardons for this terrible intrusion.

HOPE: Excuse miserable condition of pitcher's mound. Is clean-
              ing lady's day off. What is purpose of your honorable
              visit?

DANNY: It's only first inning, and already we behind eleven runs.
              You know what that means?

HOPE: Ah, so. Honorable ancestors very angry.

DANNY: Honorable manager very angry. Very regretfully, I make
              a decision.

HOPE: You mean I out of game?

DANNY: (hands him a samurai sword) Worse than that. You out
              of life!

HOPE: (using it) Tora, tora! Bonsai! Sandy Koufax!

Mountain Grinnery

Hope had learned in vaudeville that vocalists are usually adept at comedy,
too. (Bing Crosby, anyone?) Selling song lyrics utilizes the same sense of
story telling and rhythm necessary to deliver lines convincingly.

Steve Lawrence is a great sketch player. Same for Eydie Gorme, Ann
Jillian, Barbara Mandrell, Bernadette Peters, Reba McEntire, Olivia
Newton-John, Cher and Bette Midler. Sammy Davis, Jr. and John Denver were masters at it and Mac Davis and Glen Campbell rank right up
there.

Here Glen plays "Oink Smith," a potential major-league pitching
phenom recruited by scout "Branch" Hope.

                    (Up on backwoods cabin. Hope emerges through
                    the bushes.)

JOHN HARLAN: (V.O.) The least-appreciated but hardest-working
                    man in baseball is the scout, endlessly in search of
                    another Babe Ruth or Warren Spahn, someone who
                    will rewrite the record books. The scout suffers pain
                    and discomfort, hunger and thirst. Here then, is our

tribute to the scout, personified by Branch Hope. We find him closing in rapidly on another Bob Feller...

(We hear someone inside the cabin shooing chickens who come through the door, pushed by a broom. Glen emerges, wearing coveralls and has a front tooth blacked out.)

GLEN: Git outta here! Out! Out!

(The chickens scurry off the porch.)

GLEN: (spots Hope) Howdy, stranger... I'm just doin' a little house-cleanin' 'fore my wife gets home from her job shellin' peanuts over at the Carter place.

HOPE: Must be the spread I noticed coming in. That's the first time I ever seen a scarecrow made out of beer cans. Is your name Oink Smith?

GLEN: That's me.

HOPE: Isn't that kind of an unusual name?

GLEN: Well, my ol' pappy thought it up. He wanted the neighbors to think we could afford a pig.

HOPE: (to audience) And I'll bet he got away with it, too...
Are you the Oink Smith who won first place at the state Rock Throwin' Festival?

GLEN: Twarn't nothin' to it. See I just picked up a rock and flung it like this. (throws rock) (slide whistle: a dead bird drops at their feet)

GLEN: (turns it over) Well, he ain't movin' but he looks real happy, don't he?

HOPE: He should be. He's stoned... Kid, where'd you learn to throw like that?

GLEN: I was always throwin'. An apple fall off a tree, I'd throw it back up. A shingle fall off the roof, I'd throw it back up.

HOPE:	That right?
GLEN:	I got so good at it, we got a chicken that's laid the same egg two hundred times.
HOPE:	(to audience) I know the feelin'.

Like the word "bomb," the word "egg" never appeared in one of our scripts without at least a passing reference to Hope's act. Remember New Zealand's kiwi bird? "I can't fly either, and I often lay an egg bigger than myself."

Reba MacIntire, who began her career singing the "Star-Spangled Banner" at rodeos, once said to Hope in a stand-up spot, "Bob, I can't tell you how many times I had bombs bursting in air."

Hope said, "I know the feeling."

HOPE:	Sign with me and you'll be so rich, you'll be bathing in Gatorade.
GLEN:	Sounds messy. Besides, I don't need any more money. I got lucky with one of my crops.
HOPE:	Really? What did you plant?
GLEN:	I planted five thousand acres of Hamburger Helper.
HOPE:	(to audience) With a little education, this kid could be an idiot.

Throughout this sketch, Hope takes the audience into his confidence with asides like this. His look said, "How could I stoop so low as to take advantage of this poor rube?" It added another dimension that provided additional opportunities for jokes. Hope and Crosby had used this device many times in the *Road* pictures — "Time to visit the snack bar, folks. He's about to *sing*." Woody Allen, an avid fan of Hope's movies, has often employed it effectively in his films.

HOPE:	Forget all that. Just feast your eyes on this...(takes baseball jersey from suitcase)

GLEN: That's real pretty. That what they call ladies lan-ge-ree?

HOPE: Son, that's a baseball uniform. Here, try it on.

GLEN: Which end's it go on?

HOPE: In your case, it don't make much difference. (helps Glen into jersey)... now I gotta get you a hat. (to audience) Let's see what we got in the punkin section. (hands Glen a cap which he puts on)

HOPE: You look great. (pulls out a flattened, beat-up fielder's glove) Here, try this on.

GLEN: (studies it) Mercy. What happened to the *rest* of the cow?

HOPE: (to audience) This kid could run for Congress. (hands him a baseball) Here, try that.

GLEN: (takes a bite out of it): Real good... No seeds.

Hope's prop man, Al Borden, had been with him since they had worked together in *Roberta* on Broadway. A prop like an edible baseball was little challenge for Al who had to find or construct anything we requested. If we specified that smoke was to shoot out of Hope's ears, Al would have to figure out how to create the effect so it would play on camera.

Remember those chickens Glen shoos off the porch? Later, Al came over to me and said, "Why the hell did you guys ask for chickens? Since PETA complained, you can't find 'em anymore. I had to go all the way to Chinatown. I started back with four but one died in the trunk." Guess we should have ordered Peking ducks. Al was a real character and so well-liked at NBC, he was Johnny Carson's prop man and Jay Leno's until he retired.

HOPE: Son, that's called a baseball. You throw it like a rock. I'm prepared to pay you three hundred thousand dollars a year just to throw it.

GLEN: Three hundred thousand? I ain't seen that much money in my whole life.

HOPE: Who has... unless you're Korean.

This line referred to a congressional payoff scandal in the headlines at the time. The earlier references to "peanuts," "the Carter place," and the "scarecrow made out of beer cans" were Billy Carter's contributions to the current news.

This sketch had been in Hope's trunk for years — Jim Garner had played Oink in the late sixties and Steve McQueen before that. When an old standby like this was called into service, we'd update it with more timely references to make it seem new.

HOPE: (hands him a pen and paper) Just put your "X" right here.

GLEN: Shucks, I knew there was a catch to it. "X" is one of my *worst* letters.

HOPE: Let me help you. (helps him sign) Congratulations, kid, you're now a Los Angeles Angel.

GLEN: You're kidding. I thought I was takin' the *Pepsi* taste test.

HOPE: Get your things, Oink. We don't wanna miss the 4:15 mule.

GLEN: How'm I gonna break the news to my pretty ma? How can I leave that old lady? What if she don't let me go?

         (A suitcase, packed, comes flying out of the cabin and lands at Glen's feet.)

HOPE: Now you know how George Allen feels.

NFL coach Allen had recently been fired by the Washington Redskins. Three years later, he would appear as a guest on our special saluting the sixtieth anniversary of the NFL along with coaches Hank Stramm and Weeb Ewbank. (see Chapter 10). In 2007, Allen's son, Senator George Allen, Jr., launched a bid for the presidency that was cut short after a clip of him making a racist remark during a stump speech appeared on YouTube.

GLEN: Well, I gotta say goodbye to 'em. (A Daisy Mae-type blond comes out. Glen kisses her)

GLEN:	Goodbye, sis. (Another gorgeous blond comes out, and Glen kisses her.)
GLEN:	Goodbye, Maw.
HOPE:	Goodbye, *Maw*? Boy, they marry young around here, don't they!
GLEN:	Com'on, we're gonna be late!
HOPE:	(Arms around girls) You go alone. I gotta check your roots!

Multiple Grammy winner, world-class guitarist — he was for many years a studio musician — Glen Campbell was a frequent guest on our specials both home and away. He joined us at Pope Air Force Base (see Chapter 7), at West Point (see Chapter 12) and in Sweden (see Chapter 13). Whether playing a rube or a member of the first class at West Point, he could be relied upon to make our sketches come to life. It was no mystery why he remained one of Hope's favorites.

Umpire Builder

An old standby in every variety show writer's creative Rolodex was the psychiatrist sketch. We visited Dr. Freud often over the years, subjecting Hope to all manner of therapy for mental quirks ranging from delusions of winning an Oscar to job stress from coaching football (see Betty White as Dr. Freud Rice in Chapter 10) to his complaint in the following sketch with Cheryl Teigs from whom he seeks treatment for an inability to make a decision — a real career challenge for a major league umpire:

(Up on typical psychiatrist's office. Cheryl is sitting at her desk, stage right.)

CHERYL:	(into intercom) You may send in the next patient, the one with a problem making decisions.
	(HOPE enters dressed as an umpire.)
CHERYL:	(Stands) Well, I see we didn't have time to change after the game.

HOPE: There was no game today.

CHERYL: You mean you always wear that chest protector?

HOPE: I used to wear the mask, too, but I love corn-on-the-cob.
           (She leads him over to the couch.)

CHERYL: Now I want you to relax and lie down.
           (Hope brushes couch with his whisk broom before lying
           on it. Cheryl takes a seat beside him.)

HOPE: You mean for fifty dollars-an-hour you sit over *there*?

CHERYL: I must tell you before we start that male patients often
           fall in love with their female psychiatrists.

HOPE: You don't have to worry about me. No way. Not this boy.
           Uh, uh.

CHERYL: Good.

HOPE: May I plant a hickey on your neck?

Hope never saw a joke with the word "hickey" in it that he didn't pick.
He found the beaches in Tahiti so romantic, he went for a midnight
stroll by himself and "came back with three hickies." During a visit to
Honolulu, he found the Hawaiians "so romantic their official theme song
is *Don't Get Picky, I'll Give You a Hickey at the Hooky-Lau.*" As you can
sense, He was also a sucker for alliteration.

CHERYL: Tell me, do you have a happy home life? Are you happily
           married?

HOPE: Make up your mind.

CHERYL: What I'm trying to find out is something about your
           love life.

HOPE: Well, according to Tommy Lasorda, I'm an impotent,
           love-starved sissy, which is why I can't see straight.

CHERYL: That's interesting.

HOPE: And according to Sparky Anderson, I'm an oversexed, degenerate animal, which is why I can't see straight.

CHERYL: Who is right?

HOPE: I don't know, but I'm rooting for Sparky.

This was a somewhat touchy area to address in a sketch, but once in awhile we'd take a chance. This time Gig got away with it.

CHERYL: You don't seem to be making any progress.

HOPE: But I dream a lot.

CHERYL: At least you have lots of fun-filled nights.

HOPE: Well, last night I dreamt I poured marinara sauce all over Tommy Lasorda and fed him to my dog.

CHERYL: That's terrible.

HOPE: That's what my dog says. Tonight, I'll dream about Fernando Valenzuela. My dog prefers Mexican food.

CHERYL: Poor man. No wonder you look like that. Pasty complexion, twitching mouth, pitiful, frightened, whipped, defeated.

HOPE: (to audience) That's just makeup, folks!

Hope wasn't kidding. He really did like the way he looked. He applied his own makeup before personal appearances and obviously enjoyed studying the visage in the mirror staring back at him. I caught him admiring himself one day, and startled, he said to me, "You know what stars have in common?"

I said, "You're overpaid?"

He chuckled and said, "No, I mean *physically*. We all have larger heads than average."

Since then, I've been careful to check, and I have to admit, he's right. Can you think of a star with a small head? I mean *physically*.

In the same vein, it was interesting to study his reaction when viewing film clips of himself on the screen as a young man. It was as though he were looking at someone else — one whose talent he admired — but another person. He had been selling the image of Bob Hope for so long, what he saw on the screen was no longer a human being — it was a *product.*

HOPE: So there you are. We're treated like enemy aliens off the field, and we're insulted, chewed out and threatened on the field.

CHERYL: You need tenderness, care, warmth, human contact...

HOPE: I have my Teddy.

CHERYL: That's not enough. Move over. (She gets on the couch with him.)

HOPE: (Hugging her) Gee, I haven't felt such peace and satisfaction since Leo Dorocher kicked dirt on me and broke his toe.

CHERYL: Just relax. Think pleasant thoughts. Hold me tight and let the strength of my body, my confidence and self-assurance just seep into yours. How do you feel?

HOPE: Would you like to have dinner with me tonight?

CHERYL: Yes, I would. (pause) No, I wouldn't. (pause) Yes, I — Now *I* can't make a decision.

HOPE: Don't worry about it. I'll cure your condition if it takes all night. (kisses her) (then to audience) It's murder when you're a perfectionist!

Bleacher Creatures

In the midst of planning our show, Hope got a call from Steve Martin who told him he'd heard about the special, was a longtime baseball fan, and would like to offer his services as a guest. Hope was delighted, of course, because aside from *Saturday Night Live,* Steve was relatively gun shy about appearing on network television. He had big plans for a career in the movies and TV guest shots were hardly major building blocks for that. But this one, he felt, was a *special* special. Plus, he knew Don Ohlmeyer's reputation. Hope was anxious to grab Steve because he'd appeal to a considerably younger audience than we were used to. Even better as far as we were concerned, he told Hope he had written a short sketch and asked if he'd consider including it.

"Send it over," he told Steve. "I'll have the boys look at it."

Ordinarily, if a guest wanted to perform his own material, Hope would consider it, but only on the condition that we be allowed to edit and add "Hope touches" where necessary.

But when we read Steve's script, we were ecstatic, though not surprised. It was a brilliant piece of work that utilized Steve's talents as a magician. (His *Great Flydini* bit was called by Johnny Carson the "greatest magic bit" he'd ever seen on *The Tonight Show.*) The sketch would make Hope look good, too. It involved a pair of vendors in the stands competing for business and opened with Hope, alone in the nosebleed section of the cheapest bleachers above centerfield.

"So far from the diamond," he laments, that "when it's one-o'clock down there, it's two-o'clock up here." And sales have been so slow, "I may have to go back to my old job — teaching."

Enter Steve, dressed much like Hope and carrying what appears to be an ordinary sales tray supported by a strap around his neck. But he's selling something else.

"Elephant traps! Mouse ears! Elephant traps!"

Hope looks on, dismayed.

A fan comes up to Steve and asks, "Do you have any fright glasses?"

Steve reaches into his tray. "Fright glasses, right here."

The guy puts them on and the eyeballs attached by springs bounce up and down. He moves off, delighted.

Hope says, "How about that. I'm selling nuts and this guy is one."

Another fan approaches Steve. "Do you have any giraffe leg-warmers?"

Steve reaches into his tray and removes a pair of large, knitted socks. "Giraffe leg-warmers. There you go, sir."

A woman approaches both and asks, "Does anyone have a metal detector?"

Hope says, "What kind of idiot would have a metal detector?"

Steve pipes up. "I've got one!"

Hope says, "That's the kind of idiot!"

Steve removes a full-size metal detector and hands it to the woman who immediately begins using it.

Hope moves over to Steve and says, "Mind if I ask you something?"

Steve says, "Not at all."

Hope says, "Well, I've been working here all day and haven't made a sale. You come up here with all this crazy stuff, and they can't get enough of it. What's your secret?"

Steve says, "Market research. I figured if people are willing to pay to sit this far from a ball game, they'd be willing to buy my crazy stuff."

Hope grabs some items from Steve's tray — "Elephant traps! Mouse ears! Giraffe leg-warmers!" The crowd now engulfs both of them as they can't wait on people fast enough.

The visual impact of Steve's sketch was important to its success. How could anyone fit a metal detector into a vendor's tray? It wasn't an ordinary tray. Steve had rigged it so that, from the vantage point of the camera, it would *look like* an ordinary tray. As he'd done for his *Great Flydini* routine, reaching into his unzipped fly to remove an egg, a rabbit, a dove and other unexpected items, he had performed a carefully prepared, well-designed magic trick.

It was a great addition to the show, and best of all, it had a strong blackout.

Armor Star

Hope and the Muppets enjoyed a mutual admiration that came across on the screen every time they appeared on one of our specials or he guested on their syndicated series. They taped their weekly show at Elstree Studios near London, and whenever we were in England, Hope was sure to drop in. He also appeared in a cameo role as an ice cream vendor in their feature film, *The Muppet Movie*. His friendship with them had to be the warmest comedian-puppet relationship since W.C. Fields and Charlie McCarthy.

I think it was because they were so much alike. Jim Henson, the creator of the charming group of woolen wonders, was as careful about the material that he'd let come out of their mouths as Hope was about choosing jokes for himself. Both realized the importance of consistency in their characters and situations that the audience had come to expect. Whenever we submitted routines for the Muppets, Jim and his partner Frank Oz — the voice of Miss Piggy — would change any line that didn't feel just right for their latex-and-felt cohorts whom they knew intimately. Reviewing a script, Jim might say, "This joke isn't right for Kermit. Fozzy Bear might say it, but not the frog." He spoke of them as though they were human, and, after working with them, I was convinced they were, too.

As usual, they added a delightful touch to our sketch that cast Hope as a major league team owner on the lookout for talent.

KERMIT: What did you want to see me about, Mr. Hope?

HOPE: Well frankly, Kermit, I'm looking for talent.

KERMIT: I get it. You're doing another road picture, and you want me to be your co-star. You're in luck. I happen to be at liberty.

HOPE: Hold on to your lily pad, Kermit. I need someone who can hit forty homers, drive in a hundred-and-twenty runs and steal thirty bases.

MISS PIGGY: (enters from offstage) You called?

Miss Piggy was the brainchild of Henson designer Kermit Love who had accompanied Big Bird's operator, Carroll Spinney, to China in 1979. (See Chapter 8) Originally, he had modeled Miss Piggy after singer Peggy Lee, and named her "Miss Piggy Lee." She had long, flowing hair like Peggy's and a mole on her chin. After several appearances on television, the phone rang at Henson HQ — Ms. Lee's lawyer threatening to sue. But everyone on the show liked the puppet so much, Love decided to make a few adjustments. He removed the mole, made her a new curly wig and dropped the "Lee." The rest as they say...

Writing lines for Shari Lewis and her hand-puppet "Lamb Chop" held me in good stead
when coming up with convincing dialog for the Muppets. Bob Alberti wrote musical
arrangements for her, and I worked on her stage act. She was a delight and her daughter,
Mallory, carries on with the character her mother made famous. Both Shari and her
husband, Jeremy Tarcher, a publisher in Los Angeles, encouraged me to write this book.

KERMIT: Miss Piggy, this is man talk.

MISS PIGGY: I know, dear. What else could be so dull?

KERMIT: Bob was talking about me joining his team. It's nothing that would interest you.

MISS PIGGY: It would if I were your agent.

This was a theme that ran through almost every routine we wrote for the Muppets — either Hope was going to join their troupe or one of them was to become his partner. The deals invariably fell through, when both sides realized what a good thing they had going. Why tamper with the success of superstars?

Though best known for their work on the PBS children's series *Sesame Street*, the Muppets maintained a level of sophistication a few notches above that of some of our human guests. So completely convincing were they, the sound man would often hover the boom mike above their heads as they spoke, forgetting that their operators provided the voices on separate mikes located behind the stage.

MISS PIGGY: Kermit wants three-hundred grand for the season, limousine service to the ball park, caviar and champagne between innings, fresh flowers in the dugout daily and, oh yeah, a hairdresser for his agent.

In 1978, demands like these were exaggerations. How times have changed in thirty years. That would be parking meter change for today's hot prospects.

When it becomes clear that Kermit isn't willing to leave the Muppets, Miss Piggy withdraws her client's offer, but Hope manages to get in one parting-shot.

HOPE: I guess you wouldn't be interested in playing football, either, huh?

MISS PIGGY: I beg your pardon.

HOPE: You know, kicking the ol' pigskin around. (She winds
               up and punches Hope squarely in the solar plexus.)

The Muppets appeared regularly on our show throughout the eighties
and in 1995, three years following the death of Jim Henson, they landed
their own prime-time network series on ABC.

* * * *

A short spot that featured Charo as the major league's first female player
and a routine with Howard Cosell explaining baseball in Biblical terms
(a bit that, like Steve Martin, he had brought to the show) rounded out
the comedy.

Overall, the two hours offered a balance of clips, reminiscences,
player interviews, music and sketches that placed the show among the
best of Hope's sports-themed specials.

Don Ohlmeyer must have thought so, too. On the final day of taping, he gave each of us a case of vintage French and California wine worth
a bundle.

We didn't know it — what do writers know of fine wine? — until
weeks later when Charlie Lee, a non-drinker, offered his case to his son.
"Dad," he said, "what you have here is a collection of the most expensive vintages produced in the last twenty years." And we had served it to
guests like "Two Buck Chuck." Who would have guessed?

Eighteen years later, Don's loyalty would prove the equal of his gen-
erosity. A trusted friend and confidant of O.J. dating back to Ohlmeyer's
days as a sports-director, Don defended the beleaguered ex-running back
throughout the murder trial and subsequent civil suit. He hosted a victory party for the newly-freed defendant and employed O.J.'s son as his
personal chef.

A year following the acquittal, he openly criticized NBC News for
biased reporting of both trials and the public outcry following the "not
guilty" verdict in the criminal trial. While Simpson reeled from the shock

of the $35 million civil verdicts assessed against him in February 1996, Don reportedly offered his own home as a sanctuary and arranged a complete makeover for the infamous defendant, by then almost universally reviled. Whatever else can be said of Don's judgment, he's nothing if not loyal.

CHAPTER 16

Put Me on a Lukewarm Rinse Cycle

Webster defines parody as "a writing in which the language or style of an author is imitated or mimicked, especially for comic effect; a feeble or ridiculous imitation."

One could also add: "the lifeblood of every Bob Hope Show."

Feeble imitations, as Webster so aptly described them, were the Hope writer's stock-in-trade. As soon as a television series had clawed its way to the top of the Nielsen charts or a movie's box office gross had sky-rocketed, it became a sure candidate for inclusion in the writers' sketch mill. During my tenure with the show, the silver screen provided us with grist for takeoffs on *Wings, Chariots of Fire, Casablanca, Mutiny on the Bounty, The Great Escape, Rain, Coal Miner's Daughter, Tootsie, E.T. the Extraterrestrial, Reds, An Officer and a Gentleman, Star Wars* and *Superman*, among others.

The small screen gave us sendups that included *Happy Days, Charlie's Angels, The Dukes of Hazzard, Fantasy Island, Miami Vice, 60 Minutes, Shogun, Dallas, M*A*S*H, The Golden Girls* and *Cheers*. In addition, we poked fun at TV commercials, game shows, TV news, tabloid shows, TV shrinks, financial advice shows and soap operas.

Shogun's Heroes

In 1981, ABC had captured critical raves and millions of viewers with its mini-series, *Shogun*, about an English seafarer (Richard Chamberlain) who becomes Japan's first foreign-born Samurai warrior and later, a Shogun. Of course, with its period sets and colorful costumes, it was a perfect vehicle for our own transplanted Englishman. Our version, entitled *Son of Shogun*, would co-star Bruce Jenner, Merlin Olsen, Loni Anderson, Barbara Eden and Linda Evans.

> (Loni, Barbara and Linda are chatting over tea in the shogun's palace.)

BARBARA: Just think. Today, the shogun will choose one of us to be his wife.

LINDA: No, not one of us — *me*. I have what it takes to be first lady — a charge account at Bloomingdale's.

Bloomingdale's got so much air time, we should have free charge accounts there. We used the store whenever we needed a pricey, retail shopping reference.

BARBARA: I will be his choice. The shogun is an ex-naval man, and I have the best navel, although you never got to see it on *I Dream of Jeannie*.

LINDA: Before nightfall, one of us will be chosen first lady and be able to wear beautiful red kimonos designed by Oscar de la Renta-Rickshaw.

During Ronnie's first term, Nancy Reagan was criticized for wearing high-priced, custom-fitted designer gowns — red was her favorite color — without paying for them — and later was challenged by the IRS for listing them on her income tax return as charitable deductions. Maybe that was her version of the "trickle-down" theory.

Aside from providing the show with eight-to-twelve minutes of jokes, Hope sketches were also excuses to get our star into outlandish costumes, the more exaggerated the better. In many ways, he was like a kid with permission to raid his parents' closet. He took great delight in dressing as someone else, especially historical characters. Done up as George Washington, King Arthur, Robin Hood or Pope John Paul II, he'd strut up and down the halls of Studio C where we taped, popping into the guests' dressing rooms so they could preview his finery before they gathered on stage.

Several weeks into production, Warden Neil, head of the NBC Wardrobe Department, would call me for the sketch ideas Hope had approved so he could begin designing the appropriate costumes. He'd prepare two or three versions in various color combinations so Hope (who was color-blind) would have a choice. For *Son of Shogun*, Warden went all out, dressing Hope as authentically as Richard Chamberlain had been.

HOPE: Today, I must interview three beautiful women who wish to marry me. It's a dirty job, but someone must do it. (calls offstage) Houseboy, send in first candidate.

(Linda enters carrying a tray piled with plates of food)

LINDA: I will make a good wife for you because of my cooking.

HOPE: What are we waiting for? Let's start cooking.

LINDA: (pulls away) The quickest way to a man's heart is through his stomach.

HOPE: Would you consider an alternate route?

LINDA: Do you think I'm as pretty as my two rivals?

HOPE: I'd put you up against them any time, but first, I'll put you up against *me*.

We had developed an entire lexicon of these "naughty boy come-on" wisecracks from which we could draw as needed. For a co-star as glamorous as Linda, we used three in a row.

To bring you up to speed plotwise, a palace defector (Merlin Olsen) is plotting to assassinate the shogun disguised as his houseboy.

HOPE: (suspicious) Where's my regular houseboy?

MERLIN: He take day off to make transistor house*girl*.

Judging from the dialects, most of us trained at the Charlie Chan School of Far East Dialogue and nobody graduated.

          (Merlin leaves and Hope sits on the floor and begins eating.)

HOPE: Ah, my favorite — raw octopus. I like food you can arm wrestle with.

Whether referred to in monologues or sketches, Hope was always partial to food that did something. In China, his Peking duck was so fresh, when he bit into it, it flew out the window.

          (After barely avoiding injury from an exploding chopstick, Hope decides he'd better be more alert during his remaining fiancée auditions)

BARBARA: Good afternoon, Your Highness. I am Princess Barbara-san and I'm here to dance my way into your heart.

HOPE: Be my guest. It'll be a tight fit, but I'm sure there's room enough in there for both of us.

BARBARA: When you see me dance, you will lose your head over me.

HOPE: Oh, please. It's so hard to get parts.

          (Her accompanist begins to play and Barbara dances sensuously.)

HOPE: Wow. Never seen so many moving parts. Hope Japanese never try to miniaturize that.

BARBARA: Do you feel rays of love radiating from my body?

HOPE: Not yet, but I sure like your radiator.

Mechanical comparisons to the female anatomy abound in Hope sketches. At the Air Force Academy, Loni Anderson's kisses set off his afterburners.

Born in Arizona, Barbara Eden grew up in my hometown, San Francisco, where she graduated from Abraham Lincoln High School and shortly thereafter was crowned "Miss San Francisco." While pursuing a career in the movies, she took the role as the lead in *I Dream of Jeannie* and her successful TV career was launched. Over the years, she was a frequent guest on our show.

In a parody of *Coal Miner's Daughter*, his gal, Cindy Lou, has "done so much sparkin', she's on her third lip retread."

Here, it turns out that Barbara's accompanist is an assassin in jazz-man's clothing and uses the strings on his instrument to shoot a poison arrow at the shogun. He barely misses and is chased off as Loni arrives for her interview.

LONI: God afternoon, Honorable Shogun-san. I'm Princess
             Loni-san.

HOPE: Oooooo, assassin must have been successful. I think
             Shogun just arrive in heaven!

LONI:	Shogun like what he sees?
HOPE:	Like it? Figure make Mount Fuji look like Little League pitcher's mound. But why are your feet so small?
LONI:	They're bound.
HOPE:	Bound for where? Mind if I aim them toward my boudoir?

Never mind that foot-binding is strictly a Chinese custom. In Hope sketches, cultural accuracy always took a backseat to the laugh meter.

LONI:	I am honored to be in your presence, Shogan-san. I am your loyal and obedient servant.
HOPE:	Ah, good beginning. I already have cook and dancer. What is your specialty?
LONI:	I am a student in the art of love.
HOPE:	Student? Why didn't they send professor?
LONI:	Oh, you wouldn't like him — I have come to teach you the secrets of exotic, Oriental-love techniques.
HOPE:	Oh, boy! I'm going to be made in Japan!

This line had the Standards and Practices boys at NBC working their blue pencils with a fury, but not even they possessed enough power to deny the shogun. It aired as written and performed.

LONI:	(Moves away) But first...
HOPE:	But first? I've been interrupted more times than the *Tonight Show*.
LONI:	Is it true your father was an Englishman who sailed from across the sea?
HOPE:	That's true.
LONI:	Then you're half barbarian?
HOPE:	(Growls) True. Your cave or mine?

LONI:	Is it good being half Japanese and half English?
HOPE:	In my case it's a little tough. I've got a Honda engine trying to haul around a Rolls-Royce body.
LONI:	I noticed your differential was dragging.

On that line, Hope gives Loni a look a sushi chef would give a customer complaining about the uncooked fish.

Suddenly, his houseboy's attempt to subdivide the shogun's cranium with a samurai sword puts Merlin in direct sword-to-sword combat with the transplanted Englishman.

MERLIN:	I kill you, English devil!
HOPE:	But I'm only half English.
MERLIN:	Then I kill you only from the waist up!

The reemergence of the three girls with a large mallet soon sends the traitor to honorable ancestor-land and the shogun, so touched by their heroism, pledges his troth to the entire trio of lovelies. (Hey, he's a shogun.)

The sketch got good reviews, but the best news for us was that James Clavell, the author of *Shogun*, didn't sue.

Kryptonite Stalker

In 1979, *Superman* starring Christopher Reeve and Margot Kidder had been leaping tall box-office grosses in a single bound-so, faster than a speeding bullet, we decided it would be a perfect parody for Hope & Company as part of a one-hour special entitled *Hope, Women & Song* taped at the Ambassador Auditorium in Pasadena, California. Entitled *Superiorman*, the sketch featured Pat Boone and Debbie Boone, Sammy Davis, Jr. and Debbie Reynolds. Sharing writing credit with us were producer Buz Kohan and Bob Arnott.

(A mad scientist's laboratory with bubbling beakers, flashing lights. Stage right is a large metal chamber with a sealed door. Pat Boone, in smock and white fright wig is at work. Stage left, his nurse, Debbie Boone, is at desk. She answers the ringing phone.)

DEB: (into phone) Doctor Mad Doctor's office. May I help you? I'm sorry, but he can't be disturbed right now... (Off: maniacal laugh) On second thought, the doctor's already disturbed.

PAT: I've done it! My dream has come true! After tomorrow, I'll control the whole world! (maniacal laugh)

DEB: Gee, you don't look like an Arab.

Were we ahead of our time? Desert Storm was twelve years down the road and Dolly the sheep wouldn't be cloned for decades. Buz Kohan — the producer-writer who came up with the idea for this sketch — must have had some Nostradamas blood in his comedic veins.

PAT: Laugh if you will, but this time I'm going to — (aside to audience) Listen carefully. This is the plot — I'm going to make an exact duplicate of Superiorman, and soon I'll have a whole army of Superiormen to do my bidding!

DEB: Gee, and I thought it was going to be something silly. But, Doctor, how will you get Superiorman to come here to be duplicated?

PAT: I've promised the investigative reporter from the *Daily Meteor*, Lois Inane, an exclusive interview. (doorbell rings)

PAT: There she is now. (Pat answers the door and Debbie Reynolds enters.)

DEBBIE: Hi. I'm Lois Inane and you must be Dr. Mad.

PAT: Yes, but if you prefer, you can be Mad and I'll be Lois. But I warn you, if I'm Lois, I'll be mad.

DEBBIE: What a scoop! I've stumbled into the cuckoo's nest!

(She points to a large button on her jacket that reads: PRESS)

PAT: (pointing finger at it) Do I dare?

DEBBIE: I'll have you know I'm a respected member of the Fourth Estate. I'm honest, fair minded, impartial and never ask loaded questions. Now, let's get started. When did you first become a Commie, a Fascist, a pinko and a weirdo?

Even before the arrival of *Fox News* and the popularity of the tabloids, reporters ranked somewhere between politicians, lawyers and used car salesmen on the low end of the public's Trust-o-Meter.

PAT: (grabs her) Enough of this chit chat! I've got you now! If you try to escape, I'll tell everyone that you type with one finger!

DEBBIE: You call that a threat? I've been threatened by better men than you. Howard Cosell tried to bore me to death. He failed. Monte Hall tried to make a deal with me. He failed. Mork tried to na-nu-na-nu me. He failed.

Note she recites three unsuccessful attempts. Three is a funny number. Two is not funny and four is not funny. Try adding one or subtracting one. Doesn't sound right, does it? Why is three funny? Who knows?

PAT: You're right, I must be mad. But we settled that earlier, didn't we? (to Debbie) You may leave us alone now, Nurse.

            (Debbie Boone exits)

PAT: My dear, will you join me in a drink?

DEBBIE: (takes glass) Do you think we can both fit in there?

Chestnuts like this were usually holdovers from vaudeville. This is a switch on the classic line from the doctor's office sketch in which the doctor tells the patient to "Walk this way" and the patient says, "If I could walk that way, I wouldn't be here." Mel Brooks has almost single-handedly kept the line in the public consciousness.

DEBBIE: (takes a sip) Umm, that's good. What's in it?

PAT: Three parts gin, two parts vermouth and ninety-nine parts nitroglycerin.

DEBBIE: (gulps) You mean?

PAT: Yes! Tap dancing is definitely out! You are mine now!

DEBBIE: Where, oh where, is Superiorman when I need him?
           (Suddenly, Hope, dressed in tights and cape crashes through the wall.)

Note how much has gone on and how many laughs his co-stars have collected before Hope's entrance. Not many comedians were willing to allow guests so much screen time. Jack Benny was another star who believed that the more laughs his guests got, the better *he* looked.

PAT: (indicating) Look what you've done to the wall. Didn't you see the door?

HOPE: (looks) Oh, I'm sorry. I'll try again. (He goes back out through the hole he has just made and crashes through the door, splintering it.)

HOPE: Lois, what seems to be the problem here?

DEBBIE: The doctor made me drink nitroglycerine against my will and now I'm completely in his power.

HOPE: Well, what am I supposed to do about it?

DEBBIE: (to audience): I ask for Superiorman, and I get Truman Capote.

Poor Truman had to endure lines like this most of his life. The same for Liberace who was succeeded by Richard Simmons. Once labeled by comedy writers, it seems you're marked forever.

HOPE: (to Pat) Why don't you get on with your diabolical plan, and I'll foil it in the nick of time as is my custom.

            (Debbie Boone enters with a clipboard.)

DEB: (Hope) You'll need these forms filled out. Do you have medical insurance?

HOPE: Surely you're kidding. I'm a perfect physical specimen. I'm Superiorman.

DEB: (doubts) *You're* Superiorman?

HOPE: Of course. Don't you see my big "S"?

DEB: Have you tried jogging it off?

This line not only got a big laugh at the taping, but was used in a TV spot promoting the show and was quoted in the *TV Guide* listing.

HOPE: (to audience) This kid's got spunk.

            (to Pat) Release Miss Inane immediately!

PAT: I've got her now and you'll never get your hands on her!

HOPE: Big deal. I wasn't doing very well even *before* you came along.

Even as the man-of-steel, Hope is still within his well-defined character as the rejected Lothario. In the road pictures, it was Bing, you'll recall, who got the girl. Keeping Hope's well-known character consistent despite the setting was essential.

HOPE: Okay. I know when I'm licked. Let her go, and I'll do anything you want.

PAT: Anything? Could you get them to re-release *April Love* on that planet of yours?

HOPE: Are you kidding? Up there, nostalgia is a felony.

An inveterate plugger himself, Hope was always willing to allow guests the opportunity to recall a past triumph — as long as the line got a laugh.

As soon as someone was booked on our show, the standard practice was to call to find out what the guest's current projects or causes were so we could work them into show.

HOPE: Is there anything else I can do for you?

PAT: Yes. You can get into my duplicating machine.

HOPE: My super powers are powerless when it comes to saving the woman I love.

DEBBIE: You *love* me? I could jump for joy!

HOPE: (grabs her) Careful or we'll have an early Fourth of July. (to Pat) Okay, I'll be duplicated, but remember, Dr. Mad, the forces of good will always triumph over the forces of evil, although I must admit you've got a pretty good package of evil going here.

PAT: (opens door of chamber) This won't take long.

HOPE: (gets in) I'm not wearing my drip-dry suit so be sure to put me on a lukewarm rinse cycle.

We had fun coming up with lines that made the multi-millionaire appear familiar with the routine tasks of life with which we ordinary mortals are saddled. In reality, Hope probably hadn't laid eyes on a Maytag in fifty years and wouldn't have known "rinse cycle" from "fluff dry," but the audience always seemed to pick up on the irony of these references. He once asked Gig Henry what Formica was, and Gig said, "Fake wood, Bob, but don't worry — you'll never own any of it."

            (Pat closes the door and begins madly pressing buttons.)

PAT: Imagine, my very own Superiorman!

            (After several seconds of violent shaking, Pat opens the door and Hope steps out with Sammy Davis, Jr., dressed in an identical costume.)

PAT: It's a bird... it's a plane... it's Little Richard!

HOPE: Incredible! It's me right down to the last detail!

On stage, comedians know their material is working if the guys in the band laugh. For an accurate gauge on our stuff, we kept an eye on the crew. The mere sight of Hope and Sammy in skin-tight leotards hit home with a vengeance. The cameramen laughed. The floor manager laughed. The sound man laughed. We could almost hear the guys outside in the truck laughing. Even Barney McNulty laughed. We knew we had a winner here.

SAMMY: What's shakin', Bro? Slip me a high-five, Jack!

HOPE: And he even talks like me.

DEBBIE: Wait! How can we be sure which is the real Superiorman and which is the copy?

PAT: You're right. I can't tell which is my arch enemy and which is my arch support.

SAMMY: You mean you can't tell which one is the *cloner* and which is the *clonee*?

Sammy made this line literally sing with a delivery that fell somewhere between the Kingfish and his "Here come d' judge" on *Laugh In*.

HOPE: Well, obviously, I'm the real Superiorman.

DEBBIE: Look at his big "S."

SAMMY: (whining) I've got a big "S," too.

HOPE: I'm the real Superiorman and I can prove it.

SAMMY: Oh, yeah? Can you do this? (He performs a soft-shoe, tapping madly.)

HOPE: He must have been in the rhythm section while I was in line to X-ray Lois. (He tries to duplicate Sammy's dance and fails.)

SAMMY: You call that dancing?

HOPE: If you spent years leaping from tall buildings, you'd have
                 flat feet, too.

During rehearsal, Hope would ruin this gag by dancing too well. It was
like asking Doc Severensen to blow sour notes. It took a concentrated
effort for a former vaudeville hoofer to fake clumsiness, and he had to try
it about five times before it looked right.

Artists are like that, too. Ever notice how "homemade" signs carried
by picketers in movies, no matter how amateurish, always look like they
were done by the art department?

HOPE: (to Sammy) Let's test your vision. (Points) Tell me the
                 contents of that wall safe.

SAMMY: (squints) I see. . . five Twinkies. . . seven tubes of white
                 shoe polish. . . and — (Pat throws himself in front of the
                 safe)

PAT: No! No!

SAMMY: — a copy of *Playboy Magazine*!

DEB: I don't believe it! You degenerate!

DEBBIE: Criminal!

SAMMY: Lecher!

HOPE: Sickie!

PAT: Enough about me! Which one of you is the *real*
                 Superiorman?

HOPE/SAMMY: We both are! And we're taking you to jail!

                 (They each grab a leg and start pulling.)

HOPE: Make a wish!

SAMMY: Wait! Why don't we duplicate the doctor so we can
                 both take him in!

                 (They open the door, stuff Pat inside and slam the
                 door shut. Sammy presses some buttons and after

several beats, Hope opens the door revealing a giant
bottle of milk.)

HOPE: Gee, it looks just like him!

For years, Pat had been our symbol for the white-bread-and-mayonnaise
contingent of society and was currently the spokesman for the National Milk Council. Okay, so it wasn't the greatest ending in our sketch
locker. In our defense, I wanted to turn Pat into Hugh Hefner, but Hope
wouldn't spring for an extra guest with no lines. That six million in property taxes had taken its toll.

✳ ✳ ✳ ✳

Of the hundreds of guest stars I was privileged to work with over the
years, Sammy was pound-for-pound the most talented and versatile —
bar none. Everything he did, he excelled at. He was such a natural, not
even two recent knee replacements could prevent him from rocking the
deck of the aircraft carrier Lexington with a song-and-dance number
from *A Chorus Line* called "I Can Do That" and finishing with a buck-
and-wing with Hope that had the sailors on their feet. Nothing could
detract from Sammy's talent and innate love of performing — not even
a car crash in the sixties that cost him an eye. He wore a black eyepatch
for awhile, later ditching it for a glass eye that was so natural, people —
audiences and those he worked with — soon forgot about his disability.

    We were shooting a song-and-dance routine (much like the one on
the ship) with Sammy and Hope dressed as vaudevillians — straw hats,
striped red-and-white coats, white pants and a cane — in the ballroom at
the Ambassador Hotel in Los Angeles. Again, as it had for Hope and Burns
in *That's the Way It Was in Vaudeville* (see Chapter 2), a lack of enough
rehearsal coupled with a live audience would take its toll — Hope and
Sammy would wing the buck-and-wing. Sure enough, no further than two
bars into the number, Sammy was supposed to say "You dance like Fred."

Hope says, "Astaire?"

And Sam says, "No, *Flintstone.*"

Sammy could read his first line printed on Barney's card, and did. But by the time Hope got his line out, the pair had shuffled halfway across the stage and out of Barney's range. Sammy knows he must have a line, hasn't a clue what it is, so he does what any red-blooded hoofer would do in such circumstances — he falls to his knees (his old ones), and starts laughing uncontrollably. The audience, of course, joins him.

Hope looks down at Sammy and says, "What happened?"

Sam replies, "I got one eye and it was lookin' the other way!"

Sammy Davis, Jr. — he *really* was something.

CHAPTER 17

Waiting for Sharon Stone

A s the eighties drew to a close, Hope had begun showing his age. It
came as a shock to those who had worked with him, many of whom
had come to believe that he would defy the normal ravages of time forever. In what seemed a remarkably short time, he went from someone
who had perennially appeared to be fifteen years younger to a certified
octogenarian.

There were increasing signs that the mental acuity that had allowed
him to maintain almost total control of his life and his career for so long
had begun to fail him. On the telephone, he'd often become confused
— he'd repeat himself or interrupt the conversation to ask, "What did I
call about?"

But most alarming, he began to forget lines in the act he'd been
performing on stage for decades. Strutting across the footlights in the
midst of a joke or a song, his mind would suddenly short circuit. Trying
to conceal his confusion from the audience, he'd wander over to Geoff
Clarkson, his longtime pianist and music arranger, and whisper, "Where
am I? Have I done the joke about the two Aggies in the bar yet?" No
youngster himself, Geoff had been on the road with Hope for years —
recruited from the Les Brown Band — and was programmed to listen
only for his cue lines. Otherwise, while Hope delivered jokes, the pianist

and composer — he wrote the classic, "Home" — had heard countless times, Geoff's mind was elsewhere. Now he realized that he'd have to start *paying attention*. But even with Geoff helping him stay on track, Hope began to deliver abbreviated performances, sometimes leaving his prepared material to take questions from the audience. But this ploy didn't work, since he couldn't hear the questions and often tried guessing what had been asked. Promoters who had paid his standard performance fee of $50,000 to $80,000 began demanding refunds. Some even threatened breach-of-contract suits. So it was that before the decade of the nineties had barely begun, Hope's days of performing live, his favorite part of show business, came to an unpleasant and involuntary end.

✳ ✳ ✳ ✳

Throughout his life, Hope had enjoyed remarkably good health. In 1963, he received laser treatments for corneal blood clots which threatened the sight in his left eye, thanks to a carelessly held prop pistol on a movie set. Following the treatments, he compensated for his weak eye by relying on the good one. Now, almost thirty years later, his overworked right eye became cloudy, giving him the sensation — as he described it to me — "of being in a smoky room."

Over the years, as the right eye weakened, Barney McNulty printed the cue cards in progressively larger type until the lettering was almost a foot tall. An average joke could require four cards that had to be stacked on a heavy-duty easel that Barney had specially made. Ultimately, though, Hope had difficulty making out the cards no matter how large the printing.

With his eyesight and his hearing failing simultaneously, he often seemed disoriented and confused. No longer able to hear the tracks of songs, musical director Bob Alberti had to kneel just below the camera lens to help him maintain tempo. Hope's monologues became a nightmare to get on tape as he stumbled over lines, slurred his words or came to a dead stop mid-sentence when the cards suddenly drifted out of focus.

The very act of starring in and personally overseeing every facet of his specials which for so long had been such a pleasure, became a horror, not only for Hope but for those around him who were watching an American icon deteriorate before their eyes. Staffers who had been with him from the beginning began to feel like corner men administering to a once-great fighter who had taken on several bouts too many. It came as no surprise that, as his declining health prevented him from supervising the details of production, the overall quality of the specials began to decline.

In 1990, we were taping a sketch set in Sherwood Forest in which he was cast as the Sheriff of Nottingham opposite Tom Arnold's Robin Hood and Roseanne Barr's Maid Marian. The stage was darkened for Hope's entrance when, within hearing of the audience, he yelled to the producer who was standing nearby, "Why am I carrying this bow?" When reminded of the archery tournament that concluded the sketch, he looked befuddled but joked, "I have to start rehearsing more."

In 1992, during the taping of a spring special in Columbus, Ohio, guest Barbara Bush offered to read him his lines when he couldn't see the cue cards after she realized that, unless she helped him, taping her five-minute segment would take hours. Later, when he appeared as a guest on Bob Costas's late-night talk show, he couldn't hear Bob's questions even though giant speakers had been placed beside his chair. The resulting interview couldn't be aired.

The last fully staffed regular season special entitled *Bob Hope's America — Red, White and Beautiful*, aired on May 17, 1992, and based on the physical discomfort that he was obviously experiencing, the assumption of those close to him was that it would be his last as host.

In 1993, NBC honored him with a three-hour special entitled *Bob Hope, The First Ninety Years* hosted by Johnny Carson. Hope played a passive role on the show, mostly applauding the acts that had come to pay him homage — George Burns, Milton Berle, Angela Lansbury, Whoopi Goldberg, Chevy Chase and Walter Cronkite among them. Again, everyone connected with it hoped that the special would be Hope's farewell to a remarkable career on television. Sadly, it would not.

During 1993 and 1994, NBC aired several specials, compilations of clips from past shows. No longer able to walk without assistance, Hope could only be shown sitting or on the arm of a guest, most of whom had to prompt him for his lines.

With Hope now unable to oversee any phase of production, the shows appeared uneven. Between the less-than-Hope-quality production values and the star's steadily declining health, many of the old-timers who'd been with him in his prime found the specials particularly difficult to watch. The audience at home must have shared their discomfort, as one special managed to finish number 77 in the Neilsen ratings. Another was shelved as unairable.

Referring to one of the shows, David Letterman told an interviewer for *Rolling Stone*, ". . . it was tough to watch. If it had been a funeral, you would've preferred the coffin be closed."

* * * *

Meanwhile, life moved on. In the spring of 1993, Dolores decided to throw a party to celebrate Hope's ninetieth birthday. It would have a carnival theme and would take place at their sprawling estate in Toluca Lake. She would have a gigantic, three-pole circus tent erected in the backyard, beside the pool.

Around the perimeter of the house, carnival booths would beckon guests to "take a chance" on a baseball-throw, a basketball-toss and a dart booth with balloons as targets. Winners would be awarded cupie dolls and stuffed animals with ribbons around their necks that read "I celebrated Bob's 90th." Strolling among the revelers, look-alikes of the Marx Brothers, Laurel and Hardy, W. C. Fields and Charlie Chaplin would offer themselves up for free souvenir photos while a calliope near the house wheezed carney tunes.

Inside the tent, which featured at one end a fully stocked Ben & Jerry's ice cream shop with stools, four hundred guests would enjoy a sit-down dinner (main course: rack of lamb). Among them would be family members, former co-stars, staff members, friends, colleagues — everyone he liked. The guest list would include his writers, Ronald and Nancy Reagan, Gerald and Betty Ford, and over a hundred Secret Service agents.

At the center of the tent was a stage on which the Les Brown Band would back the evening's slate of entertainers that included Don Rickles, Milton Berle, Phyllis Diller, Jack Carter, Shecky Green (Hope's favorite comedian), Jane Russell, and a host of others.

During the finale, while the guests sang "Happy Birthday," hundreds of multicolored balloons were released to float upward until they reached the overhead klieg lights where they went *pop! pop! pop!* while Secret Service agents, cocked-Glocks in hand, glanced around frantically to locate the shooter.

As we were saying our goodnights to Dolores, I said, "This whole thing was magnificent. It must have cost a fortune." She smiled and said, "When I tell Bob how much, you'll hear him scream at your house." She knew we lived a mile and a half away.

In the summer of 1998, Hope attended a party celebrating Barney McNulty's seventy-fifth birthday at a church hall in North Hollywood. Scores of Barney's friends and colleagues stopped by, including Angela Lansbury, with whom he had worked on *Murder, She Wrote.* Hundreds of photos that he had taken over the years were tacked on bulletin boards.

The event would turn out to be the last time most of us would see Hope. He now had assistance twenty-four-seven and looked all of his ninety-five years. After about an hour and a half, he was helped into a van and waved feebly out the window as it drove off. Barney ran alongside. "Thanks for coming, boss!"

Ironically, his fifty-year reign as NBC's longest-running radio and television star, which for so long had been such a blessing, now became a curse. The network, fearing negative public reaction were they to do otherwise, allowed him to continue appearing on the screen.

No one in the network's executive suite dared cancel someone who had been one of their giants — least of all entertainment chief Warren Littlefield, who hadn't yet been born when Hope signed his first contract with the peacock.

* * * *

Meanwhile, public relations man Ward Grant worked overtime denying rumors — due in large part to Hope's appearance on the specials — that his boss was at death's door, while NBC cheerily announced that there would be no 1995 Christmas special "... in order to allow Mr. Hope to concentrate his efforts on upcoming specials."

On July 30, 1996, the tabloid magazine *Star* ran a photo of a frail and shockingly aged Hope on its cover with the headline: "Bob Hope Tragedy. He's Gone Blind, Deaf and Needs Your Prayers." In the cover story by Deidre Hall and Beverly Williston, Hope was described during a visit to Milton Berle's eighty-eighth birthday party as "a virtually helpless invalid [who] has to be led around by the hand." Within days, NBC dispatched sitcom actor Tony Danza to deny the grim picture that the article had painted. Danza also announced that he would co-host with Hope an election year special that would air in the fall.

Two weeks later, the tabloid magazine *Globe* followed up the *Star's* revelations with yet another disturbing cover story on Hope's rapidly deteriorating health. Entitled "Bob Hope's Tragic Last Wish," the article by Diane Albright quoted unnamed friends describing him as "almost ready for the final curtain," "feeling that the end is near" and ". . .knocking himself out to attend tributes and birthday parties of his oldest and dearest friends, telling them this could be the last time they're together." Another long-time pal was quoted in the article as saying, "Everyone close to Bob feels he may be running out of time. They fear he may not see next Christmas." The article, complete with family photos of happier times past, went on to detail "Frail Bob Hope's last wish: to co-star with his gorgeous dream girl, Sharon Stone."

Describing his excitement at the prospect, the author quotes him as saying, "I've had every hot screen siren in the last sixty years on stage or overseas with me — everyone but Marilyn Monroe, who tragically died before I could book her — and Sharon Stone. I can't get Marilyn back, but I haven't given up hope of getting Sharon." The author then

The last opportunity most of us had to bid Hope goodbye occurred at a
Studio City church hall during a party celebrating Barney McNulty's
seventy-fifth birthday in 1998. From left: Gene Perret, Si Jacobs, me.
Seated: Barney McNulty, Bob Hope, Hal Kanter. Hal wrote the Hope movies *Off
Limits, Here Come the Girls, Casanova's Big Night,* and *Bachelor in Paradise.*

concluded that "Friends hope Sharon doesn't take too long to make up
her mind."

Hope's final television special, *Laughing With the Presidents,* was
billed as his "farewell to NBC." The network took out full-page ads in
Variety, The Hollywood Reporter and *The Los Angeles Times* to promote
the show which aired on November 23, 1996. *Washington Post* television
critic Tom Shales wrote of it:

"It has to rank as one of the strangest TV specials in years. The star of
it barely moves, barely speaks, and seems at best semi-conscious. . . The
special is more than mortifying and the fact that Bill and Hillary Clinton,
George and Barbara Bush and Gerald and Betty Ford were dragged into

it seems unfortunate. . . Of course, despite America's fixation with youth, living to a ripe old age is anything but a disgrace. But the comedian's abilities as a performer have dimmed now almost to the point of invisibility. The few lines he does have on the special are recited mechanically. Hope is mortal and therefore cannot spring eternal. . . For some time Hope's specials have been tributes to Hope mounted by Hope's own production company. . . When the inevitable strains of 'Thanks for the Memory' sneak in near the end of the show, one can't help thinking that, perhaps, after all these years, Hope has now been thanked enough."

* * * *

Meanwhile, the honors continued to pour in. The Navy christened a ship the *USNS Bob Hope* and the Air Force named one of their new C-17 bombers "The Spirit of Bob Hope." In October, 1997, President Bill Clinton signed a bill naming him an honorary veteran, the first in the nation's history.

Ironically, Hope may have had a premonition that crippling old age would not present him in his finest hour. Back in 1981, he had flown to Washington to present a Lifetime Achievement Medal to World War II's five-star General Omar Bradley who was then eighty-eight and in frail health. The old warrior, totally incapacitated by a stroke, could barely manage a smile as Hope pinned the medal on his dress blue uniform. The presentation at the Kennedy Center received extensive coverage by all three networks, and after Hope returned from the capital, I told him how stirring it had appeared on television.

"Maybe," he replied, "but they didn't warn me that he'd be in a wheelchair — paralyzed and completely helpless. He looked pathetic." Even so, I assured him, it had been a touching and heartwarming presentation.

"Yeah," he said, "I just hope that never happens to *me*."

* * * *

Bob Hope died on July 27, 2003.

A memorial High Mass was celebrated at St. Charles Borromeo, the church a few blocks from his house that he had helped build. ("Every time I drive up, they try to auction off my car.") NBC News covered the services, sending Ashleigh Banfield, who stood near the steps of the church, to file a live report.

Following the mass attended by about thirty princes of the Catholic Church, bishops and cardinals that included the embattled Roger Mahoney, close friends and family were invited to the Lakeside Country Club where Hope had been a member and played countless rounds of golf. It was a sunny day and guests mingled among the tables set up outside the clubhouse.

Later in the day, a memorial tribute was staged at the Academy of Television Arts & Sciences in North Hollywood. Produced by Gary Smith who, with his partner Dwight Hemion had produced Hope specials, it was filled with remembrances from Hope's friends and professional colleagues including Larry King, Angela Lansbury, Johnny Grant, Katherine Crosby, Michael Feinstein, Sid Caesar, Red Buttons, Tom Selleck, Phyllis Diller, Jack Jones, Jim Lipton, Ward Grant, Lee Iococca, Brooke Shields, Mort Lachman, Jane Russell, Connie Stevens, Tony Orlando, Loni Anderson, Rick Ludwin, Barbara Eden, Rhonda Fleming, Carole Lawrence, Ed McMahon, Janice Page, Mickey Rooney and Linda Hope.

The memorial lasted over three hours.

Bob Hope was buried at the Mission San Fernando Cemetery, Mission Hills, California.

✳ ✳ ✳ ✳

Hope's birth at the turn of the last century couldn't have been more fortuitously timed. It allowed him to take advantage of a "perfect storm" of American popular entertainment that's unlikely to recur. When vaudeville died, he was ready to move on to radio. When radio died, he conquered television — all the while making successful movies.

His unprecedented, decades-long tenure as the elder member of TV's royal family may have ended sadly, but nothing could detract from the real joy of his truly remarkable career captured in the lyrics of a song he sang at the conclusion of a 1978 tribute to vaudeville's Palace Theater. Sitting on a stool backstage, he dedicated the song — written by Sol Weinstein — to the memory of the performer he credited with inspiring him to become an entertainer — Charlie Chaplin — who had died several weeks earlier. As the footlights slowly dimmed, he sang:

Off comes the makeup
Off comes the clown's disguise
The curtain's falling
The music softly dies

To play the Palace
When vaudeville reigned supreme
Made up for bad times
Brought glad times
'Twas every trouper's dream

We've shared a memory
And as the evening ends
I've got a feeling
We're parting now as friends

To a performer
There's nothing warmer
Than taking his curtain calls

If I had this to do again
And the Palace were new again
I would play it for you again
But now the curtain falls

Your cheers and laughter
Will linger after
They've torn down these dusty walls

People say I was made for this
Nothing else would I trade for this
And to think I get paid for this...

The world will not soon see the likes of Bob Hope again.

June 6, 2008
Studio City, California

Postscript

While the twentieth century ground inexorably toward its extinction, I became involved with several unsuccessful television pilots, the first of which was initiated by a call from Jim McCauley, former talent-coordinator for *The Tonight Show Starring Johnny Carson* and a member of Carson's inner circle who had followed my career with Hope. (Johnny's producer, Fred De Cordova, had long assured me that I "had a job waiting" on the Tonight Show, but Johnny retired in 1992.) Jim had recommended that I be hired as head writer on a late-night talk show that would star comedian Paul Rodriguez. Financed by KingWorld which also produced *Jeopardy* and *Wheel of Fortune*, the show would compete with Leno and Letterman and would attempt to capture Latino-American viewers in the coveted 18–35 demographic.

Surveys had shown that Rodriquez, who was familiar to audiences through his commercials for tortilla chips and talk show appearances, appealed to both Mexican-American and non-ethnic viewers. His act focused on his Chicano upbringing and life in the *barrio*, but did so from a white American's point of view. He was smart, fluent in both languages, and seemed to the brothers who owned KingWorld, the perfect challenge to the established late-night hosts who hadn't faced a possible usurper since Arsenio Hall had called it a night.

Not that some hadn't tried — remember the Chevy Chase fiasco or *The Joan Rivers Show*? *The Paul Rodriguez Late Night Show* would change all that and, it was hoped, make TV history.

The four-man writing staff had been signed as well as the show's musical director, Sheila E. Pre-launch meetings went on for several weeks at a small production office near Rodeo Drive in Beverly Hills. The show was set to be unveiled at the week-long meeting of the National Association of Television Producers and Exhibitors (NATPE) in Las Vegas, to which station owners and sponsors are invited each year to sample fresh offerings for the upcoming season. The headline entertainer on the Saturday night variety show capping the week of parties, screenings, and business meetings was to be our star, Paul Rodriguez.

Since the show had been pre-sold to several big city affiliates, the convention was just a formality as far as KingWorld was concerned — an opportunity to showcase our affable host and maybe sign more outlets for the fledgling late-night entry. MaCauley would drive to Nevada with Paul on Friday, settle in at Caesar's Palace and ready themselves for the big Saturday night.

On Sunday morning, my phone rang. It was McCauley.

"Are you sitting down?" I wasn't, but I did.

Sadness in his voice, he told me that the night before, just as Paul was about to go on stage, he announced that he'd had a sudden change-of-heart. He told Jim he felt he was in over his head, that too many people were relying on him to be successful in a timeslot where so many before him had failed. He wanted out. And, when informed of Paul's cold feet about hosting the show, so did the King brothers.

It happens.

A similar scenario would unfold a decade later when comedian Dave Chappell would walk away from a $30 million dollar deal to star in his own TV series, leaving hundreds of staffers in the lurch. Six installments of the show had already aired, leaving viewers hungry for more which would not be forthcoming. Dave fled to South Africa, telling no one where he was going. Not until weeks later did he explain what had happened: He'd been happy doing stand-up and felt the new show was making him sick and had been a terrible mistake.

It happens often.

In the late-nineties, Dick Cavett was signed to host a syndicated radio talk show, the producers of which had lined up hundreds of stations and signed contracts with sponsors. On the Monday morning it was to debut, Dick couldn't get out of bed. A longtime manic depressive (a condition he discussed in several of his books) he was paralyzed with fear. The project was aborted.

Today, Paul Rodriguez continues his career as a stand-up comic and appears occasionally on television. I wonder if he ever thinks about what might have been. I know I do.

The second pilot I became involved with was called *From the Hip* and had a format similar to Bill Maher's canceled ABC series, *Politically Incorrect*. The show was hosted by comedian Argus Hamilton, whose regular guests included comedians Kathy Griffin and Paul Mooney. We shot the pilot at a theater in Beverly Hills, and audience reaction was positive.

But the show didn't sell.

In 2000, I became a plaintiff along with 150 other *Writers Guild of America* members, in a class action lawsuit that alleged age-discrimination in employment of writers over age forty. Titled *Tracy Keenan Wynn, et al.* vs. *National Broadcasting Company, Inc., et al.*, the suit named as defendants virtually every major television network, film studio and talent agency in Hollywood. For the next eight years, the suit wound its way through the state and federal courts and on August 19, 2008, International Creative Management (ICM) became the first defendant to agree to a settlement. The talent agency will pay $4.5 million in damages, among other concessions that include a "job relief program" for older television writers. "We still have a lot of work ahead of us," declared the lead attorney, Steve Sprenger of Sprenger & Lang in Washington, D.C.. At this writing, hopes are high of settling with the twenty-three remaining defendants, including among others, NBC, CBS, ABC, Fox, Universal, and Disney. Wish us luck.

In September 1994, *The Los Angeles Times* hired me to contribute to a daily, topical humor column called *Laugh Lines*. The syndicated feature, which occupied about a half page in the *Life & Style* section, appeared five-days-a-week and included an essay every other day along with a cartoon. The impressive group of essayists included Carrie St. Michel who also wrote for *Good Housekeeping* and *Family Circle* magazines — former *Tonight Show* writer Roy Teischer, who was also a script consultant on *Mork and Mindy* and contributed to the development of *Mad About You*. Among my fellow contributors providing lines gleaned from the current headlines were comedian Argus Hamilton, a fixture at The Comedy Store in Los Angeles, Tony Peyser, who also wrote for Jay Leno and Joan Rivers and drew the daily cartoon, and Mark Miller, a writer for Roseanne Barr, Garry Shandling and Dana Carvey. The column was edited by Charlie Waters who also edited *The Best of Laugh Lines*, a compilation from the columns, published by the *Los Angeles Times* Syndicate in 1996.

Shortly thereafter, when a change in ownership of the *Times* spelled doom for the column, former Editor Shelby Coffey III said of it, "Here was a colorful set of essays and quips, of wise guys and wiser women, who gave Angelenos the small smiles and longer laughs that made the day less daunting."

In 1996, I began publishing a topical comedy newsletter intended for disc jockeys and speakers called *Funny Side Up*. The early subscribers received it daily by fax and later on the internet where it still resides, updated weekly at www.topica.com/lists/funnysideup/read and serves about 5,000 subscribers who now receive it free.

A blog version is also available at www.bereftontheleft.blogspot.com.

In 1998, I launched *Podium Productions @ Sea,* providing hour-long cruise ship lectures based on stories and anecdotes contained in this book and illustrated with video clips of sketches and routines described here. Over the next nine years, my wife, Shelley, and I would sail to New Zealand, South America, Africa, Europe, the Bahamas, Alaska and the Mexican Riviera aboard ships that included the Crystal Symphony and Harmony, the Celebrity Mercury and the Princesses Diamond, Island, and Pacific .

In June 2007, we flew to Beijing and visited many of the locations

In November, 2000, the Pacific Pioneer Broadcasters, a professional group of radio and television veterans that was founded by Edgar Bergen and Jim Jordan (Fibber McGee), honored TV comedy writers at one of their bi-monthly luncheons at the Sportsmens Lodge in Studio City. Almost half of the honorees had been Hope staff writers. (L to R) Kneeling, Arthur Marx (Hope movies *I'll Take Sweden, Eight on the Lamb, Cancel My Reservation*), Bill Idelson (*Love American Style, The Bob Newhart Show*), me, Gil Stratton (PPB President), Jeanne DeVivier Brown (PPB Secretary), Sam Denoff (*The Dick Van Dyke Show, That Girl* with partner Bill Persky), Gene Perret, Seaman Jacobs and Bill Persky.

described and pictured in the book. Sailing on a riverboat up the Yangtze past the Three Gorges Dam toward Shanghai, I was struck by the vast changes that had transformed the People's Republic since my last visit twenty-eight years before; the bicycles are now automobiles, the dusty roads, modern freeways.

In Shanghai, I was told the Chi Ching Hotel where Gig and I sat with Hope in the room where Nixon had signed the 1974 trade agreement no longer exists, razed to make room for an 85-story hotel.

I'm still in touch with many of the friends and colleagues I worked with on the Hope Show.

Linda Hope runs Hope Enterprises and most recently oversaw a Julian's Auction House sale of Hope memorabilia aboard the Queen Mary en route to England.

Dolores Hope is 99 and lives in the Toluca Lake mansion that, upon her death, will become a Catholic girls school.

Ward Grant died in 2007 while still working as a publicist for the Hope family.

Elliott Kozak suffers from early-stage Alzheimer's and is in the process of moving to the Motion Picture Country Home and Hospital in Woodland Hills, California.

Announcer John Harlan lives in Woodland Hills, is a past president of the Pacific Pioneer Broadcasters, and works the annual "Mrs. America Pageant."

Don Marando, lives in South Bend, Indiana. He sold his house in Hawaii following the death of his wife, Rosie.

Barney McNulty died in 2000 at age 77 from a long-standing heart condition.

Bob Alberti lives with his wife, Shirley, on Hilton Head Island, South Carolina, where he produces jazz concerts for the Hilton Head Symphony Orchestra.

Geoff Clarkson lives in Toluca Lake, California about a block from Hope's house.

Production coordinator Sil Caranchini died in 1993.

Bob Keene, our set designer, died in 2002. He was in his 50s and — along with his wife, Sharon — succumbed to a mysterious viral disease.

Warden Neil, wardrobe-master, moved back home to New Zealand.

Hal Kanter is 95 and the "Resident Humorist" of the Pacific Pioneer Broadcasters.

Bernie Weintraub (Robinson-Weintraub Agency), who negotiated my yearly contracts, is retired. His office was in Beverly Hills and I lived in the San Fernando Valley so we had no occasion to meet. We never did.

Producer Jane Upton Bell lives in Los Angeles, calls occasionally, and we reminisce about the old days.

Producer Don Ohlmeyer is an independent producer in Los Angeles.

Producer-writer Sheldon Keller died in 2008 of complications of Alzheimer's Disease.

Producer Buz Kohen writes for the annual Oscar presentations and other award shows.

Producer James Lipton lives in Manhattan with his wife, Kedakai, and hosts *Inside the Actors Studio* on Bravo.

The Laugh Makers

The Officers:

Gene Perret founded a workshop for beginning writers called "Gene Perret's Round Table." The author of many books on comedy writing and career development, he lives in Westlake Village, California where he plays golf, lectures occasionally, writes magazine columns, and is working on his first novel.

Martha Bolton lives in Brentwood, Tennessee, and has written seventy motivational books including her latest, with former *Tonight Show* writer Brad Dixon, entitled *Race You to the Fountain of Youth*. She writes a column for *Brio Magazine* called "Cafeteria Lady."

Charlie Lee died in 1988, suffering a series of strokes. After retiring in 1979, he was hired by Johnny Carson, but quit after a week and spent his remaining years writing irate letters to the editor of the *Los Angeles Times*.

Gig Henry died in 1989 of a cerebral hemorrhage while walking his dog. He was scheduled for surgery the following day for a blocked carotid artery.

Jeffrey Barron died of a heart attack in 1995 at age 43.

Fred Fox died in 2006 from complications of Alzheimer's disease.

Seaman Jacobs died in 2008 at age 95 after suffering a fall on an escalator.

Both Si and Freddy were memorialized by scores of friends and colleagues at the Writers Guild Theater in Beverly Hills.

The Enlisted Personnel

Sol Weinstein lives with his son in New Zealand and still writes music and spec scripts.

Howard Albrecht lives in Encino, California, and edits a comedy newsletter, *Funny Stuff from the Gags Gang,* which he started with Sheldon Keller in 1993.

Bryan Blackburn returned to England in 1986 and had a successful career on several British variety shows. He died in 2006 at age 78.

Bob Keane lives in Burbank, California where he's working on a biography of St. Thomas More.

Doug Gamble lives in Carmel, California, where he works as a freelance writer.

Joe Madieros became head writer on *The Tonight Show with Jay Leno.*

Tom Shadyac graduated from the USC Film School and wrote and directed movies starring Jim Carrey, beginning with *Ace Ventura, Pet Detective.*

Cathy Green wrote scripts for *Married... with Children* and *The Bob Newhart Show* where she was responsible for "Darryl and his other brother, Darryl."

John Markus wrote for and later produced *Taxi* and *The Cosby Show.*

Ron Burla, wrote for *Alf* and *Married... with Children.*

Phil Lasker produced *Joe Bash* with Peter Boyle and wrote the film *The Man from Elysian Fields* with Mick Jagger and James Coburn.

Casey Keller and Richard Albrecht wrote for *The Love Boat, Who's the Boss?* and *The Hogan Family.*

Dennis Snee wrote for *The New Leave It to Beaver, In Living Color* and *Mr. Belvedere.*

Bob Arnott wrote for *The Annual Emmy Awards, The Annual Grammy Awards* and *The Annual People's Choice Awards.*

Marty Farrell wrote for *The Annual Emmy Awards.*

Peter Rich and Gail Lawrence wrote for *The Doctors* and *Guiding Light.*

Pat Proft, wrote *The Naked Gun, The Naked Gun 2-1/2* and *Police Academy I.*

Dick Vosburgh and Gary Chambers wrote the Broadway hit, *A Day in Hollywood, A Night in the Ukraine.*

Steve Martin (*75th Anniversary of the World Series*) is a successful actor, writer and producer.

David Letterman (*Bob Hope Down Under*) hosts a late-night talk show on CBS.

I can't tell you how much I miss them all and how often I think back on the wonderful times we shared working for Bob Hope. I titled this book "The Laugh Makers" because I hope we made you laugh. If we did, well... it doesn't get any better than that, does it?

About the Author

A native of San Francisco, Bob Mills served in the Navy from 1956 to 1959, graduated from San Francisco State University in 1962 and the University of California Hastings Law in 1965 and practiced in Palo Alto, California from 1966 until becoming a television writer in 1976, whereupon he ceased all contact with lawyers. In 1973, he married his wife, Shelley, with whom he lives in Studio City, California. He writes a topical blog entitled *Bereft on the Left* online at www.bereftontheleft. blogspot. com. He is a volunteer reader at Recording for the Blind and Dyslexic in Hollywood and hosts a weekly program entitled *Inside Television* for the Los Angeles Radio Reading Service in Northridge, California, streamed live online at www.larrs.org. He is an *emeritus* member of the Writers Guild of America and holds memberships in two organizations: Yarmy's Army, a group of veteran writers and entertainers who meet monthly for dinner and produce fund-raisers for worthy causes including the Motion Picture and Television House and Hospital in Woodland Hills, California, and in The Pacific Pioneer Broadcasters, a social club made up of former radio and television professionals that meets bimonthly for lunch and a celebrity "roast." Neither club meets after ten p.m.

Index

Note: The page numbers of photos are italics.

Printed in the United States
141223LV00003B/2/P

9 781593 933234